# A More Perfect Union

## Volume 2: Since 1865

# A More Perfect Union

DOCUMENTS IN U.S. HISTORY

SEVENTH EDITION

## Volume 2: Since 1865

### Ronald Story

*University of Massachusetts, Amherst*

### Paul F. Boller, Jr.

*Professor Emeritus, Texas Christian University*

HOUGHTON MIFFLIN HARCOURT PUBLISHING COMPANY

Boston ■ New York

Executive Publisher: Patricia A. Coryell
Publisher: Suzanne Jeans
Senior Sponsoring Editor: Ann West
Senior Marketing Manager: Katherine Bates
Senior Discipline Product Manager: Lynn Baldridge
Senior Development Editor: Jeffrey Greene
Senior Project Editor: Margaret Park Bridges
Senior Media Producer: Lisa Ciccolo
Senior Content Manager: Janet Edmonds
Art and Design Manager: Jill Haber
Cover Design Director: Tony Saizon
Senior Photo Editor: Jennifer Meyer Dare
Senior Composition Buyer: Chuck Dutton
New Title Project Manager: Susan Peltier
Editorial Assistant: Sareeka Rai
Marketing Coordinator: Lauren Bussard

Cover Image: Seal from the treaty to establish NATO
North Atlantic Treaty
This treaty created the North Atlantic Treaty Organization as a bulwark against Communist expansion. Leaders from the United States, Canada, Iceland, Britain, France, Denmark, Norway, Belgium, the Netherlands, Luxembourg, Italy, and Portugal signed this treaty in 1949. They pledged assistance against aggression within the North Atlantic area and promised cooperation in military training, strategic planning, and arms production.
Credit: © Corbis

Printed in the U.S.A.

Library of Congress Control Number: 2008928060

ISBN-10: 0-547-15057-1
ISBN-13: 978-0-547-15057-4

1 2 3 4 5 6 7 8 9-CRS-12  11  10  09  08

# CONTENTS

★═══★═══★

★ CHAPTER THREE

# Economic Growth and Social Reform

★────────────
## CHAPTER FOUR

# Expansion and War

★────────────
## CHAPTER FIVE

# Interlude

Chapter Six

★————————————————————

# Crisis and Hope

Chapter Seven

★————————————————————

# Protracted Conflict

CHAPTER NINE

★─────────────────

# Conservative Resurgence

# PREFACE

This two-volume reader, *A More Perfect Union: Documents in U.S. History*, presents students with the original words of speeches and testimony, political and legal writings, diary entries and literature that have reflected, precipitated, and implemented pivotal events of the past four centuries. The readings in Volume 1 cover the era from first settlement to Reconstruction. Volume 2 begins with the post-Civil War period and concludes with selections that relate to recent history. We are pleased with the reception that *A More Perfect Union* has received and have worked to refine the contents of this new edition.

## Changes to the Seventh Edition

The seventh edition incorporates a number of significant changes. Forty percent of the documents are new to this edition. There are still, as always, major statements that all students should know, particularly from political history. But there are also more items from social, economic, and cultural history—an early planter's will, letters from a working woman, a Southern defense of slavery, anti-immigration speeches, a description of assembly line production, trial testimony about evolution, a resolution against homosexuality.

Volume 1 contains more documents from the colonial era, on early national expansionism, on early labor organization, from the Civil War years, and from the Reconstruction period. There is a greater variety of voices—Native Americans, African Americans, women, workers, Southerners. There are separate chapters on ante-bellum reform, the antislavery struggle, and the experience of the war—seven chapters in all.

Volume 2 includes material from women and African Americans and also, in this edition, from Catholics, business leaders, Hispanics, and conservatives. There are completely new chapters on the 1920s and on modern conservatism—nine in all.

## Goal and Format

The readings in these volumes represent a blend of social and political history, along with some cultural and economic trends, suitable for introductory courses in American history. We made our selections with three thoughts in mind. First we looked for famous documents with a lustrous place in the American tradition—the Gettysburg Address, for example, or Franklin D. Roosevelt's First Inaugural Address. These we chose for their great mythic quality, as expressions of fundamental sentiments with which students should be familiar. Second, we looked for writings that caused something to happen or had an impact when they appeared. Examples include the Virginia slave statutes, Andrew Jackson's Bank Veto Message, and Earl Warren's opinion in *Brown* v. *Board of Education of Topeka*—all of them influential pieces, some of them famous as well. Third, we looked for documents that seem to reflect important attitudes or developments. Into this group fall the writings of Upton Sinclair on industrial Chicago and Reinhold Niebuhr on the 1920s. In this category, where the need for careful selection from a wide field was most apparent, we looked especially for thoughtful pieces with a measure of fame and influence. Horace Mann's statement on schools reflected common reform attitudes; it also caused something to happen and is a well-known reform statement. We have also tried to mix a few unusual items into the stew, as with the "Report of the Joint Committee on Reconstruction."

We have edited severely in places, mostly when the document is long or contains extraneous material or obscure references. We have also, in some cases, modernized spelling and punctuation.

Each document has a lengthy head note that summarizes the relevant trends of the era, provides a specific setting for the document, and sketches the life of the author. In addition, "Questions to Consider" guide students through the selections and suggest ways to think about them.

## Acknowledgements

We would like to thank the following people who reviewed the sixth edition in preparation for the seventh edition: Carter Jones Myer, Ramapo College of New Jersey; Paul O'Hara, Xavier University; George D. Price, University of Florida; Nikki Taylor, University of Cincinnati; and Karol K. Weaver, Susquehanna University.

We would also like to thank the following people who reviewed the manuscript in prior editions: John K. Alexander, University of Cincinnati; June G. Alexander, University of Cincinnati; Jonathan M. Atkins, Berry College; Judith L. Demark, Northern Michigan University; Kurk Dorsey, University of New Hampshire; Paul G. Faler, University of Massachusetts at Boston; Lorri Glover, University of Tennessee; Harvey Green, Northeastern University; Carol Sue Humphrey, Oklahoma Baptist University; Andrew McMichael, Western Kentucky University; Richard H. Peterson, San Diego State University; Ben Rader, University of Nebraska at Lincoln; C. Elizabeth Raymond, University of Nevada–Reno; Steven E. Siry, Baldwin-Wallace

College; Thomas Templeton Taylor, Wittenberg University; and John Scott Wilson, University of South Carolina.

We also wish to express our appreciation to the editorial staff of Houghton Mifflin Company for their hard and conscientious work in producing these volumes. We owe a special debt of gratitude to our sponsoring editor, Ann West.

R. S.
P. F. B

**Former slave children at a Freedmen's Bureau school.** The Freedmen's Bureau, created by Congress in March 1865 to help the former slaves adjust to freedom, provided emergency food and shelter at first. Later on it helped the freedmen obtain work, conducted military courts to hear complaints, established schools at both the elementary and college levels, and registered black voters. By 1872, when the bureau was abolished, it had spent more than $21 million in aiding the freedmen and had established many schools. (Valentine Museum, Cook Collection)

CHAPTER ONE

# The Agony of Reconstruction

# 1

## A HUNGER FOR LITERACY

■═══■═══■

The Thirteenth Amendment, which became part of the Constitution in 1865, freed about four million former slaves in the South. But with freedom came uncertainty, insecurity, and perplexity. Unlike the peasants of France and Russia, who retained the land on which they had been working when they were freed from serfdom, the former American slaves were cast adrift at the end of the Civil War with no means of livelihood. They found themselves without property, legal rights, education, training, or any experience as independent farmers or laborers. Thousands began roaming the countryside looking for work and ways to survive. The first year of freedom meant hunger, disease, suffering, and death for many blacks. Thousands died of disease and starvation during 1865 and 1866.

The freedmen did receive some assistance from the federal government after the war. In March 1865, Congress established the Bureau of Refugees, Freedmen, and Abandoned Lands (commonly called the Freedmen's Bureau) to provide them with food, clothing, shelter, and medical aid. Under the direction of General Oliver O. Howard (the "Christian General"), the Freedmen's Bureau also established schools and colleges for young African Americans, founded savings banks, set up courts to protect their civil rights, and tried to get them jobs and fair contracts of employment. During its seven years of existence (1865–1872), the bureau spent more than fifteen million dollars for food and other aid and over six million dollars on schools and educational work and gave medical attention to nearly half a million patients. Bureau agents also registered black voters and encouraged political participation. There is no doubt that the bureau did much to help Southern blacks during the Reconstruction period. When Reconstruction came to an end, however, the hostility of Southern whites and the growing indifference of whites in the North negated most of the bureau's work. For example, corrupt political appointees in Washington embezzled the funds of the Freedmen's Savings Bank. Every bank failed, and every dollar the impoverished freedmen had deposited was lost.

**Questions to Consider.** In February 1866 President Andrew Johnson vetoed a bill expanding the powers of the Freedmen's Bureau. Although Congress overrode his veto he continued to regard the bill as unconstitutional. He was especially critical of the authority it gave bureau agents to conduct courts to safeguard the freedmen's rights; he said it involved "military jurisdiction" in time of peace. Was there any merit in his opinion? According to the congressional report appearing below, how involved was the army in education for the former slaves? What did the Freedmen's Bureau accomplish in the field of education? From what sources did the bureau draw teachers and funds? How did J. W. Alvord explain the great "desire of the freedmen for knowledge"? What was the reaction of Southern whites to efforts to educate the former slaves?

■━━■━━■

# Congressional Report on the Freedmen's Bureau (1868)

When our armies entered the South two facts became apparent; first, a surprising thirst for knowledge among the negroes; second, a large volunteer force of teachers for their instruction.

Without delay schools were successfully established and the earliest efforts to impart knowledge found the freedmen ready for its reception. Teachers of character and culture were ready from the first. To some extent the army had carried its own instructors. Negro servants of officers studied at the campfires of fellow servants. Chaplains of colored troops became instructors. In the campaigns of 1864 and 1865 the Christian Commission employed 50 teachers in colored camps and regiments.

At the close of the war it is believed that 20,000 colored soldiers could read intelligently, and a much larger number were learning their first lessons.

Really wonderful results had been accomplished through the disinterested efforts of benevolent associations working in connection with the government. But arrangements were soon made to give, on a larger scale, systematic and impartial aid to all of them. This consisted in turning over for school use temporary government buildings no longer needed for military purposes, and buildings seized from disloyal owners; also transportation for teachers, books, and school furniture, with quarters and rations for teachers and superintendants when on duty.

Schools were taken in charge by the Bureau, and in some States carried on wholly (in connection with local efforts) by use of the "refugees and

*Report of the Joint Committee on Reconstruction,* 1st Session, 40th Congress (Government Printing Office, Washington, D.C., 1868), 369–388.

**A visit of the Ku Klux Klan.** This popular drawing from the early 1870s renders its black subjects with exaggerated, stereotyped features. But the one-room cabin—small, sparsely furnished, with food dangling from the ceiling—rings true to life. The illustrator effectively captured the aura of invasion without warning and the startled terror that accompanied Ku Klux Klan raids. These succeeded so well partly because they reached directly into black homes in this way. Faced with assaults on their children as well as themselves and lacking weaponry and military or police protection, the freedmen eventually buckled to Klan terror, although total segregation and disfranchisement did not take place until the 1890s. (Library of Congress)

freemen's fund." Teachers came under the general direction of the assistant commissioners, and protection through the department commanders was given to all engaged in the work. . . .

Whenever our troops broke through the lines of the enemy, schools followed. At Hampton, Beaufort, North Carolina, Roanoke Island, and New Orleans, they were soon in operation. A very efficient system was instituted for Louisiana in the early part of 1864, by Major General Banks, then in command of that State. It was supported by a military tax upon the whole population. Schools were opened in Savannah, Georgia, on the entrance of General Sherman, in December, 1864, and 500 pupils were at once enrolled. Ten intelligent colored persons were the first teachers, and nearly $81,000 were immediately contributed by the negroes for their support. This work was organized by the Secretary of the American Tract Society, Boston. Two of the largest of these schools were in "Bryan's slave mart," where platforms occupied a few days before with bondmen for sale became crowded with children learning to read. . . .

Some change of sentiment had, at this time, been observed among the better classes of the South; those of higher intelligence acknowledging that education must become universal. Still, multitudes bitterly opposed the schools. Teachers were proscribed and ill-treated; school-houses were burned; many schools could not be opened, and others, after a brief struggle, had to be closed. Nevertheless, the country began to feel the moral power of this movement. Commendations came from foreign lands, and the universal demand of good men was that the work should go on.

As showing the desire for education among the freedmen, we give the following facts: When the collection of the general tax for colored schools was suspended in Louisiana by military order, the consternation of the colored population was intense. Petitions began to pour in. I saw one from the plantations across the river, at least thirty feet in length, representing ten thousand negroes. It was affecting to examine it, and note the names and marks [X] of such a long list of parents, ignorant themselves, but begging that their children might be educated, promising that from beneath their present burdens, and out of their extreme poverty, they would pay for it.

In September, 1865, J. W. Alvord, the present general superintendant, was appointed "Inspector of Schools." He traveled through nearly all the States lately in insurrection, and made the first general report to the Bureau on the subject of education, January 1, 1866.

Extracts from this report give the condition of the freedmen throughout the whole South. He says, "The desire of the freedmen for knowledge has not been overstated. This comes from several causes.

"1. The natural thirst for knowledge common to all men.
"2. They have seen power and influence among white people always coupled with *learning*; it is the sign of that elevation to which they now aspire.
"3. Its mysteries, hitherto hidden from them in written literature, excite to the special study of *books*.
"4. Their freedom has given wonderful stimulus to *all effort*, indicating a vitality which augurs well for their whole future condition and character.
"5. But, especially, the practical business of life now upon their hands shows their immediate need of education.

"This they all feel and acknowledge; hence their unusual welcome of and attendance upon schools is confined to no one class or age. Those advanced in life throw up their hands at first in despair, but a little encouragement places *even these* as pupils at the alphabet.

"Such as are in middle life, the laboring classes, gladly avail themselves of evening and Sabbath-schools. They may be often seen during the intervals of toil, when off duty as servants, on steamboats, along the railroads, and when unemployed in the streets in the city, or on plantations, with some fragment of a spelling-book in their hands, *earnestly* at study." . . .

The report goes on to say, "Much opposition has been encountered from those who do not believe in the elevation of the negro. A multitude of facts might be given. It is the testimony of all superintendants that if military power should be withdrawn, our schools would cease to exist.

"This opposition is sometimes ludicrous as well as inhuman. A member of the legislature, in session while I was at New Orleans, was passing one of the schools with me, having at the time its recess, the grounds about the building being filled with children. He stopped and looked intently, then earnestly inquired 'Is this a school?' 'Yes,' I replied. 'What! of niggers?' 'These are colored children, evidently,' I answered. 'Well! Well!' said he, and raising his hands, 'I have seen many an absurdity in my lifetime, but *this is the climax of absurdities!*' I am sure he did not speak from effect, but as he felt. He left me abruptly, and turned the next corner to take his seat with legislators similarly prejudiced."

There are now 35 industrial schools, giving instruction to 2,124 pupils in the various kinds of female labor, not including 4,185 in the day schools, who are taught needle-work. The average daily attendance in all the above schools has been nearly 75 per cent of the enrollment.

There are now connected with these schools 44 children's temperance societies, called the "Vanguard of Freedom," having, in the aggregate, 3,000 members. These societies are constantly increasing, and doing much to train children in correct moral habits.

Education in thrift and economy is effected through the influence of the "Freedmen's Savings and Trust Company," chartered by Congress, and placed under the protection of this Bureau. Twenty branches of this institution, located in as many of the central cities and larger towns of the Southern States, are now in operation. Six of these banks have, at this time (January 1, 1868), on deposit an average of over $50,000 each, the whole amount now due depositors at all the branches being $585,770.17. Four times this amount has been deposited and drawn out for use in important purchases, homesteads etc. Both the business and the influence of the banks are rapidly increasing. Multitudes of these people never before had the first idea of saving for future use. Their former industry was only a hard, profitless task, but under the instructions of the cashiers the value of money is learned, and they are stimulated to earn it.

# 2

# The Politics of Intimidation

★━━★━━★

Reconstruction developed in a series of moves and countermoves. In a white Southern backlash to Union victory, emancipation and the Freedmen's Bureau came "black codes" for coercing black laborers and President Johnson's pardon of Confederate landowners. Then in a Northern backlash to these codes and pardons came the Civil Rights bills, the sweeping Reconstruction Acts, and the Fourteenth and Fifteenth Amendments, all designed to guarantee black political rights. White Southerners now reacted to these measures with secret nightriding forces aiming to shatter Republican political power. Congress, in turn, tried to protect Republican voters and the freedmen with the Force Acts, which allowed the use of army troops to prevent physical assaults. But Northern willingness to commit troops and resources to the struggle was waning. By the mid-1870s, only three Southern states remained in Republican hands, and within three years, racist Democrats controlled these, too. The night riders had turned the tide.

By far the largest and most influential of the secret terrorist societies was the Ku Klux Klan, the so-called "Invisible Empire." The Klan began in Tennessee in the late 1860s as a men's social club with peculiar costumes and rituals similar to the Odd Fellows and other men's clubs of the nineteenth century. Anti-Republican racists began to see the usefulness of such a spookily secret order, and the Klan was reorganized to provide for "dens," "provinces" (counties), and "realms" (states), all under the authority of a "Grand Wizard," a post filled originally by Nathan B. Forrest, a former slave trader and Confederate general.

The Klan structure was probably never fully established because of the disorganized conditions of the postwar South, and the Reconstruction-era "KKK" may have disbanded as a formal entity in the 1870s. But it clearly survived in spirit and in loose informal groups, continuing to terrorize Republicans and their allies among the newly enfranchised freedmen and sowing fear among the black families who composed the labor force on which white planters still depended. In 1872 a Joint Select Committee of Congress held hearings in an attempt to find out and publicize the facts about anti-black intimidation. Below is testimony from Elias Hill, a South Carolina man victimized by the "knights" of a local den of the Klan.

**Questions to Consider.** Elias Hill's story shone an unaccustomed spotlight on the KKK's behavior. Congressmen found Hill's testimony unusually moving and persuasive. What was there in his testimony that would give it credibility? Klansmen later claimed that they did not use violence because they could intimidate the superstitious freedmen with ghostly sheets and masks; opponents have called them basically sadists acting irrationally. Does Elias Hill's testimony support either of these conflicting claims? What position did Hill hold in the black community? Why did they ask Hill to pray for the Klan? Would it be fair to call the Ku Klux Klan a political terrorist organization that succeeded?

★━━★━━★

# Report of the Joint Committee on Reconstruction (1872)

A select committee of the Senate, upon the 10th of March, 1871, made a report of the result of their investigation into the security of person and property in the State of North Carolina. . . . A sub-committee of their number proceeded to the State of South Carolina, and examined witnesses in that State until July 29. . . .

Elias Hill of York County, South Carolina, is a remarkable character. He is crippled in both legs and arms, which are shriveled by rheumatism; he cannot walk, cannot help himself . . . ; was in early life a slave, whose freedom was purchased by his father. . . . He learned his letters and to read by calling the school children into the cabin as they passed, and also learned to write. He became a Baptist preacher, and after the war engaged in teaching colored children, and conducted the business correspondence of many of his colored neighbors. . . . We put the story of his wrongs in his own language:

"On the night of the 5th of May, after I had heard a great deal of what they had done in that neighborhood, they came . . . to my brother's door, which is in the same yard, and broke open the door and attacked his wife, and I heard her screaming and mourning. I could not understand what they said, for they were talking in an outlandish and unnatural tone, which I had heard they generally used at a negro's house. They said, 'Where's Elias?' She said, 'He doesn't stay here; yon is his house.' I had heard them strike her five or six licks. Someone then hit my door. . . .

*Report of the Joint Select Committee to Inquire into the Condition of Affairs in the Late Insurrectionary States* (Government Printing Office, Washington, D.C., 1872), 25–27, 44–47.

"They carried me into the yard between the houses, my brother's and mine, and put me on the ground. . . . 'Who did that burning? Who burned our houses?' I told them it was not me. I could not burn houses. Then they hit me with their fists, and said I did it, I ordered it. They went on asking me didn't I tell the black men to ravish all the white women. No, I answered them. They struck me again. . . . 'Haven't you been preaching and praying about the Ku-Klux? Haven't you been preaching political sermons? Doesn't a [Republican Party newspaper] come to your house? Haven't you written letters?' Generally one asked me all the questions, but the rest were squatting over me—some six men I counted as I lay there. . . . I told them if they would take me back into the house, and lay me in the bed, which was close adjoining my books and papers, I would try and get it. They said I would never go back to that bed, for they were going to kill me. . . . They caught my leg and pulled me over the yard, and then left me there, knowing I could not walk nor crawl. . . .

"After they had stayed in the house for a considerable time, they came back to where I lay and asked if I wasn't afraid at all. They pointed pistols at me all around my head once or twice, as if they were going to shoot me. . . . One caught me by the leg and hurt me, for my leg for forty years has been drawn each year, more and more, and I made moan when it hurt so. One said, 'G–d d—n it, hush!' He had a horsewhip, [and] I reckon he struck me eight cuts right on the hip bone; it was almost the only place he could hit my body, my legs are so short. They all had disguises. . . . One of them then took a strap, and buckled it around my neck and said, 'Let's take him to the river and drown him.' . . .

"Then they said, 'Look here! Will you put a card in the paper to renounce all republicanism? Will you quit preaching?' I told them I did not know. I said that to save my life. . . . They said if I did not they would come back the next week and kill me. [After more licks with the strap] one of them went into the house where my brother and sister-in-law lived, and brought her to pick me up. As she stooped down to pick me up one of them struck her, and as she was carrying me into the house another struck her with a strap. . . . They said, 'Don't you pray against Ku-Klux, but pray that God may forgive Ku-Klux. Pray that God may bless and save us.' I was so chilled with cold lying out of doors so long and in such pain I could not speak to pray, but I tried to, and they said that would do very well, and all went out of the house. . . ."

Satisfied that he could no longer live in that community, Hill wrote to make inquiry about the means of going to Liberia. Hearing this, many of his neighbors desired to go also. . . . Others are still hoping for relief, through the means of this sub-committee.

# 3

## AFTERMATH

Frederick Douglass regarded the Declaration of Independence as a "watchword of freedom." But he was tempted to turn it to the wall, he said, because its human rights principles were so shamelessly violated. A former slave himself, Douglass knew what he was talking about. Douglass thought that enslaving blacks fettered whites as well and that the United States would never be truly free until it ended chattel slavery. During the Civil War, he had several conversations with Lincoln, urging him to make emancipation his major aim. He also put unremitting pressure on the Union army to accept black volunteers, and after resistance to admitting blacks into the army gave way, he toured the country encouraging blacks to enlist and imploring the government to treat black and white soldiers equally in matters of pay and promotion.

Douglass had great hopes for his fellow blacks after the Civil War. He demanded they be given full rights—political, legal, educational, and economic—as citizens. He also wanted to see the wall of separation between the races crumble and see "the colored people of this country, enjoying the same freedom [as whites], voting at the same ballot-box, using the same cartridge-box, going to the same schools, attending the same churches, travelling in the same street cars, in the same railroad cars, on the same steam-boats, proud of the same country, fighting the same war, and enjoying the same peace and all its advantages." He regarded the Republican Party as the "party of progress, justice and freedom" and at election time took to the stump and rallied black votes for the party. He was rewarded for these services by appointment as marshal of the District of Columbia in 1877, as recorder of deeds for the District in 1881, and as minister to Haiti in 1889. But he was also asked by Republican leaders to keep a low profile, was omitted from White House guest lists, and was excluded from presidential receptions even though one duty of the District marshal was to introduce the guests at White House state occasions.

Douglass was puzzled and then upset by the increasing indifference of Republican leaders to conditions among blacks after the Civil War. In 1883 he attended a convention of blacks in Louisville, Kentucky, which met to discuss their plight and reaffirm their demand for full civil rights. In his keynote address, which is reprinted here, Douglass vividly portrayed the discrimination and persecution his people encountered, but he continued to believe that "prejudice, with all its malign accomplishments, may yet be removed by peaceful means."

Born into slavery in Maryland in 1817, Frederick Augustus Washington Bailey learned to read and write despite efforts to keep him illiterate. In 1838 he managed to escape to freedom and adopted the name Frederick Douglass. Shortly afterward he became associated with William Lloyd Garrison and developed into such an articulate spokesman for the antislavery cause that people doubted he had ever been a slave. In 1845 he published his *Narrative of the Life of Frederick Douglass, an American Slave,* naming names, places, dates, and precise events to convince people he had been born in bondage. Douglass continued to be an articulate spokesman for the black cause throughout his life. Shortly before his death in 1895 a college student asked him what a young black could do to help the cause. Douglass is supposed to have told him, "Agitate! Agitate! Agitate!"

**Questions to Consider.** In the following address Douglass was speaking to a convention of blacks in Louisville, but his appeal was primarily to American whites. How did he try to convince them that blacks deserved the same rights and opportunities as all Americans? How powerful did he think the color line was? What outrages against his people did he report? What was his attitude toward the Republican Party, which he had so faithfully served? Were the grievances he cited largely economic or were they social and political in nature?

■══■══■

# Address to the Louisville Convention (1883)

### FREDERICK DOUGLASS

Born on American soil in common with yourselves, deriving our bodies and our minds from its dust, centuries having passed away since our ancestors were torn from the shores of Africa, we, like yourselves, hold ourselves to be in every sense Americans, and that we may, therefore, venture to speak to you in a tone not lower than that which becomes earnest men and American citizens. Having watered your soil with our tears, enriched it with our blood,

Philip Foner, ed., *The Life and Writings of Frederick Douglass* (4 v., International Publishers, New York, 1955), IV: 373–392. Reprinted by permission.

performed its roughest labor in time of peace, defended it against enemies in time of war, and at all times been loyal and true to its best interests, we deem it no arrogance or presumption to manifest now a common concern with you for its welfare, prosperity, honor and glory. . . .

It is our lot to live among a people whose laws, traditions, and prejudices have been against us for centuries, and from these they are not yet free. To assume that they are free from these evils simply because they have changed their laws is to assume what is utterly unreasonable and contrary to facts. Large bodies move slowly. Individuals may be converted on the instant and change their whole course of life. Nations never. Time and events are required for the conversion of nations. Not even the character of a great political organization can be changed by a new platform. It will be the same old snake though in a new skin. Though we have had war, reconstruction and abolition as a nation, we still linger in the shadow and blight of an extinct institution. Though the colored man is no longer subject to be bought and sold, he is still surrounded by an adverse sentiment which fetters all his movements. In his downward course he meets with no resistance, but his course upward is resented and resisted at every step of his progress. If he comes in ignorance, rags, and wretchedness, he conforms to the popular belief of his character, and in that character he is welcome. But if he shall come as a gentleman, a scholar, and a statesman, he is hailed as a contradiction to the national faith concerning his race, and his coming is resented as impudence. In the one case he may provoke contempt and derision, but in the other he is an affront to pride, and provokes malice. Let him do what he will, there is at present, therefore, no escape for him. The color line meets him everywhere, and in a measure shuts him out from all respectable and profitable trades and callings. In spite of all your religion and laws he is a rejected man.

He is rejected by trade unions, of every trade, and refused work while he lives, and burial when he dies, and yet he is asked to forget his color, and forget that which everybody else remembers. If he offers himself to a builder as a mechanic, to a client as a lawyer, to a patient as a physician, to a college as a professor, to a firm as a clerk, to a Government Department as an agent, or an officer, he is sternly met on the color line, and his claim to consideration in some way is disputed on the ground of color.

Not even our churches, whose members profess to follow the despised Nazarene, whose home, when on earth, was among the lowly and despised, have yet conquered this feeling of color madness, and what is true of our churches is also true of our courts of law. Neither is free from this all-pervading atmosphere of color hate. The one describes the Deity as impartial, no respecter of persons, and the other the Goddess of Justice as blindfolded, with sword by her side and scales in her hand held evenly between high and low, rich and low, white and black, but both are the images of American imagination, rather than American practices.

Taking advantage of the general disposition in this country to impute crime to color, white men *color* their faces to commit crime and wash off the hated color to escape punishment. In many places where the commission of crime is alleged against one of our color, the ordinary processes of law are set aside as too slow for the impetuous justice of the infuriated populace. They take the law into their own bloody hands and proceed to whip, stab, shoot, hang, or burn the alleged culprit, without the intervention of courts, counsel, judges, juries, or witnesses. In such cases it is not the business of the accusers to prove guilt, but it is for the accused to prove his innocence, a thing hard for him to do in these infernal Lynch courts. A man accused, surprised, frightened, and captured by a motley crowd, dragged with a rope about his neck in midnight-darkness to the nearest tree, and told in the coarsest terms of profanity to prepare for death, would be more than human if he did not, in his terror-stricken appearance, more confirm suspicion of guilt than the contrary. Worse still, in the presence of such hell-black outrages, the pulpit is usually dumb, and the press in the neighborhood is silent or openly takes side with the mob. There are occasional cases in which white men are lynched, but one sparrow does not make a summer. Every one knows that what is called Lynch law is peculiarly the law for colored people and for nobody else. If there were no other grievance than this horrible and barbarous Lynch law custom, we should be justified in assembling, as we have now done, to expose and denounce it. But this is not all. Even now, after twenty years of so-called emancipation, we are subject to lawless raids of midnight riders, who, with blackened faces, invade our homes and perpetrate the foulest of crimes upon us and our families. This condition of things is too flagrant and notorious to require specifications or proof. Thus in all the relations of life and death we are met by the color line.

While we recognize the color line as a hurtful force, a mountain barrier to our progress, wounding our bleeding feet with its flinty rocks at every step, we do not despair. We are a hopeful people. This convention is a proof of our faith in you, in reason, in truth and justice—our belief that prejudice, with all its malign accomplishments, may yet be removed by peaceful means; that, assisted by time and events and the growing enlightenment of both races, the color line will ultimately become harmless. When this shall come it will then only be used, as it should be, to distinguish one variety of the human family from another. It will cease to have any civil, political, or moral significance, and colored conventions will then be dispensed with as anachronisms, wholly out of place, but not till then. Do not marvel that we are discouraged. The faith within us has a rational basis, and is confirmed by facts. When we consider how deep-seated this feeling against us is; the long centuries it has been forming; the forces of avarice which have been marshaled to sustain it; how the language and literature of the country have been pervaded with it; how the church, the press, the play-house, and other influences of the country have been arrayed in its support, the progress toward its extinction must be considered vast and wonderful. . . .

We do not believe, as we are often told, that the Negro is the ugly child of the national family, and the more he is kept out of sight the better it will be for him. You know that liberty given is never so precious as liberty sought for and fought for. The man outraged is the man to make the outcry. Depend upon it, men will not care much for a people who do not care for themselves. Our meeting here was opposed by some of our members, because it would disturb the peace of the Republican party. The suggestion came from coward lips and misapprehended the character of that party. If the Republican party cannot stand a demand for justice and fair play, it ought to go down. We were men before that party was born, and our manhood is more sacred than any party can be. Parties were made for men, not men for parties.

The colored people of the South are the laboring people of the South. The labor of a country is the source of its wealth; without the colored laborer to-day the South would be a howling wilderness, given up to bats, owls, wolves, and bears. He was the source of its wealth before the war, and has been the source of its prosperity since the war. He almost alone is visible in her fields, with implements of toil in his hands, and laboriously using them to-day.

Let us look candidly at the matter. While we see and hear that the South is more prosperous than it ever was before and rapidly recovering from the waste of war, while we read that it raises more cotton, sugar, rice, tobacco, corn, and other valuable products than it ever produced before, how happens it, we sternly ask, that the houses of its laborers are miserable huts, that their clothes are rags, and their food the coarsest and scantiest? How happens it that the land-owner is becoming richer and the laborer poorer?

The implication is irresistible—that where the landlord is prosperous the laborer ought to share his prosperity, and whenever and wherever we find this is not the case there is manifestly wrong somewhere. . . .

Flagrant as have been the outrages committed upon colored citizens in respect to their civil rights, more flagrant, shocking, and scandalous still have been the outrages committed upon our political rights by means of bulldozing and Kukluxing, Mississippi plans, fraudulent courts, tissue ballots, and the like devices. Three States in which the colored people outnumber the white population are without colored representation and their political voice suppressed. The colored citizens in those States are virtually disfranchised, the Constitution held in utter contempt and its provisions nullified. This has been done in the face of the Republican party and successive Republican administrations. . . .

This is no question of party. It is a question of law and government. It is a question whether men shall be protected by law, or be left to the mercy of cyclones of anarchy and bloodshed. It is whether the Government or the mob shall rule this land; whether the promises solemnly made to us in the constitution be manfully kept or meanly and flagrantly broken. Upon this vital point we ask the whole people of the United States to take notice that whatever of political power we have shall be exerted for no man of any party who will not, in advance of election, promise to use every power given him by the Government, State or National, to make the black man's path to the ballotbox as straight, smooth and safe as that of any other American citizen. . . .

We hold it to be self-evident that no class or color should be the exclusive rulers of this country. If there is such a ruling class, there must of course be a subject class, and when this condition is once established this Government of the people, by the people, and for the people, will have perished from the earth.

**Anti-Chinese riot.** This wood engraving from *Frank Leslie's Illustrated Newspaper* depicts an anti-Chinese riot in Denver, Colorado, in 1880. Initially welcomed in the Western states as cheap labor for railroad construction and service work in the mining towns, immigrants from China were commonly perceived as a threat to the jobs and social mores of white Americans and became the targets of intense, sometimes violent hostility. (Library of Congress)

CHAPTER TWO

# Minorities

# 4

# A SISTER ON THE FRONTIER

Roman Catholics found a niche in predominantly Protestant North America when Charles I granted Lord Baltimore a charter to establish the colony of Maryland. But prejudice compelled even Lord Baltimore to enjoin Catholics to worship "as privately as may be" and to avoid public discussion of their beliefs. Elsewhere, Catholics often faced hostility, and persevered by keeping their religious convictions to themselves. With the Revolution and the religious freedom it promised, Catholics expected their position to improve—after all, they had fought enthusiastically for the cause, and the Catholic Count Pulaski, the top cavalry commander in the southern campaign, had died a hero of the Revolution.

Things did get better. With greater numbers of European Catholic immigrants, churches and dioceses multiplied, missionaries went west, and schools were founded. As the Catholic population increased, however, so again did nativist suspicions. By the 1830s anti-Catholicism was so virulent that in Boston a mob burned the Ursuline convent school. The huge influx of Irish Catholics in the 1840s and 1850s further aroused American prejudices.

Yet Catholics remained intent on spreading their faith. And in contrast to their reception in some urban areas, they were often welcome on the frontier. Of Catholic schools in the Ohio and Indiana wilderness one observer reported:

> Everywhere in America, in the best society, the most accomplished and influential ladies have been educated in convents, and though they may never go over to Rome they love and respect their teachers. . . . Education is removing prejudices, and the chaotic condition of the Protestant community, divided into warring sects, increases the power of a Church whose characteristic is unity, and whose claim is infallibility.

Sister Blandina Segale was a Catholic missionary and teacher who found herself in the rough cowboy country of the Colorado Territory in the 1870s. Sent by the Sisters of Charity to the town of Trinidad, she labored in the Southwest (in what is today Colorado and New Mexico) among the predominantly Mexican population for twenty-one years. Hers was hardly a monastic existence; Sister Blandina's experiences included an encounter with Billy the Kid, whom she charmed into inviting her to call on him should she ever need assistance, and the rescue of a man about to be lynched by a mob. Her indomitable spirit, shrewd insight, and quick-wittedness are illustrated in the document below, a fragment from a journal she kept in the form of letters to her sister, Sister Justina, in Cincinnati. Here she records how she was able to get a new school built, a tale that reflects both her resourcefulness as an individual and the self-sufficient fashion in which the Catholic church established itself on the frontier.

Following her days in the territory, Sister Blandina returned to Cincinnati, where she and her sister established the Santa Maria Institute, the oldest aid society for Italian immigrants. There she labored for thirty-five years, personally instructing nearly 80 percent of the Italian population in the Catholic faith.

**Questions to Consider.** What qualities made Sister Blandina particularly well suited to life in a frontier situation? What kind of relationship did she have with the people she served? To what extent did she respect local wisdom and customs? How would you describe the relationship between local people and women?

★━━★━━★

# Letter from Colorado (1876)

### BLANDINA SEGALE

Dear Sister Justina:

To-day I asked Sister Eulalia if, in her opinion, we did not need a new school building, which would contain a hall and stage for all school purposes. She said: "Just what we need, Sister. Do you want to build it?" I answered, "Yes, I do." She added, "We have not enough cash to pay interest on our indebtedness. Have you a plan by which you can build without money? If so, I say build."

"Here is my plan, Sister. Borrow a crowbar, get on the roof of the schoolhouse and begin to detach the adobes. The first good Mexican who sees me will ask, "What are you doing, Sister?" I will answer, "Tumbling down this structure to rebuild it before the opening of the fall term of school."

You should have seen Sister Eulalia laugh! It did me good. After three days' pondering how to get rid of low ceilings, poor ventilation, acrobats

From Sister Blandina Segale, *At the End of the Santa Fe Trail* (Milwaukee, 1948), 62–65.

from log-rafters introducing themselves without notice, and now here is an opportunity to carry out a test on the good in human nature, so I took it. I borrowed a crowbar and went on the roof, detached some adobes and began throwing them down. The school building is only one story high.

The first person who came towards the schoolhouse was Doña Juanita Simpson, wife of the noted hero of Simpson's Rest. When she saw me at work, she exclaimed, *"Por amor de Dios, Hermana, qué está Vd. haciendo?"* (For the love of God, Sister, what are you doing?)

I answered, "We need a schoolhouse that will a little resemble those we have in the United States, so I am demolishing this one in order to rebuild."

"How many men do you need, Sister?"

"We need not only men, but also straw, moulds, hods, shovels—everything it takes to build a house with a shingle roof. Our assets are good-will and energy."

Earnestly Mrs. Simpson said: "I go to get what you need."

The crowbar was kept at its work. In less than an hour, Mrs. Simpson returned with six men. One carried a mould, another straw, etc. The mould carrier informed me at once that women only know how to *encalar* (whitewash), the men had the trades and they would continue what I began. In a few days the old building was thrown down, the adobes made and sun-burnt. In two weeks all the rubbish was hauled away. The trouble began when we were ready for the foundation. Keep in mind it was only by condescension I was permitted to look on. At this juncture I remarked to the moulder:

"Of course, we will have a stone foundation."

"Oh, no!" he answered, "we use adobes laid in mud."

"Do you think if we laid a foundation with stone laid in mortar, the combination would resist the rainy season better than adobes laid in mud?"

"No, no, Sister we never use stone for any of our houses," he replied.

I was at the mercy of the good natives and my best move was to let them have their way. Moreover, I recalled the fact that in the Far East there are mud structures centuries old in a good state of preservation. No mistake would be made by not changing their mode of building in that one point. We got the necessary lumber, sashes and shingles from Chené's mill, sixty miles from Trinidad. Wagons hauled the material. As the Chené family has a daughter at our boarding school, there will be no difficulty in meeting our bill. Mr. Hermann's daughter is a resident student, and Mr. Hermann is a carpenter and will pay his bill by work.

When the schoolhouse was ready for roofing, a number of the town carpenters offered to help. The merchants gave nails, paints, brushes, lime, hair, etc.

But now came the big obstacle. There is but one man who calls himself a plasterer, and his method is to plaster with mud. It is impossible to get a smooth surface with mud. I remarked to the plasterer: "You will use lime, sand and hair to plaster the schoolrooms."

His look plainly said: "What do women know of men's work?" Yet he condescended to explain: "I am the plasterer of this part of the country; if I should use any material but mud, my reputation would be lost."

I said to him, "But if lime, sand and hair made a better job, your reputation would gain."

He made answer, "Sister, I'll make a bargain with you. I will do as you suggest, but I will tell my people I carried out your American idea of plastering."

We both agreed to this. Meanwhile, the other men had shouldered their implements and were on their way home. The plasterer had to mix the sand, lime and hair following my directions. All that was done satisfactorily to me, at least. But there was not a man to carry the mortar to the plasterer, so I got the bucket and supplied a man's place. The comedy follows:

Rev. Charles Pinto, S.J., pastor, took pleasure in telling his co-religionists that the study of human nature, combined with good will and tactfulness, were building a schoolhouse.

On this day of my hod-carrying, the Rt. Rev. Bishop Machebeuf of Denver, Colorado, arrived on his visitation. The first place to which he was taken was the schoolhouse being built without money. Bishop and Pastor had just turned the kitchen corner when the three of us came face to face. Both gentlemen stood amazed. I rested my hod-bucket. Father Pinto looked puzzled. The Bishop remarked:

"I see how you manage to build without money." I laughed and explained the situation.

They took the bucket, and the three of us went to where the plasterer was working. After the welcome to the Bishop, the plasterer said:

"Your Reverence, look at me, the only Mexican plasterer, and I am putting aside my knowledge to follow American ways of doing my trade; but I told Sister the failure will not be pointed at me." The Rt. Rev. Bishop analyzed the material at a glance, then said: "Juan, if this method of plastering is better than yours, come again to help Sister when she needs you. If it fails, report to me and between us we shall give her the biggest penance she ever received."

The schoolroom walls turned out smooth, the plaster adhesive, and the plasterer will now make a lucrative living at his American method of plastering.

# 5

## Indian Autumn

Conflict between whites and Native Americans began with the first colonial landings and continued undiminished into the late nineteenth century. At that time, the United States finally completed its conquest of the continent and extended its authority over all the lands formerly held by the indigenous peoples. After the Civil War, whites began moving in large numbers along the new rail lines west of the Mississippi River. As part of this movement, the U.S. Army fought continuous wars against the larger and more combative Native American nations— notably the Comanche, Apache, Kiowa, Cheyenne, and Sioux. The army also harassed most of the smaller nations. Native Americans won occasional victories, for example, the Sioux victory over former Civil War General George A. Custer at the Little Bighorn in 1876. Most of the time, however, the tribespeople fell victim to the U.S. Army's superior organization, supplies, and firepower. Whites' slaughter of the vast buffalo herds on which the Native Americans had based their lives— thirteen million buffalo had been killed by 1883—virtually ensured that the tribes would be crushed. The last major military clash between the government and the Native Americans came with the slaughter of scores of Sioux families in 1890 at Wounded Knee, South Dakota.

The Plains peoples were confined almost entirely to reservations. These large tracts of land had been set aside by the U.S. government as places where, with the protection and economic aid of the Indian Office, the Plains peoples might continue their nomadic communal ways. But this policy was a failure. Tribal ranks, already severely depleted by the Plains wars, were further thinned by the growing scarcity of buffalo. Moreover, large tribes were often widely divided on scattered reservations, where resident U.S. government agents usually proved unwilling or unable to prevent looting by white settlers and theft of funds earmarked for tribal assistance.

"Chief Joseph's Story," excerpted below, is a commentary on events during the 1870s. It describes both the encounters—peaceful and otherwise—of the Nez Percés[1] of the Oregon and Idaho country with

1. "Nez Percé," like "Joseph," was a European-American name imposed by American explorers in place of the tribal name.

U.S. settlers and authorities and the betrayals that accompanied those encounters. Born about 1840, "Young Joseph" was the son of a chief of a major Nez Percé band, who had also been christened Joseph by white missionaries. The father had refused to cede tribal lands to the U.S. government following the discovery of gold in the Oregon country, and he passively resisted white efforts to settle the area. When his father died in 1873, "Young Joseph"—named Hinmatonyalatkit, or Thunder Traveling Over The Mountains, in his native tongue—continued the policy of noncooperation. In early 1877 General O. O. Howard ordered the Nez Percés off the land, promising them a reservation elsewhere in the Oregon region. "Young Joseph," seeking to protect his people, agreed to leave, but other Nez Percés did not. A skirmish quickly escalated into a series of pitched battles that decimated the tribe. After armed resistance and a masterly retreat of 1,500 miles, "Young Joseph" surrendered in October 1877. He and his band were sent to Indian Territory, then in 1885 to Washington state. Chief "Young Joseph," by now a figure of legendary proportions to Native Americans and whites alike, died in 1904.

**Questions to Consider.** What were the key features in the history of relations between Native Americans and whites, as "Young Joseph" told it? In "Young Joseph's" eyes, was the U.S. Army merely an arm of westward expansion or was it an autonomous agent? Given the Nez Percé beliefs (as the chief summarized them), do you think the Americans' westward advance could have occurred without wrecking the tribal nations? In his policy proposals at the end of the passage, was "Young Joseph" advocating a policy of assimilation, separate but equal status, ethnic autonomy, or simple justice? Was his vision practical at that time? Can you see any alternative that might have suited both sides?

★ ▬ ★ ▬ ★

# Chief Joseph's Story (1879)

## YOUNG JOSEPH

My friends, I have been asked to show you my heart. I am glad to have a chance to do so. I want the white people to understand my people. Some of you think an Indian is like a wild animal. This is a great mistake. I will tell you about our people, and then you can judge whether an Indian is a man or not. I believe much trouble and blood would be saved if we opened our hearts more. I will tell you in my way how the Indian sees things. The white

From "Chief Joseph's Own Story," *North American Review* (April 1879), 415–433.

man has more words to tell you how they look to him, but it does not require many words to speak the truth. What I have to say will come from my heart, and I will speak with a straight tongue. Ah-cum-kin-i-ma-me-hut (the Great Spirit) is looking at me, and will hear me.

My name is In-mut-too-yah-lat-lat (Thunder-traveling-over-the-mountains). I am chief of the Wal-lam-wat-kin band of Chute-pa-lu, or Nez Percés (nose-pierced Indians). I was born in eastern Oregon, thirty-eight winters ago. My father was chief before me. When a young man he was called Joseph by Mr. Spalding, a missionary. He died a few years ago. There was no stain on his hands of the blood of a white man. He left a good name on the earth. He advised me well for my people.

Our fathers gave us many laws, which they had learned from their fathers. These laws were good. They told us to treat all men as they treated us; that we should never be the first to break a bargain; that it was a disgrace to tell a lie; that we should speak only the truth; that it was a shame for one man to take from another his wife, or his property, without paying for it. We were taught to believe that the Great Spirit sees and hears everything, and that He never forgets; that hereafter He will give every man a spirit-home according to his deserts; if he has been a good man, he will have a good home; if he has been a bad man, he will have a bad home. This I believe, and all my people believe the same.

The first white men of your people who came to our country were named Lewis and Clarke. They also brought many things that our people had never seen. They talked straight, and our people gave them a great feast, as a proof that their hearts were friendly. These men were very kind. They made presents to our chiefs and our people made presents to them. We had a great many horses of which we gave them what they needed, and they gave us guns and tobacco in return. All the Nez Percés made friends with Lewis and Clarke, and agreed to let them pass through their country, and never to make war on white men. This promise the Nez Percés have never broken. . . .

Next there came a white officer who invited all the Nez Percés to a treaty council. After the council was opened he made known his heart. He said there were a great many white people in the country, and many more would come; that he wanted the land marked out so that the Indians and white men could be separated. If they were to live in peace it was necessary, he said, that the Indians should have a country set apart for them, and in that country they must stay. My father, who represented his band, refused to have anything to do with the council, because he wished to be a free man. He claimed that no man owned any part of the earth, and a man could not sell what was not his own. . . .

For a short time we lived quietly. But this could not last. White men had found gold in the mountains around the land of the winding water. They stole a great many horses from us, and we could not get them back because we were Indians. . . . We could have avenged our wrongs many times, but we did not. Whenever the Government has asked us to help them against other

Indians we have never refused. When the white men were few and we were strong we could have killed them off, but the Nez Percés wished to live at peace. . . .

Year after year we have been threatened, but no war was made upon my people until General [O. O.]. Howard came to our country two years ago and told us that he was the white war-chief of all that country. He said: "I have a great many soldiers at my back. I am going to bring them up here, and then I will talk to you again. I will not let white men laugh at me the next time I come. The country belongs to the Government, and I intend to make you go upon the reservation."

I remonstrated with him against bringing more soldiers to the Nez Percé country. He had one house full of troops all the time at Fort Lapwei. . . .

When the party arrived there General Howard sent out runners and called all the Indians to a grand council. In the council General Howard informed us in a haughty spirit that he would give my people thirty days to go back home, collect all their stock, and move on to the reservation, saying, "If you are not here in that time, I shall consider that you want to fight, and will send my soldiers to drive you on." . . .

When I returned to Wallowa I found my people very much excited upon discovering that the soldiers were already in the Wallowa Valley. We held a council, and decided to move immediately to avoid bloodshed. . . .

We gathered all the stock we could find, and made an attempt to move. We left many of our horses and cattle in Wallowa, and we lost several hundred in crossing the river. All my people succeeded in getting across in safety. Many of the Nez Percés came together in Rocky Cañon to hold a grand council. . . .

Again I counseled peace, and I thought the danger was past. We had not complied with General Howard's order because we could not, but we intended to do so as soon as possible. I was leaving the council to kill beef for my family when news came that a young man whose father had been killed had gone out with several hot-blooded young braves and killed four white men. He rode up to the council and shouted: "Why do you sit here like women? The war has begun already." [Following many battles] I went to General [Colonel Nelson] Miles and gave up my gun, and said, "From where the sun now stands I will fight no more." . . .

Words do not pay for my dead people. They do not pay for my country, now overrun by white men. They do not protect my father's grave. They do not pay for my horses and cattle. Good words will not give me back my children. Good words will not make good the promise of your War Chief, General Miles, [of reservation land in Idaho]. Good words will not give my people good health and stop them from dying. Good words will not get my people a home where they can live in peace and take care of themselves. I am tired of talk that comes to nothing. . . .

I know that my race must change. We cannot hold our own with the white men as we are. We only ask an even chance to live as other men live. We ask to be recognized as men. We ask that the same law shall work alike on all men. If the Indian breaks the law, punish him by the law. If the white man breaks the law, punish him also.

Let me be a free man—free to travel, free to stop, free to work, free to trade where I choose, free to choose my own teachers, free to follow the religion of my fathers, free to think and talk and act for myself—and I will obey every law, or submit to the penalty.

Whenever the white man treats the Indian as they treat each other, then we shall have no more wars. We shall be all alike—brothers of one father and one mother, with one sky above us and one country around us, and one government for all. Then the Great Spirit Chief who rules above will smile upon this land, and send rain to wash out the bloody spots made by brothers' hands upon the face of the earth. For this time the Indian race are waiting and praying. I hope that no more groans of wounded men and women will ever go to the ear of the Great Spirit Chief above, and that all people may be one people. . . .

In-mut-too-yah-lat-lat has spoken for his people.

Young Joseph

# 6

## Newcomers

❖══❖══❖

The sprawling city was as fundamental a fact of life as the great West or the bitter South in the late nineteenth century, and most Americans found it simultaneously exciting and unsettling. Cities were exciting because they symbolized prosperity and progress, cardinal virtues of the country for decades if not centuries. These urban centers were full of good and novel things to buy and do in a land lusting to do both. But cities were also unsettling—seething (so it seemed) with greedy landlords, corrupt politicians, and radical workers. Most unsettling of all, they were populated by foreigners, not "real" Americans—immigrants from a dozen lands, speaking as many languages and exhibiting as many objectionable habits. These newcomers spilled out from the waterfronts of New York, Baltimore, or Chicago into vast impoverished tenement districts that strained not only public morality but also public order and public health. They may have been lovers of liberty "yearning to be free," as it said on the Statue of Liberty, but they were also "huddled masses."

For most Americans, New York City—the country's largest city and chief port of European debarkation—was the epitome of the immigrant city. No U.S. city could claim more foreign-born inhabitants or more crowded housing conditions. Relatively little open space remained for new residential or business construction. But New York was more than an immigrant center; it was also the publishing and literary capital of the United States. By 1890, hundreds of reporters and writers lived in the city, working for dozens of newspapers and magazines, not counting the foreign-language press. When the United States developed an appetite for urban coverage, New York had a thriving industry to supply it.

Jacob Riis, a Danish immigrant, was a pioneer in the field of urban exposé journalism. Riis, who arrived in New York in 1870, wandered in semipoverty for several years before becoming a city police reporter, first for the *New York Tribune,* then for the *Evening Sun*. His beat was the Lower East Side, a teeming immigrant district. For twenty-two years, until 1899, his office was directly across from police headquarters. Here, he wrote, "I was to find my lifework." But Riis was more than a reporter; he became a reformer, determined not only to describe slum life but to improve it. His goal was partly to establish better building codes, but chiefly to ensure that all immigrants learned English and were assimilated thoroughly into American life. This path, after all, was the one that Jacob Riis himself had followed. *How the Other Half Lives,* which first appeared as a series of newspaper essays (one of which is excerpted below), was a weapon in Riis's crusade.

Jacob Riis, born in Ribe, Denmark, in 1849, was educated by his father and became an apprentice carpenter before emigrating to the United States in 1870. By 1890 he had become one of the best-known, most colorful newspapermen in New York. *How the Other Half Lives,* which Riis illustrated with startling photographs of slum conditions, made him a byword in the nation as well. Among its readers was another budding reformer and member of the New York City police board—Theodore Roosevelt, who befriended Riis, accompanied him on forays into the slums, and supported his reform efforts. Riis carried on his crusade in later books, including several on immigrant children, and saw significant improvements in slum schools and recreational facilities. He died in Barre, Massachusetts, in 1914.

**Questions to Consider.** Modern readers will instantly notice Riis's constant use of stereotypes in discussing various immigrant groups. Why might an intelligent, sympathetic reporter of the 1890s resort to such stereotypes? How could such an author be seen (as Riis was) as a champion of liberal social reform? Riis was a reporter, not a social scientist. Are his descriptions and explanations of group social mobility persuasive? When he explains why immigrant groups tend to form separate enclaves, is he persuasive?

# How the Other Half Lives  (1890)

### JACOB RIIS

When once I asked the agent of a notorious Fourth Ward alley how many people might be living in it I was told: One hundred and forty families, one hundred Irish, thirty-eight Italian, and two that spoke the German tongue. Barring the agent herself there was not a native-born individual in the court. The answer was characteristic of the cosmopolitan character of lower New York, very nearly so of the whole of it, wherever it runs to alleys and courts. One may find for the asking an Italian, a German, a French, African, Spanish, Bohemian, Russian, Scandinavian, Jewish, and Chinese colony. Even the Arab, who peddles "holy earth" from the Battery as a direct importation from Jerusalem, has his exclusive preserves at the lower end of Washington Street. The one thing you shall vainly ask for in the chief city of America is a distinctively American community. . . .

Jacob Riis, *How the Other Half Lives* (Scribner's, New York, 1907), 14–21.

**Bandit's Roost, Mulberry Street, Manhattan.** Jacob Riis took this photograph of the toughest, most dangerous denizens of the Lower East Side in 1890, about the time he enlisted the assistance of Theodore Roosevelt, then chairman of the New York Police Commission. (Museum of the City of New York)

They are not here. In their place has come this queer conglomerate mass of heterogeneous elements, ever striving and working like whiskey and water in one glass, and with the like result: final union and a prevailing taint of whiskey. The once unwelcome Irishman has been followed in his turn by the Italian, the Russian Jew, and the Chinaman, and has himself taken a hand at opposition, quite as bitter and quite as ineffectual, against these later hordes. Wherever these have gone they have crowded him out, possessing the block, the street, the ward with their denser swarms. But the Irishman's revenge is complete. Victorious in defeat over his recent as over his more ancient foe, the one who opposed his coming no less than the one who drove him out, he dictates to both their politics, and, secure in possession of the offices, returns the native his greeting with interest, while collecting the rents of the Italian whose house he has bought with the profits of his saloon. . . .

In justice to the Irish landlord it must be said that like an apt pupil he was merely showing forth the result of the schooling he had received, reenacting, in his own way, the scheme of the tenements. It is only his frankness that shocks. The Irishman does not naturally take kindly to tenement life, though with characteristic versatility he adapts himself to its conditions at once. It does violence, nevertheless, to the best that is in him, and for that very reason of all who come within its sphere soonest corrupts him. The result is a sediment, the product of more than a generation in the city's slums, that, as distinguished from the larger body of his class, justly ranks at the foot of tenement dwellers, the so-called "low Irish." . . .

An impulse toward better things there certainly is. The German ragpicker of thirty years ago, quite as low in the scale as his Italian successor, is the thrifty tradesman or prosperous farmer of today.

The Italian scavenger of our time is fast graduating into exclusive control of the corner fruit-stands, while his black-eyed boy monopolizes the boot-blacking industry in which a few years ago he was an intruder. The Irish hod-carrier in the second generation has become a bricklayer, if not the Alderman of his ward, while the Chinese coolie is in almost exclusive possession of the laundry business. The reason is obvious. The poorest immigrant comes here with the purpose and ambition to better himself and, given half a chance, might be reasonably expected to make the most of it. To the false plea that he prefers the squalid homes in which his kind are housed there could be no better answer. . . .

As emigration from east to west follows the latitude, so does the foreign influx in New York distribute itself along certain well-defined lines that waver and break only under the stronger pressure of a more gregarious race or the encroachments of inexorable business. A feeling of dependence upon mutual effort, natural to strangers in a strange land, unacquainted with its language and customs, sufficiently accounts for this.

The Irishman is the true cosmopolitan immigrant. All-pervading, he shares his lodging with perfect impartiality with the Italian, the Greek, and the "Dutchman," yielding only to sheer force of numbers, and objects equally to them all. A map of the city, colored to designate nationalities, would show more stripes than on the skin of a zebra, and more colors than any rainbow. The city on such a map would fall into two great halves, green for the Irish prevailing in the West Side tenement districts, and blue for the Germans on the East Side. But intermingled with these ground colors would be an odd variety of tints that would give the whole the appearance of an extraordinary crazy-quilt. From down in the Sixth Ward, upon the site of the old Collect Pond that in the days of the fathers drained the hills which are no more, the red of the Italian would be seen forcing its way northward along the line of Mulberry Street to the quarter of the French purple on Bleecker Street and South Fifth Avenue, to lose itself and reappear, after a lapse of miles, in the "Little Italy" of Harlem, east of Second Avenue. Dashes of red, sharply defined, would be seen strung through the Annexed District, northward to the city line. On the West Side the red would be seen overrunning the old Africa of Thompson Street, pushing the black of the negro rapidly uptown, against querulous but unavailing protests, occupying his home, his church, his trade, and all with merciless impartiality.

Hardly less aggressive than the Italian, the Russian and Polish Jew, having overrun the district between Rivington and Division Streets, east of the Bowery, to the point of suffocation, is filling the tenements of the old Seventh Ward to the river front, and disputing with the Italian every foot of available space in the back alleys of Mulberry Street. The two races, differing hopelessly in much, have this in common: they carry their slums with them wherever they go, if allowed to do it. Little Italy already rivals its parent, the "Bend," in foulness. Other nationalities that begin at the bottom make a fresh start when crowded up the ladder. Happily both are manageable, the one by rabbinical, the other by the civil law. Between the dull gray of the Jew, his favorite color, and the Italian red, would be seen squeezed in on the map a sharp streak of yellow, marking the narrow boundaries of Chinatown. Dovetailed in with the German population, the poor but thrifty Bohemian might be picked out by the sombre hue of his life as of his philosophy, struggling against heavy odds in the big human bee-hives of the East Side. Colonies of his people extend northward, with long lapses of space, from below the Cooper Institute more than three miles. The Bohemian is the only foreigner with any considerable representation in the city who counts no wealthy man of his race, none who has not to work hard for a living, or has got beyond the reach of the tenement.

Down near the Battery the West Side emerald would be soiled by a dirty stain, spreading rapidly like a splash of ink on a sheet of blotting paper, headquarters of the Arab tribe, that in a single year has swelled from the original dozen to twelve hundred, intent, every mother's son, on trade and barter. Dots and dashes of color here and there would show where the Finnish sailors worship their djumala (God), the Greek pedlars the ancient name of their race, and the Swiss the goddess of thrift. And so on to the end of the long register, all toiling together in the galling fetters of the tenement. Were the question raised who makes the most of life thus mortgaged, who resists most stubbornly its levelling tendency—knows how to drag even the barracks upward a part of the way at least toward the ideal plane of the home—the palm must be unhesitatingly awarded the Teuton. The Italian and the poor Jew rise only by compulsion. The Chinaman does not rise at all; here, as at home, he simply remains stationary. The Irishman's genius runs to public affairs rather than domestic life; wherever he is mustered in force the saloon is the gorgeous centre of political activity. The German struggles vainly to learn his trick; his Teutonic wit is too heavy, and the political ladder he raises from his saloon usually too short or too clumsy to reach the desired goal. The best part of his life is lived at home, and he makes himself a home independent of the surroundings, giving the lie to the saying, unhappily become a maxim of social truth, that pauperism and drunkenness naturally grow in the tenements. He makes the most of his tenement, and it should be added that whenever and as soon as he can save up money enough, he gets out and never crosses the threshold of one again.

# 7

## FROM ANOTHER SHORE

★━━★━━★

In 1882, Congress passed the Chinese Exclusion Act, prohibiting Chinese workers from entering this country for a period of ten years. As the date of expiration approached, however, pressure from powerful sources mounted for renewing the law. Leading the fight was the Immigration Committee of the House of Representatives, under the chairmanship of Representative Herman Stump of Maryland, who produced a stream of witnesses describing how the Chinese used drugs, committed crimes, and lusted after American women. Stump distilled the most important parts of this testimony in the report, reprinted below, that accompanied the committee's recommendation that the exclusion act be renewed.

The committee and its witnesses were persuasive. Not only did Congress extend the law for another ten years, but in 1893 President Grover Cleveland named Representative Stump superintendent of immigration. The exclusion act and Stump's appointment in turn set the stage for a treaty between the United States and China, signed in 1894, barring the immigration of Chinese laborers for ten years from the date of the exchange of ratifications. Those who had left the United States were permitted to return, provided they had wives, children, parents, or property worth $1,000 in this country. The treaty gave China the right to exclude American workers (of which there were none in China), but not American merchants and officials (who were numerous and important there). Chinese were thus all but barred from American soil, even as the Statue of Liberty (a gift of France) was unveiled in 1886 to welcome immigrants from Europe.

By 1900, Japanese workers, too, were entering the United States in sizable numbers; outcries against the "yellow peril" were again raised in the West. The so-called Gentleman's Agreement of 1907 between Washington and Tokyo instantly reduced the flow of unskilled Japanese laborers into the United States.

**Questions to Consider.** The congressional report of 1892 argued that the Chinese presence in the United States was a threat to American "institutions." What institutions did the Immigration Committee seem most concerned about? Why does the report mention the "vegetable"

# 8

## New South, Old South

✯═══✯═══✯

Following the Civil War, the South suffered two ordeals: racism and poverty. The problem of race touched all Southerners, from oppressed former slaves to anxious white farmers and city dwellers. Poverty, especially the bleak agricultural poverty characteristic of the South, intensified the already severe problem of race. These twin cauldrons finally boiled over in the 1890s, when more than one hundred and fifty blacks were lynched per year, and collapsing farm prices drove many thousands of families—black and white—into bankruptcy.

The Cotton States Exposition of Industry and the Arts, held in Atlanta in 1895, was designed to address the problem of poverty. Mainly the brainchild of Atlanta publishers and bankers, the exposition made much of the prospects for railroad expansion, iron and textile manufacturing, and lumber and tobacco processing. It was hoped their success would reduce the South's unhappy dependence on agriculture and tie the region to the rest of industrial America. But the explosive issue of race also loomed. To address it, the exposition organizers, almost as an afterthought, invited Booker T. Washington, head of the Tuskegee Institute, a black vocational school in Tuskegee, Alabama, to speak to the mostly white exposition gathering. The exposition produced only a slight effect on Southern industrialization—manufacturing did not become widespread there until the 1920s and industrial prosperity has barely arrived even today. Washington's speech, however, was of major importance. His moderate message, accommodating tone, and stress on business and hard work generally pleased his listeners, who marked him as a worthy spokesman for his race. His reputation soon spread to the white North and to blacks as well. Thus, almost overnight, Washington became a prominent figure whose message mattered to everyone, especially in the South.

Not everyone agreed with Washington's approach. Black intellectuals and reformers still found their inspiration in Frederick Douglass, the great abolitionist and stalwart of Radical Reconstruction and equal rights. In their eyes, Washington's acceptance of disfranchisement and segregation seemed a betrayal. They thought his refusal to condemn lynching was a surrender and viewed his influence as mostly negative.

One of the most forceful of these critics was Ida B. Wells, a Chicago woman born to Mississippi slaves. Wells's *A Red Record,* excerpted below, told the gruesome story of antiblack violence in the South in persuasive, compelling terms. It thus formed an important counterpoint to Washington's conservative views.

Ida B. Wells was born a slave in Holly Springs, Mississippi, in 1862. She was educated in a freedmen's school, became a teacher herself, and eventually moved to Memphis, Tennessee, where she taught school and attended Fisk University. She turned to journalism in 1891 after losing her teaching post for refusing to give up her seat in a "whites-only" railroad car. When she wrote against antiblack violence, whites retaliated by burning her newspaper office. She left the South in 1892, in time marrying Ferdinand Barnett, a prominent black Chicagoan. A tireless writer and speaker for both women's and black's rights, Wells encouraged the Niagara Movement, a 1909 initiative of W. E. B. Du Bois and other militants opposed to the Tuskegee Machine. She refused to support its successor organization, the National Association for the Advancement of Colored People (NAACP), on the grounds that it was too moderate. She died in Chicago in 1931.

**Questions to Consider.** Why did Ida B. Wells go to such enormous pains in *A Red Record* to establish the record, from white sources, of antiblack atrocities in the post–Civil War South? For whom does she appear to have been writing? Were there models elsewhere in American society for this kind of "exposé" journalism? In this excerpt, she also takes care to refute the arguments given by white Southerners to justify the violence. Do these passages constitute an attack on paternalism— male chauvinism—as well as on racism? If Wells wrote, as she said, "in no spirit of vindictiveness," why did whites burn her newspaper office for printing similar stories? Was vindictiveness inherent in the material, bound inevitably to provoke outrage and assault? What strategies did Wells devise to avoid this?

# A Red Record (1895)

### IDA B. WELLS

Not all nor nearly all of the murders done by white men, during the past thirty years in the South, have come to light, but the statistics as gathered and preserved by white men, and which have not been questioned, show that

Ida B. Wells, *A Red Record: Tabulated Statistics and Alleged Causes of Lynchings in the United States, 1892–1893–1894* (Chicago, n.d.), 9–15, 20, 43, 45–48.

**Four sharecroppers hanging from a tree in Russellville, Kentucky, 1908.** Their "crime" was to express sympathy for a black man who had killed his white employer in self-defense. Thousands of black lynching victims died the same way, prompting the anti-lynching crusade of Ida B. Wells and other reformers. (Gilman Paper Company Collection)

during these years more than ten thousand Negroes have been killed in cold blood, without the formality of judicial trial and legal execution. And yet, as evidence of the absolute impunity with which the white man dares to kill a Negro, the same record shows that during all these years, and for all these murders only three white men have been tried, convicted, and executed. As no white man has been lynched for the murder of colored people, these three executions are the only instances of the death penalty being visited upon white men for murdering Negroes.

Naturally enough the commission of these crimes began to tell upon the public conscience, and the Southern white man, as a tribute to the nineteenth century civilization, was in a manner compelled to give excuses for his barbarism.

The first excuse given to the civilized world for the murder of unoffending Negroes was the necessity of the white man to repress and stamp out alleged "race riots." For years immediately succeeding the war there was an appalling slaughter of colored people, and the wires usually conveyed to northern people and the world the intelligence, first, that an insurrection was being planned by Negroes, which, a few hours later, would prove to have been vigorously resisted by white men, and controlled with a resulting loss of several killed and wounded. It was always a remarkable feature in these insurrections and riots that only Negroes were killed during the rioting, and that all the white men escaped unharmed. . . .

Then came the second excuse, which had its birth during the turbulent times of reconstruction. By an amendment to the Constitution the Negro was given the right of franchise, and, theoretically at least, his ballot became his invaluable emblem of citizenship. In a government "of the people, for the people, and by the people," the Negro's vote became an important factor in all matters of state and national politics. But this did not last long. The southern white man would not consider that the Negro had any right which a white man was bound to respect, and the idea of a republican form of government in the southern states grew into general contempt.

The white man's victory soon became complete by fraud, violence, intimidation and murder. The franchise vouchsafed to the Negro grew to be a "barren ideality," and regardless of numbers, the colored people found themselves voiceless in the councils of those whose duty it was to rule. With no longer the fear of "Negro Domination" before their eyes, the white man's second excuse became valueless. With the Southern governments all subverted and the Negro actually eliminated from all participation in state and national elections, there could be no longer an excuse for killing Negroes to prevent "Negro Domination."

Brutality still continued; Negroes were whipped, scourged, exiled, shot and hung whenever and wherever it pleased the white man so to treat them, and as the civilized world with increasing persistency held the white people of the South to account for its outlawry, the murderers invented the third excuse—that Negroes had to be killed to avenge their assaults upon women. There could be framed no possible excuse more harmful to the Negro and more unanswerable if true in its sufficiency for the white man.

Humanity abhors the assailant of womanhood, and this charge upon the Negro at once placed him beyond the pale of human sympathy. With such unanimity, earnestness, and apparent candor was this charge made and reiterated that the world has accepted the story that the Negro is a monster which the Southern white man has painted him. . . .

A word as to the charge itself. In considering the third reason assigned by the Southern white people for the butchery of blacks, the question must be asked, what the white man means when he charges the black man with rape. Does he mean the crime which the statutes of the civilized states describe as such? Not by any means. With the Southern white man, any mésalliance existing between a white woman and a black man is a sufficient foundation for the charge of rape. The Southern white man says that it is impossible for a voluntary alliance to exist between a white woman and a colored man, and therefore, the fact of an alliance is a proof of force. In numerous instances where colored men have been lynched on the charge of rape, it was positively known at the time of lynching, and indisputably proven after the victim's death, that the relationship sustained between the man and woman was voluntary and clandestine, and that in no court of law could even the charge of assault have been successfully maintained.

It was for the assertion of this fact, in the defense of her own race, that the writer hereof became an exile; her property destroyed and her return to her home forbidden under penalty of death. . . .

But threats cannot suppress the truth, and while the Negro suffers the soul deformity, resultant from two and a half centuries of slavery, he is no more guilty of this vilest of all vile charges than the white man who would blacken his name.

During all the years of slavery, no such charge was ever made, not even during the dark days of the rebellion, when the white man, following the fortunes of war went to do battle for the maintenance of slavery. While the master was away fighting to forge the fetters upon the slave, he left his wife and children with no protectors save the Negroes themselves. And yet during those years of trust and peril, no Negro proved recreant to his trust and no white man returned to a home that had been despoiled.

Likewise during the period of alleged "insurrection," and alarming "race riots," it never occurred to the white man, that his wife and children were in danger of assault. Nor in the Reconstruction era, when the hue and cry was against "Negro Domination," was there ever a thought that the domination would ever contaminate a fireside or strike to death the virtue of womanhood. . . .

In his remarkable apology for lynching, Bishop Haygood, of Georgia, says: "No race, not the most savage, tolerates the rape of women, but it may be said without reflection upon any other people that the Southern people are now and always have been most sensitive concerning the honor of their women—their mothers, wives, sisters and daughters." It is not the purpose of this defense to say one word against the white women of the South. Such need not be said, but it is their misfortune that the chivalrous white men of that section, in order to escape the deserved execration of the civilized world, should shield themselves by their cowardly and infamously false excuse, and call into question that very honor about which their distinguished priestly apologist claims they are most sensitive. To justify their own barbarism they assume a chivalry which they do not possess. . . .

When emancipation came to the Negroes, there arose in the northern part of the United States an almost divine sentiment among the noblest, purest and best white women of the North, who felt called to a mission to educate and Christianize the millions of southern ex-slaves. From every nook and corner of the North, brave young white women answered that call and left their cultured homes, their happy associations and their lives of ease, and with heroic determination went to the South to carry light and truth to the benighted blacks. It was a heroism no less than that which calls for volunteers for India, Africa, and the Isles of the sea. To educate their unfortunate charges; to teach them the Christian virtues and to inspire in them the moral sentiments manifest in their own lives, these young women braved dangers whose record reads more like fiction than fact. They became social outlaws in the South. The peculiar sensitiveness of the southern white men for women, never shed its protecting influence about them. No friendly word from their own race cheered them in their work; no hospitable doors gave them the companionship like that from which they had come. No chivalrous white man doffed his hat in honor or respect. They were "Nigger teachers"— unpardonable offenders in the social ethics of the South, and were insulted, persecuted and ostracized, not by Negroes, but by the white manhood which boasts of its chivalry toward women.

And yet these northern women worked on, year after year, unselfishly, with a heroism which amounted almost to martyrdom. Threading their way through dense forests, working in schoolhouse, in the cabin and in the church, thrown at all times and in all places among the unfortunate and lowly Negroes, whom they had come to find and to serve, these northern women, thousands and thousands of them, have spent more than a quarter of a century in giving to the colored people their splendid lessons for home and heart and soul. Without protection, save that which innocence gives to every good woman, they went about their work, fearing no assault and suffering none. . . . Before the world adjudges the Negro a moral monster, a vicious assailant of womanhood and a menace to the sacred precints of home, the colored people ask the consideration of the silent record of gratitude, respect, protection, and devotion of the millions of the race in the South, to the thousands of northern white women who have served as teachers and missionaries since the war. . . .

These pages are written in no spirit of vindictiveness, for all who give the subject consideration must concede that far too serious is the condition of that civilized government in which the spirit of unrestrained outlawry constantly increases in violence, and casts its blight over a continually growing area of territory. We plead not for the colored people alone, but for all victims of the terrible injustice which puts men and women to death without form of law. During the year 1894, there were 132 persons executed in the United States by due form of law, while in the same year, 197 persons were put to death by mobs who gave the victims no opportunity to make a lawful defense. No comment need be made upon a condition of public sentiment responsible for such alarming results.

# 9

## Bearing Gifts

⬛══⬛══⬛

Nativist bigotry was widespread in turn-of-the-century America, attaching itself with special force to immigrants from Eastern or Catholic Europe and perhaps most venomously to Jews. Anti-Semitism was a powerful current from czarist Russia to the democratic United States in the late nineteenth century, intensifying in the United States with the beginning of large-scale Jewish immigration in the 1880s. Thereafter, anti-Semitism emerged in all regions, classes, and parties. Resort hotels and exclusive men's clubs barred Jewish businessmen, and upper-class colleges established quota systems. Small-town Midwesterners and Southern farmers criticized not just Wall Street bankers but international Jewish bankers. Radical writers like Jack London cast a racist net that snared Jews as well as blacks. Even urban Catholic immigrants, who themselves experienced religious and nativist discrimination, harassed the "Christ-killers" and "Shylocks" who shared their ethnic slums.

Spokespersons for the various immigrant groups labored hard to counter nativist bigotry. They challenged stereotypes where they could, chiefly by publicizing their group's successes, including successful examples of Americanization. They also tried to portray the group's distinctive characteristics in positive terms, stressing how the country would benefit from Italian musical genius, for example, or Polish religious fervor. The Jewish community had no finer advocate than Mary Antin, a young writer and political activist whose speech before a New York convention of the General Federation of Women's Clubs is excerpted below.

Mary Antin was born in Russia in 1881 and emigrated with her parents to the United States in 1894. When she was still a teenager, Antin wrote her first book—in Yiddish—about the Jewish immigrant experience. After studying at Teachers College and Barnard College in New York City, she published *The Promised Land* (1912), perhaps our most beautiful version of the immigrant saga. An ardent socialist and union supporter, Antin continued to write and lecture on the subject of immigration; she was a notable opponent of congressional efforts to pass restrictive immigration laws. She died in Suffern, New York, on May 15, 1949.

**Questions to Consider.** Why didn't Mary Antin argue for the value of Jewish immigration by offering case studies, as immigrant defenders sometimes did, of successful individual Jews? What point was she trying to make by implicitly reinforcing a stereotype about Jews—that as a group they produced a disproportionate number of scholars, lawyers, and debaters? How did she attempt to connect the discussion about Jews and the law with her discussion later about the organization of the clothing industry? Was she right to argue that the passion for justice was fundamental to being a Jew, so that Jews were, in a sense, heirs to the "Spirit of '76" and therefore naturally American? What were the "false gods" Antin referred to in her final sentence?

★══★══★

# Russian Jews (1916)

### MARY ANTIN

On the whole the Russian immigrant in this country is the Jewish immigrant, since we are the most numerous group out of Russia. But to speak for the Jews—the most misunderstood people in the whole of history—ten minutes, in which to clear away 2,000 years of misunderstanding! Your President has probably in this instance, as in other instances, been guided by some inspiration, the source of which none of us may know. I was called by name long before your President notified me that she would call me to this assembly. I was called by name to say what does the Jew bring to America—by a lady from Philadelphia. Miss Repplier, not long ago, in an article in her inimitable fashion, called things by their name, and sometimes miscalled them, spoke of "the Jew in America who has received from us so much and has given us so little." This comment was called down by something that I had said about certain things in American life that did not come up to the American standard. "The Jew who has given so little." Tonight I am the Jew—you are the Americans. Let us look over these things.

What do we bring you besides our poverty and our rags? Men, women, and children—the stuff that nations are built of. What sort of men and women? I shall not seek to tire you with a list of shining names of Jewish notables. If you want to know who's who among the Jews, I refer you to your biographical dictionary. You are as familiar as I am with the name of Jews who shine in the professions, who have done notable service to the state, in politics, in diplomacy, and where you will. . . .

You know as well as I what numbers of Jewish youth are always taking high ranks, high honors in the schools, colleges and universities. You know

General Federation of Women's Clubs, *Thirteenth Biennial Convention* (New York, 1916).

as well as I do in what numbers our people crowd your lecture halls and your civic centers, in all those places where the spiritual wine of life may be added to our daily bread. These are things that you know. I don't want you to be thinking of any list of Jewish notables.

A very characteristic thing of Jewish life is the democracy of virtue that you find in every Jewish community. We Jews have never depended for our salvation on the supreme constellations of any chosen ones. . . . Our shining ones were to us always examples by means of which the whole community was to be disciplined to what was Jewish virtue.

Take a group of Jews anywhere, and you will have the essence of their Jewishness, though there be not present one single shining luminary. The average Jew presents the average of whatsoever there is of Jewish virtue, talent or capacity.

What is this peculiar Jewish genius? If I must sum it up in a word, I will say that the Jewish genius is a love for living out the things that they believe. What do we believe? We Jews believe that the world is a world of law. Law is another name for our God, and the quest after the law, the formulation of it, has always permeated our schools, and the incorporation of the laws of life, as our scholars noted it down, has been the chief business of the Jewish masses. No wonder that when we come to America, a nation founded as was our ancient nation, a nation founded on law and principle, on an ideal— no wonder that we so quickly find ourselves at home, that presently we fall into the regulation habit of speaking of America as our own country, until Miss Repplier reproves us, and then we do it no more. I used formerly when speaking of American sins, tribulations, etc., I used to speak of them as "ours"; no more—your sins. I have been corrected.

Why then, now that we have come here, to this nation builded on the same principle as was our nation, no wonder that we so quickly seize on the fundamentals. We make no virtue of the fact—it is the Jewishness in us—that has been our peculiar characteristics, our habit. We need no one from outside of our ranks to remind us of the goodly things we have found and taken from your hands. We have been as eloquent as any that has spoken in appreciation of what we have found here, of liberty, justice, and a square deal. We give thanks. We have rendered thanks, we Jews, some of you are witnesses. We know the value of the gifts that we have found here.

Who shall know the flavor of bread if not they that have gone hungry, and we, who have been for centuries without the bread of justice, we know the full flavor of American justice, liberty, and equality.

To formulate and again formulate, and criticise the law,—what do our Rabbis in the Ghetto besides the study of law? To them used to come our lawyers, to our Rabbis, not to find the way how to get around the law, but to be sure that we were walking straight in the path indicated by the law. So today in America we are busy in the same fashion.

The Jewish virtues, such as they are, are widespread throughout the Jewish masses. Here in New York City is congregated the largest Jewish community in the whole world, and what is true of the Jews of New York, is true of the Jews of America, and the Jews of the world. If I speak of the characteristics of Jewish life on the East side, one of the great characteristics is its restlessness in physical form, due to the oppression of city life, and the greater restlessness, due to the unquenchable, turbulent quest for the truth, and more truth. You know that the East side of New York is a very spawning ground for debate, and debating clubs. There are more boys and girls in debating clubs than in boys' basket ball teams, or baseball teams. I believe in boys playing baseball, but I also believe in that peculiar enthusiasm of our Jewish people for studying the American law, just as they used to study their own law, to see whether any of the American principles find incorporation in American institutions and habits. We are the critics. We are never satisfied with things as they are. Go out and hear the boys and girls. They like to go to school and learn the names of liberty, and equality and justice, and after school they gather in their debating circles and discuss what might be the meaning of these names, and what is their application to life. That is the reason there is so much stirring, rebellion, and protest that comes out of the East side.

In the great labor movement, it is the effort of the people to arrive at a program of economic justice that shall parallel the political justice. Consider for a moment the present condition of the garment-making trade. That is a Jewish trade. Ages ago when the lords of the nations, among whom we lived, were preventing us from engaging in other occupations, they thrust into the hands of our people the needle, and the needle was our tool, why through the needle we have still thought to give expression to the Jewish genius in our life.

This immense clothing industry—a Jewish industry primarily—is today in a better condition as regards unionization, is further on the road to economic justice than any other great industry that you could name. Mind you, the sweatshop we found here when we came here. We took it just as it was, but the barring of the sweatshop and the organization of the clothing industry in such fashion that it is further in advance, more nearly on a basis that affords just treatment to all concerned—that has been the contribution of our tailor men and tailor women. We have done this thing. . . . The Protocol[1] is a piece of machinery for bringing about justice in this great industry. We have invented that thing, we Jews. We are putting it in operation, we are fighting for its perpetuation. Whatsoever good comes from it, we have done it. . . .

Consider us, if you will, in the most barbarous sense, but I point to this as our great contribution, we are always protesting, and if you want to know the value of that contribution, I remind you that the formulae of the rights of men, which was a criticism of things as they used to be, and a formularizing of things as they ought to be, was at least as efficient as all the armies of the continent put together in the revolutionary war. The Spirit of '76 is the spirit of criticism. We Jews in America are busy at our ancient business of pulling down false gods.

---

1. **The Protocol:** A labor–management agreement recognizing union rights and providing for improved working conditions in the garment industry.—*Eds.*

# 10

## CLOSING THE DOOR

For most of its history the United States maintained an unrestrictive policy toward immigration from Europe, allowing the assimilation of a steady flow of nineteenth-century immigrants, particularly from Germany, Ireland, and Britain. People spoke with some pride of the U.S. as a "nation of immigrants." But this was about to change. The coming of so many millions of immigrants who were neither Protestant nor northern European caused growing alarm among "old-stock" Americans, who associated the newcomers with various social ills.

The first broad twentieth-century effort to curtail immigration was the Literacy Test of 1917. But this did not impose a cap on total immigration or differentiate according to national origins. In 1921, Congress limited immigration from any country to 3 percent of that country's proportion of the American population as of 1910, which still allowed many newcomers from Southern and Eastern Europe. By 1924 the public favored additional restrictive measures. The National Origins Act of 1924 established a quota system based on the U.S. population of 1890 and a total cap of 164,000 persons from outside the Western Hemisphere. (A separate act banned Asians altogether.) The 1924 Act brought the long tradition of unrestricted entry by Europeans to a definitive close.

Below are excerpts from the speeches of three supporters of the 1924 Act. The national-origins standard, though modified, persisted until 1965, when Congress began to exempt refugees, relatives, and occupational skills from the caps and quotas.

**Questions to Consider.** In what specific ways, according to these supporters of the 1924 Act, did recent immigrants differ from those who arrived before 1890? Why did they endanger American society? Were the dangerous traits of the new immigrants a reflection of learned non-American attitudes that might change over time? Or were they inherent traits that would never change? In what ways did immigrant political attitudes worry supporters of the restriction bill? If the newcomers' political attitudes had been different, would supporters of the restriction bill have changed their vote? In the eyes of restriction supporters, what two recent developments within the U.S. itself made the problem greater? What part of the country did these three Senators represent? Does that help explain their antagonism to Southern and Eastern Europeans?

★▬▬★▬▬★

# Senate Speeches on Immigration Restriction (1924)

*Mr. Shields.* [Tenn.] Mr. President, the future immigration policy of the United States is challenging the most serious attention of the American people. They demand that this policy be changed from one of practically the open door to all peoples of the world to one of rigid restriction if not absolute prohibition of immigration. . . . The immigrants we are receiving to-day are of different character from those that came in the early history of our country, and the great numbers in which they are arriving is a cause of serious alarm and menaces the purity of the blood, the homogeneity, and the supremacy of the American people and the integrity and perpetuity of our representative form of government. . . .

The great majority of the present-day immigrants do not, like the old ones, distribute themselves over the States, mingle with and become absorbed in the great body of American people, and build homes, cultivate lands, or, in other words, become permanent and loyal American citizens. They do not have the social characteristics of the original stock. They are not assimilable and do not seem to desire to be assimilated. They bring with them lower standards of living and labor conditions and strange customs and ideals of social justice and government. Civil and religious liberty do not attract them, but they come here to enjoy our prosperity and possess the country our forefathers redeemed from the wilderness and improved as none other in the world.

They largely congregate in cities and form communities of their several foreign nationalities; they speak their own languages and train their children to do so. . . . [M]ore than half of them remain unnaturalized and owe allegiance to foreign governments. . . . There are whole wards in New York and Chicago where the English language is seldom heard and no newspapers printed in it read. . . .

Mr. President, these undesirable immigrants are seriously endangering the peace and tranquillity of our people and the supremacy of our laws and Government. . . . There are many who are intolerant of all restraint and all law and would introduce into this country the wildest doctrines of

*Congressional Record,* April 16–28, 1924.

Bolshevism. We get the majority of the communists, the I.W.W.'s, the dy-
namiters, and the assassins of public officers from the ranks of the present-
day immigrant. . . .

*Mr. Sheppard.* [Texas] . . . As long as a stream of migrating peoples rushes
over the gangways of the ships that bear them from other lands to this they
produce a swirling, turbulent, disordered mass that is never permitted to
reach an angle of racial, political, intellectual, or spiritual repose. While fer-
tile lands in public or in private possession remained available on fairly easy
terms and while the cities were still small the new accessions were distributed with a minimum of disturbance and maladjustment. With the disap-
pearance, however, of the public-land frontier, the rise in price and the
almost complete occupation of the habitable, cultivable, and readily obtain-
able areas until they are beyond the reach of the masses, who have only their
labor to exchange, the extensive concentration of people in the factory
districts and the cities, a condition has developed whereby the American
standard of living . . . is being seriously imperiled, and whereby the discord
and the turmoil of former years are rendered tenfold more dangerous and
intense. . . .

*Mr. Heflin.* [Alabama] . . . Mr. President, down at Fort Mims, in my State . . .
there was a fort in which the white people of that section dwelt . . . [T]here
was a big gate in the wall around the fort, and when they closed that mighty
gate to this walled-in place they were safe from the Indians. But they grew
careless and indifferent, as some Americans have done on this question. One
day . . . one of the girls living in the houses within this inclosure, looked down
and saw the big gate open, and she said, "Who left that gate open?" They
said, "That don't make any difference. There isn't an Indian in 50 miles of
here." . . . Just then a little white boy . . . ran through the open gate and said,
"I saw a man down by the river side with red paint on his face and feathers in
his hair." They screamed with one voice, "Indians! Close the gates!" They
started with a rush to the gate, but the Red Eagle, with his Creek warriors,
had already entered. It was too late! Too late! . . . With the exception of two or
three prisoners, they massacred the whole white population at Fort Mims.

I am appealing to the Senate of the United States to close the gates, close
them now while we can. If we do not close them now, the time will come
when we will be unable to close them at all. And in that sad day we will cry
in vain, "Close the gates."

**The conveyor-belt assembly line at a Ford factory** in Highland Park, Michigan, just after World War I. (Brown Brothers)

CHAPTER THREE

# Economic Growth and Social Reform

# 11

## PRODUCTION AND WEALTH

✪━━✪━━✪

During the late nineteenth century the United States experienced remarkable industrial development. In 1860 it was largely a nation of farms, villages, small businesses, and small-scale manufacturing establishments; by 1900 it had become a nation of cities, machines, factories, offices, shops, and powerful business combinations. Between 1860 and 1900, railroad trackage increased, annual production of coal rose steadily, iron and steel production soared, oil refining flourished, and development of electric power rapidly expanded. "There has never been in the history of civilization," observed economist Edward Atkinson in 1891, "a period, or a place, or a section of the earth in which science and invention have worked such progress or have created such opportunity for material welfare as in these United States in the period which has elapsed since the end of the Civil War." By the end of the century, America's industrial production exceeded that of Great Britain and Germany combined, and the United States was exporting huge quantities of farm and factory goods to all parts of the world. The country had become one of the richest and most powerful nations in history.

More than any other single element, steel permitted and laid the foundation for industrialization. The process of steel production powered industrial development, because it was from steel that railroad tracks and cars, bridges and girders, machines and farm equipment, elevators, ships, and automobiles were all manufactured. One key to rising steel production was the adaptation of the so-called Bessemer process to American conditions. The emergence of mass steel manufacture by this method involved a dynamic interplay between foreign and domestic production ideas, patent law, firm capitalization and competition, creative marketing, and, perhaps most important, constant technical improvement on the factory floor.

At the other end of the production scale was Andrew Carnegie, the "King of Steel." Carnegie liked to boast of the accomplishments of efficient business organization in the American steel industry, as he did in the excerpt below from *Triumphant Democracy* (1886), a best seller. "Two pounds of ironstone mined upon Lake Superior and transported nine hundred miles to Pittsburgh; one pound and a half of coal mined and manufactured into coke, and transported to Pittsburgh; one-half pound of lime, mined and transported to Pittsburgh; a small amount of manganese ore mined in Virginia and brought to Pittsburgh—and these four pounds of materials manufactured into one pound of steel, for which the consumer pays one cent."

Carnegie preached what he called a "gospel of wealth." His gospel emphasized individual initiative, private property, competition, and the accumulation of wealth in the hands of those with superior ability and energy. But in the last quarter of the nineteenth century, less than 1 percent of the population controlled more than 50 percent of the nation's wealth, the highest concentration in U.S. history up to that time, and the benefits of spectacular industrial growth were hardly shared equitably. The nation had been built on the assumption that all men were created equal, and most Americans took for granted that in a republican society property and power would be widely distributed. Yet the disparity between the very rich and the very poor had grown extreme.

Thoughtful observers, troubled by the concentration of wealth and power in the hands of so few, raised their voices in protest. Andrew Carnegie was unusual in that, on the one hand, he defended the absolute right of the entrepreneur to accumulate wealth and also the Social Darwinist notion of "survival of the fittest." But at the same time, like some of the radicals of his era, Carnegie argued that the rich should dispense their wealth in ways that would benefit society. The "man who dies rich," he asserted, "dies disgraced."

Andrew Carnegie, the son of a handloom weaver, was born in Scotland in 1835. With his family, he moved to Allegheny, Pennsylvania, at the age of twelve and got a job in a textile mill at $1.20 a week. During this period he studied telegraphy, a skill that landed him a position as the personal secretary and telegrapher of a leading raiload executive. Carnegie was himself a railroad executive for a time, and then amassed a fortune selling bonds, dealing in oil, and building bridges. In 1873 he concentrated his efforts on steel and gradually built his Carnegie Steel Company into a massive industrial giant. In 1901 he sold the firm to J. P. Morgan, who made it the core of the world's first billion-dollar company, the United States Steel Corporation. Over the next two decades Carnegie gave away some $350 million for libraries and other public works. He died in Lenox, Massachusetts, in 1919.

**Questions to Consider.** The excerpt from *Triumphant Democracy* is typical of the many articles and books Andrew Carnegie wrote celebrating the American system. Why did Carnegie think life "has become vastly better worth living" than it had been a century before? What particular aspects of American life did he single out for special mention? In what ways did he think life in the United States was better than life in Europe? Was he writing mainly about the life of the average or of the well-to-do American? How did he relate America's economic achievements to democracy?

■==■==■

# Triumphant Democracy (1886)

### ANDREW CARNEGIE

A community of toilers with an undeveloped continent before them, and destitute of the refinements and elegancies of life—such was the picture presented by the Republic sixty years ago. Contrasted with that of today, we might almost conclude that we were upon another planet and subject to different primary conditions. The development of an unequaled transportation system brings the products of one section to the doors of another, the tropical fruits of Florida and California to Maine, and the ice of New England to the Gulf States. Altogether life has become vastly better worth living than it was a century ago.

Among the rural communities, the change in the conditions is mainly seen in the presence of labor-saving devices, lessening the work in house and field. Mowing and reaping machines, horse rakes, steam plows and threshers, render man's part easy and increase his productive power. Railroads and highways connect him with the rest of the world, and he is no longer isolated or dependent upon his petty village. Markets for his produce are easy of access, and transportation swift and cheap. If the roads throughout the country are yet poor compared with those of Europe, the need of good roads has been rendered less imperative by the omnipresent railroad. It is the superiority of the iron highway in America which has diverted attention from the country roads. It is a matter of congratulation, however, that this subject is at last attracting attention. Nothing would contribute so much to the happiness of life in the country as such perfect roads as those of Scotland. It is a difficult problem, but its solution will well repay any amount of expenditure necessary. [British historian Thomas] Macaulay's test of the civilization of a people—the condition of their roads—must be interpreted, in this age of steam, to include railroads. Communication between great cities is now cheaper and more comfortable than in any other country. Upon the principal railway lines, the cars—luxurious drawing-rooms by day, and sleeping chambers by night—are ventilated by air, warmed and filtered in winter, and cooled in summer. Passenger steamers upon the lakes and rivers are of gigantic size, and models of elegance.

Andrew Carnegie, *Triumphant Democracy* (Scribner's, New York, 1886), 164–183.

It is in the cities that the change from colonial conditions is greatest. Most of these—indeed all, excepting those upon the Atlantic coast—have been in great measure the result of design instead of being allowed, like Topsy, to "just grow." In these modern days cities are laid out under definite, far-seeing plans; consequently the modern city presents symmetry of form unknown in mediaeval ages. The difference is seen by contrasting the crooked cowpaths of old Boston with the symmetrical, broad streets of Washington or Denver. These are provided with parks at intervals for breathing spaces; amply supplied with pure water, in some cases at enormous expense; the most modern ideas are embodied in their sanitary arrangements; they are well lighted, well policed, and the fire departments are very efficient. In these modern cities an extensive fire is rare. The lessening danger of this risk is indicated by the steady fall in the rate of fire insurance.

The variety and quality of the food of the people of America excels that found elsewhere, and is a constant surprise to Europeans visiting the States. The Americans are the best-fed people on the globe. Their dress is now of the richest character—far beyond that of any other people, compared class for class. The comforts of the average American home compare favorably with those of other lands, while the residences of the wealthy classes are unequaled. The first-class American residence of today in all its appointments excites the envy of the foreigner. One touch of the electric button calls a messenger; two bring a telegraph boy; three summon a policeman; four give the alarm of fire. Telephones are used to an extent undreamt of in Europe, the stables and other out-buildings being connected with the mansion; and the houses of friends are joined by the talking wire almost as often as houses of business. Speaking tubes connect the drawing-room with the kitchen; and the dinner is brought up "piping hot" by a lift. Hot air and steam pipes are carried all over the house; and by the turning of a tap the temperature of any room is regulated to suit the convenience of the occupant. A passenger lift is common. The electric light is an additional home comfort. Indeed, there is no palace or great mansion in Europe with half the conveniences and scientific appliances which characterize the best American mansions. New York Central Park is no unworthy rival of Hyde Park and the Bois de Boulogne in its display of fine equipages; and in winter the hundreds of graceful sleighs dashing along the drives form a picture. The opera-houses, theatres, and public halls of the country excel in magnificence those of other lands, if we except the latter constructions in Paris and Vienna, with which the New York, Philadelphia, and Chicago opera-houses rank. The commercial exchanges, and the imposing structures of the life insurance companies, newspaper buildings, hotels, and many edifices built by wealthy firms, not only in New York but in the cities of the West, never fail to excite the Europeans' surprise. The postal system is equal in every respect to that of Europe. Mails are taken up by express trains, sorted on board, and dropped at all important points without stopping. Letters are delivered several times a day in every considerable town, and a ten-cent special delivery stamp insures delivery at once by special messenger in the large cities. The uniform rate of postage for all distances, often exceeding three thousand miles, is only two cents . . . per ounce.

In short, the conditions of life in American cities may be said to have approximated those of Europe during the sixty years of which we are speaking. Year by year, as the population advances, the general standard of comfort in the smaller Western cities rises to that of the East. Herbert Spencer [an English philosopher] was astonished beyond measure at what he saw in American cities. "Such books as I had looked into," said he, "had given me no adequate idea of the immense developments of material civilization which I have found everywhere. The extent, wealth, and magnificence of your cities, and especially the splendors of New York, have altogether astonished me. Though I have not visited the wonder of the West, Chicago, yet some of your minor modern places, such as Cleveland, have sufficiently amazed me by the marvelous results of one generation's activity. Occasionally, when I have been in places of some ten thousand inhabitants, where the telephone is in general use, I have felt somewhat ashamed of our own unenterprising towns, many of which, of fifty thousand inhabitants and more, make no use of it."

Such is the Democracy; such its conditions of life. In the presence of such a picture can it be maintained that the rule of the people is subversive of government and religion? Where have monarchical institutions developed a community so delightful in itself, so intelligent, so free from crime or pauperism—a community in which the greatest good of the greatest number is so fully attained, and one so well calculated to foster the growth of self-respecting men—which is the end civilization seeks?

> "For ere man made us citizens
> God made us men."

The republican is necessarily self-respecting, for the laws of his country begin by making him a man indeed, the equal of other men. The man who most respects himself will always be found the man who most respects the rights and feelings of others.

The rural democracy of America could be as soon induced to sanction the confiscation of the property of its richer neighbors, or to vote for any violent or discreditable measure, as it could be led to surrender the President for a king. Equal laws and privileges develop all the best and noblest characteristics, and these always lead in the direction of the Golden Rule. These honest, pure, contented, industrious, patriotic people really do consider what they would have others do to them. They ask themselves what is fair and right. Nor is there elsewhere in the world so conservative a body of men; but then it is the equality of the citizen—just and equal laws—republicanism, they are resolved to conserve. To conserve these they are at all times ready to fight and, if need be, to die; for, to men who have once tasted the elixir of political equality, life under unequal conditions could possess no charm.

To every man is committed in some degree, as a sacred trust, the manhood of man. This he may not himself infringe or permit to be infringed by others. Hereditary dignities, political inequalities, do infringe the right of man, and hence are not to be tolerated. The true democrat must live the peer of his fellows, or die struggling to become so.

The American citizen has no further need to struggle, being in possession of equality under the laws in every particular. He has not travelled far in the path of genuine Democracy who would not scorn to enjoy a privilege which was not the common birthright of all his fellows.

# 12

# LABOR'S VISION

The decades following the Civil War brought an enormous expansion of activity in railroads, coal, steel, and other basic industries. This rapid rise in the development of America's natural resources was accompanied by a sharp rise in the country's per capita wealth and income and, in the long run, a higher standard of living for most people. But it resulted in other things as well: greater wealth and power for "capitalists," as the new leaders of industry were called; a deterioration in conditions for many workers; and a society repeatedly torn by class conflict.

The Noble Order of the Knights of Labor, formed as a secret workingmen's lodge in 1869, represented an early response to these trends. Secrecy seemed essential at first because of the hostility of employers toward labor unions. Not until 1881 did the Knights of Labor abandon secrecy and announce its objectives to the world. Its slogan was "An injury to one is the concern of all." The Knights took pride in their admission of all workers—regardless of race, sex, or level of skill—and in their moderate, public-spirited vision of a cooperative economic order. These factors, together with their support of successful railroad strikes, swelled the Knights of Labor membership rolls to nearly 800,000 by 1886. After that, however, a wave of antiradicalism, combined with internal problems and the loss of several bitter industrial struggles, sent membership plummeting. By 1900 the organization was gone. It was replaced by two other labor organizations: the American Federation of Labor (AFL), founded in 1886, which organized skilled labor and struck over wages and working conditions, and the Industrial Workers of the World (IWW), founded in 1905, which appealed to the unskilled and stood for industrial reorganization. The AFL, which opposed most of the Knights' principles, endured; the IWW, which shared many of them, did not.

The American Federation of Labor was a combination of national craft unions with an initial membership of about 140,000. It was the result of craft disagreement with the Knights of Labor partly over tactics and partly over leadership. The unions that constituted the AFL were central players in a nationwide campaign in support of an eight-hour workday. Centered in Chicago but spreading rapidly to other cities, the campaign (whose major statement appears below) culminated in a series of mass strikes and demonstrations on May 1, 1886. The campaign failed in its efforts to impose a uniform eight-hour day throughout American industry. It succeeded, however, in making a shortened workday one of the cardinal ongoing demands of union organizers and negotiators. When major breakthroughs in union representation and influence came during the 1930s and 1940s, eight hours—"nine to five" with an hour for lunch—became in fact the standard workday everywhere.

Samuel Gompers was the president of the AFL in 1886 and a key figure in the Eight-Hour Association. Gompers was a London-born cigar maker who emigrated to New York City with his parents at age thirteen. At first a strong socialist, he became a leader of the Cigar Makers' Union in the 1870s, moving it away from social and political reform and toward "pure and simple unionism" based on demands for higher wages, benefits, and security. Gompers was president of the AFL every year but one from 1886 to 1924. During this time, he built an organization that was both powerful and conservative—one that was hostile to radicalism, party alignments, and the admission of the unskilled. He died in San Antonio, Texas, in 1924.

**Questions to Consider.** In this May Day speech, what impression of American workers was Gompers eager to convey? What arguments did he use to try to make this point? What different arguments did he use to support the demand for an eight-hour workday? Which of these do you find most persuasive? Which do you find most surprising? What was Gompers's purpose in mentioning foreign countries, from England to China, so frequently in this speech? Gompers did not mention governmental action. How, then, did he hope to achieve a standard eight-hour day? May Day (May 1) became Labor Day across the entire industrializing world except for the United States, where in 1894 Congress, following the lead of certain New York trade unions, declared the first Monday in September as Labor Day, a legal holiday. Why might the U.S. government have picked a different day from the rest of the world?

# What Does the Working Man Want? (1890)

### SAMUEL GOMPERS

My friends, we have met here today to celebrate the idea that has prompted thousands of working-people of Louisville and New Albany to parade the streets . . . ; that prompts the toilers of Chicago to turn out by their fifty or

*Labor Tribune,* April 1890.

**Police provide** safe conduct to a streetcar during a New York City streetcar workers' strike, March 1883. (Library of Congress)

hundred thousand of men; that prompts the vast army of wage-workers in New York to demonstrate their enthusiasm and appreciation of the importance of this idea; that prompts the toilers of England, Ireland, Germany, France, Italy, Spain, and Austria to defy the manifestos of the autocrats of the world and say that on May the first, 1890, the wage-workers of the world will lay down their tools in sympathy with the wage-workers of America, to establish a principle of limitations of hours of labor to eight hours for sleep, eight hours for work, and eight hours for what we will.

It has been charged time and again that were we to have more hours of leisure we would merely devote it to debauchery, to the cultivation of vicious habits—in other words, that we would get drunk. I desire to say this in answer to that charge: As a rule, there are two classes in society who get drunk. One is the class who has no work to do in consequence of too much money; the other class, who also has no work to do, because it can't get any, and gets drunk on its face. I maintain that that class in our social life that exhibits the greatest degree of sobriety is that class who are able, by a fair number of hours of day's work to earn fair wages—not overworked. . . .

. . . They tell us that the eight-hour movement can not be enforced, for the reason that it must check industrial and commercial progress. I say that the history of this country, in its industrial and commercial relations, shows the reverse. I say that is the plane on which this question ought to be discussed—that is the social question. As long as they make this question an economic one, I am willing to discuss it with them. I would retrace every step I have taken to advance this movement did it mean industrial and commercial stagnation. But it does not mean that. It means greater prosperity; it means a greater degree of progress for the whole people; it means more advancement and intelligence, and a nobler race of people. . . .

They say they can't afford it. Is that true? Let us see for one moment. If a reduction in the hours of labor causes industrial and commercial ruination, it would naturally follow increased hours of labor would increase the prosperity, commercial and industrial. If that were true, England and America ought to be at the tail end, and China at the head of civilization.

Is it not a fact that we find laborers in England and the United States, where the hours are eight, nine and ten hours a day—do we not find that the employers and laborers are more successful? Don't we find them selling articles cheaper? We do not need to trust the modern moralist to tell us those things. In all industries where the hours of labor are long, there you will find the least development of the power of invention. Where the hours of labor are long, men are cheap, and where men are cheap there is no necessity for invention. How can you expect a man to work ten or twelve or fourteen hours at his calling and then devote any time to the invention of a machine or discovery of a new principle or force? If he be so fortunate as to be able to read a paper he will fall asleep before he has read through the second or third line.

Why, when you reduce the hours of labor, say an hour a day, just think what it means. Suppose men who work ten hours a day had the time lessened to nine, or men who work nine hours a day have it reduced to eight hours; what does it mean? It means millions of golden hours and opportunities for thought. Some men might say you will go to sleep. Well, some men might sleep sixteen hours a day; the ordinary man might try that, but he would soon find he could not do it long. He would have to do something. He would probably go to the theater one night, to a concert another night, but he could not do that every night. He would probably become interested in some study and the hours that have been taken from manual labor are devoted to mental labor, and the mental labor of one hour will produce for him more wealth than the physical labor of a dozen hours.

I maintain that this is a true proposition—that men under the short-hour system not only have opportunity to improve themselves, but to make a greater degree of prosperity for their employers. Why, my friends, how is it in China, how is it in Spain, how is it in India and Russia, how is it in Italy? Cast your eye throughout the universe and observe the industry that forces nature to yield up its fruits to man's necessities, and you will find that where the hours of labor are the shortest the progress of invention in machinery and the prosperity of the people are the greatest. It is the greatest impediment to progress to hire men cheaply. Wherever men are cheap, there you find the least degree of progress. It has only been under the great influence of our great republic, where our people have exhibited their great senses, that we can move forward, upward and onward, and are watched with interest in our movements of progress and reform. . . .

The man who works the long hours has no necessities except the barest to keep body and soul together, so he can work. He goes to sleep and dreams of work; he rises in the morning to go to work; he takes his frugal lunch to work; he comes home again to throw himself down on a miserable apology for a bed so that he can get that little rest that he may be able to go to work again. He is nothing but a veritable machine. He lives to work instead of working to live. . . .

My friends, you will find that it has been ascertained that there is more than a million of our brothers and sisters—able-bodied men and women—on the streets, and on the highways and byways of our country willing to work but who cannot find it. You know that it is the theory of our government that we can work or cease to work at will. It is only a theory. You know that it is only a theory and not a fact. It is true that we can cease to work when we want to, but I deny that we can work when we will, so long as there are a million idle men and women tramping the streets of our cities, searching for work. The theory that we can work or cease to work when we will is a delusion and a snare. It is a lie.

What we want to consider is, first, to make our employment more secure, and, secondly, to make wages more permanent, and, thirdly, to give these poor people a chance to work. The laborer has been regarded as a mere producing machine . . . but back of labor is the soul of man and honesty of purpose and aspiration. Now you can not, as the political economists and college professors, say that labor is a commodity to be bought and sold. I say we are American citizens with the heritage of all the great men who have stood before us; men who have sacrificed all in the cause except honor. . . . I say the labor movement is a fixed fact. It has grown out of the necessities of the people, and, although some may desire to see it fail, still the labor movement will be found to have a strong lodgment in the hearts of the people, and we will go on until success has been achieved!

# 13

## PROHIBITION AND REFORM

★▬▬★▬▬★

The Women's Christian Temperance Union (WCTU) arose from the "Women's Crusade" against the heavy drinking of alcoholic beverages in the early 1870s. Founded in Cincinnati in 1874, the WCTU at first advocated temperance—moderate drinking—but with the election of Frances Willard as president in 1879 shifted to a demand for outright prohibition. Although membership waxed and waned, in the late 1880s the organization had 150,000 members, making it the largest women's organization in the world. There were affiliates in the states and specialized "departments" that urged, for example, "scientific temperance instruction" in the schools (very successful for a time) and women's suffrage, which Willard and other leaders felt was essential if women were to be taken seriously and make their influence felt.

WCTU leaders saw the crusade against alcohol as a fight on behalf of the American family. They therefore quickly came to advocate much broader social goals than simply persuading people to quit drinking. In the 1880s, under Willard, these goals, included support for the eight-hour work day (good for families) and equal wages for men and women (good for women). Much of this reflected a sense that women were different from men and had special responsibilities for the health and well-being of the family. By the turn of the century, the more narrowly focused Anti-Saloon League, run by male ministers, was starting to displace the WCTU in the prohibition crusade, and the National American Woman Suffrage Association, working exclusively to gain the right to vote for women, was supplanting it in the suffrage movement. But the WCTU was the early driving force behind these causes, and in the run-up to the passage after World War I of the prohibition and suffrage amendments, the organization, with membership of nearly 300,000, contributed mightily to both causes.

Frances Willard was born in upstate New York in 1839 and grew up on a Wisconsin farm. She attended college, taught school, and was president of Evanston College for Women and a dean of women, early evidence of her leadership qualities. She became a convert to the anti-alcohol cause while assisting Dwight L. Moody, a famous Chicago evangelist, and she maintained close ties to the Protestant churches throughout her life. She served as president of the Women's Christian Temperance Union for almost 20 years, proving to be a powerful public speaker, a brilliant organizer and a role model for women reformers. She was keenly aware of the importance of politics, which led her to attend conventions of the male-only Prohibition party and meet with Republican stalwarts in rooms suffused (she wrote) with the "loathsome" stench of tobacco smoke and whiskey. An effort to unite the WCTU with the Knights of Labor and the Populist party came to naught, but at the time of her death in 1898, Willard was probably late nineteenth-century America's best-known woman. The document below is a passage from her 1889 autobiography.

**Questions to Consider.** What, according to Willard, were the main differences between men and women, and how did those differences show themselves in politics and reform? Are her arguments about the innate character of men and women still persuasive? To what did she attribute the growth and influence of the WCTU? How important to her was individual leadership—what she called "personality"? How significant for Willard was the "Christian" part of the organization's name? How did Christianity influence her goals?

★━━★━━★

# The Woman's Christian Temperance Union (1889)

### FRANCES WILLARD

Nothing is more suggestive in all the national gatherings of the Woman's Christian Temperance Union . . . than the wide difference between these meetings and any held by men. The beauty of decoration is specially noticeable; banners of silk, satin and velvet, usually made by the women themselves, adorn the wall; the handsome shields of states; the great vases bearing aloft grains, fruits and flowers; the moss-covered well with its old bucket; or the setting of a platform to present an interior as cozy and delightful as a parlor could afford, are features of the pleasant scene. The rapidity of movement with which business is conducted, the spontaneity of manner, the originality of plan, the perpetual freshness and ingenuity of the convention, its thousand unexpectednesses, its quips and turns, its wit and pathos, its impromptu eloquence and its perpetual good nature—all these

Frances E. Willard, *Glimpses of Fifty Years* (Woman's Temperance Publication Association, 1889), 263–281.

elements, brought into condensed view in the National Conventions, are an object-lesson of the new force and unique method that womanhood has contributed to the consideration of the greatest reform in Christendom. It is really . . . the home going forth into the world. Its manner is not that of the street, the court, the mart, or office; it is the manner of the home. Men take one line, and travel onward to success; with them discursiveness is at a discount. But women in the home must be mistresses, as well as maids of all work; they have learned well the lesson of unity in diversity; hence by inheritance and by environment, women are varied in their methods; they are born to be "branchers-out." Men have been in the organized temperance work not less than eighty years—women not quite fifteen. Men pursued it at first along the line of temperance, then total abstinence; license, then prohibition; while women have already over forty distinct departments of work, classified under the heads of preventive, educational, evangelistic, social, and legal. Women think in the concrete. The crusade showed them the drinking man, and they began upon him directly, to get him to sign the pledge and seek "the Lord behind the pledge." The crusade showed them the selling man, and they prayed over him and persuaded him to give up his bad business, often buying him out, and setting him up in the better occupation of baker, grocer, or keeper of the reading-room into which they converted his saloon after converting him from the error of his ways.

But oftentimes the drinking man went back to his cups, and the selling man fell from his grace; the first one declaring, "I can't break the habit I formed when a boy," and the last averring, "Somebody's bound to sell, and I might as well make the profit." Upon this the women, still with their concrete ways of thinking, said, "To be sure, we must train our boys, and not ours only, but everybody's; what institution reaches all?—the Public Schools." . . .

To the inane excuse of the seller that he might as well do it since somebody would, the quick and practical reply was, "To be sure; but suppose the people could be persuaded not to let anybody sell? why, then that would be God's answer to our crusade prayers." So they began with petitions to municipalities, to Legislatures and to Congress, laboriously gathering up, doubtless, not fewer than ten million names in the great aggregate, and through the fourteen years. Thus the Woman's Christian Temperance Union stands as the strongest bulwark of prohibition, state and national, by constitutional amendment and by statute. Meanwhile, it was inevitable that their motherly hearts should devise other methods for the protection of their homes. Knowing the terrors and the blessings of inheritance, they set about the systematic study of heredity, founding a journal for that purpose. Learning the relation of diet to the drink habit, they arranged to study hygiene also; desiring children to know that the Bible is on the side of total abstinence, they induced the International Sunday-school Convention to prepare a plan for lessons on this subject; perceiving the limitless power of the Press, they did their best to subsidize it by sending out their bulletins of temperance facts and news items, thick as the leaves of Vallambrosa, and incorporated a publishing company of women. . . .

They have become an army, drilled and disciplined. They have a method of organization, the simplest yet the most substantial known to temperance annals. It is the same for the smallest local union as for the national society with its ten thousand auxiliaries. Committees have been abolished, except the executive, made up of the general officers, and "superintendencies" substituted, making each woman responsible for a single line of work in the local, state and national society. This puts a premium upon personality, develops a negative into a positive with the least loss of time, and increases beyond all computation the aggregate of work accomplished. Women with specialties have thus been multiplied by tens of thousands, and the temperance reform introduced into strongholds of power hitherto neglected or unthought of. Is an exposition to be held, or a state or county fair? there is a woman in the locality who knows it is her business to see that the W. C. T. U. has an attractive booth with temperance literature and temperance drinks; and that, besides all this, it is her duty to secure laws and by-laws requiring the teetotal absence of intoxicants from grounds and buildings. Is there an institution for the dependent or delinquent classes? there is a woman in the locality who knows it is her duty to see that temperance literature is circulated, temperance talking and singing done, and that flowers with appropriate sentiments attached are sent the inmates by young ladies banded for that purpose. Is there a convocation of ministers, doctors, teachers, editors, voters, or any other class of opinion-manufacturers announced to meet in any town or city? there is a woman thereabouts who knows it is her business to secure, through some one of the delegates to these influential gatherings, a resolution favoring the temperance movement, and pledging it support along the line of work then and there represented. Is there a Legislature anywhere about to meet, or is Congress in session? there is a woman near at hand who knows it is her business to make the air heavy with the white, hovering wings of petitions gathered up from everywhere asking for prohibition, for the better protection of women and girls, for the preventing of the sale of tobacco to minors, for the enforcement of the Sabbath, or for the enfranchisement of women. . . .

"No sectarianism in religion," "no sectionalism in politics," "no sex in citizenship"—these are the battle-cries of this relentless but peaceful warfare. We believe that woman will bless and brighten every place she enters, and that she will enter every place on the round earth. We believe in prohibition by law, prohibition by politics, and prohibition by woman's ballot. After ten years' experience, the women of the crusade became convinced that until the people of this country divide at the ballot-box on the foregoing issue, America can never be nationally delivered from the dram-shop. . . .

While their enemy has brewed beer, they have brewed public opinion; while he distilled whisky, they distilled sentiment; while he rectified spirits, they rectified the spirit that is in man. They have had good words of cheer alike for North and South, for Catholic and Protestant, for home and foreign born, for white and black, but gave words of criticism for the liquor traffic and the parties that it dominates as its servants and allies.

While the specific aims of . . . women everywhere are directed against the manufacture, sale and use of alcholic beverages, it is sufficiently apparent that the indirect line of their progress is, perhaps, equally rapid, and involves social, governmental, and ecclesiastical equality between women and men. By this is meant such financial independence on the part of women as will enable them to hold men to the same high standards of personal purity in the habitudes of life as they have required of women, such a participation in the affairs of government as shall renovate politics and make home questions the paramount issue of the state, and such equality in all church relations as shall fulfill the gospel declaration, "There is neither male nor female, but ye are all one in Christ Jesus."

# 14

## WOMEN'S SUFFRAGE

★═══★═══★

Abigail Adams and other isolated voices urged voting rights for women at the time of the American Revolution, to no avail. In 1848 women convened at Seneca Falls, New York, to demand legal and political rights, including the vote, and they kept up their demand during the postwar debate on the enfranchisement of the freedmen. In 1869 two organizations emerged, the National Woman Suffrage Association, which fought for federal voting rights via a Constitutional amendment, and the American Woman Suffrage Association, which sought victories in the states. A woman suffrage amendment was introduced in the Senate in 1878 but gained little backing and was seldom debated. By the 1890s nineteen states allowed women to vote on school issues; three allowed them to vote on tax and bond issues; Wyoming, Colorado, Utah, and Idaho allowed full political rights.

In 1890, fearing (correctly) that the movement was about to stall in the face of the typical male view that "equal suffrage is a repudiation of manhood," the two main suffrage organizations combined in the National American Woman Suffrage Association, which focused its efforts on the most promising states and on Congress. Raising the level of argument and agitation as best they could, suffrage leaders met annually to resolve, write, speak, and strategize. Several more states now gave women the vote, including the key battlegrounds of Illinois and New York. Pressure thus built in Congress to pass a suffrage amendment.

World War I proved the turning point. President Woodrow Wilson, an opponent of woman suffrage, wanted women's organizations to support the war. Most of them did so and even served in the government—but only after he promised to support a suffrage amendment. Wilson told the Senate in 1918 that the vote for women was "vital to the winning of the war." In 1919 Congress passed the Nineteenth Amendment. Ratification came the next year. After a century of struggle, women had the vote.

Born in Wisconsin in 1859, Carrie Chapman Catt, whose presidential address to the Woman Suffrage Association in 1902 is reprinted below, worked her way through Iowa State Agricultural College, read law, was a high-school principal, and in 1883 became one of the country's first female school superintendents. Twice widowed, in the

1880s Catt became an organizer for women's suffrage in Iowa, and in 1900 succeeded the great suffragist, Susan B. Anthony, as president of the National American Woman Suffrage Association. In 1915 she led a drive to make New York the first eastern state to give the vote to women. She then helped lead the campaign that finally resulted in the Nineteenth Amendment that gave the vote to women everywhere in the country. Increasingly committed to the struggle for world peace, Catt was a staunch supporter of the League of Nations and later the United Nations. When she died in New York in 1947, she was widely recognized as one of the outstanding women of her time.

**Questions to Consider.** Why did Catt in this address argue that women faced twice the obstacles to popular voting that ordinary men had faced previously? Did it strengthen or weaken her argument for suffrage to mention specific instances of sex prejudice, as she did in paragraph four? Was she right to describe such prejudice as "outside the domain of reason"? What did Catt mean by the "New Woman"? Were the opponents of women's suffrage all male? Catt's last paragraph argues that the liberty from male domination that women had finally achieved in their homes should now logically be extended to freedom from male domination in politics. Was Catt right that all women as of 1902 had achieved domestic independence? If so, do you find this reasoning persuasive?

★══★══★

## Address to the Woman Suffrage Association (1902)

### CARRIE CHAPMAN CATT

The question of woman suffrage is a very simple one. The plea is dignified, calm and logical. Yet, great as is the victory over conservatism which is represented in the accomplishment of man suffrage, infinitely greater will be the attainment of woman suffrage. Man suffrage exists through the surrender of many a stronghold of ancient thought, deemed impregnable, yet these obstacles were the veriest Don Quixote windmills compared with the opposition which has stood arrayed against woman suffrage.

Woman suffrage must meet precisely the same objections which have been urged against man suffrage, but in addition, it must combat sex-prejudice, the oldest, the most unreasoning, the most stubborn of all human idiosyncrasies.

Ida Husted Harper, ed., *The History of Woman Suffrage* (National American Woman Suffrage Association, New York, 1922), V: 29–30.

What *is* prejudice? An opinion, which is not based upon reason; a judgment, without having heard the argument; a feeling, without being able to trace from whence it came. And sex-prejudice is a pre-judgment against the rights, liberties and opportunities of women. A belief, without proof, in the incapacity of women to do that which they have never done. Sex-prejudice has been the chief hindrance in the rapid advance of the woman's rights movement to its present status, and it is still a stupendous obstacle to be overcome.

In the United States, at least, we need no longer argue woman's intellectual, moral and physical qualification for the ballot with the intelligent. The Reason of the best of our citizens has long been convinced. The justice of the argument has been admitted, but sex-prejudice is far from conquered.

When a great church official exclaims petulantly, that if women are no more modest in their demands men may be obliged to take to drowning female infants again; when a renowned United States Senator declares no human being can find an answer to the arguments for woman suffrage, but with all the force of his position and influence he will oppose it; when a popular woman novelist speaks of the advocates of the movement as the "shrieking sisterhood"; when a prominent politician says "to argue against woman suffrage is to repudiate the Declaration of Independence," yet he hopes it may never come, the question flies entirely outside the domain of reason, and retreats within the realm of sex-prejudice, where neither logic nor common sense can dislodge it. . . .

Four chief causes led to the subjection of women, each the logical deduction from the theory that men were the units of the race—obedience, ignorance, the denial of personal liberty, and the denial of right to property and wages. These forces united in cultivating a spirit of egotism and tyranny in men and weak dependence in women. . . . In fastening these disabilities upon women, the world acted logically when reasoning from the premise that man is the race and woman his dependent. The perpetual tutelage and subjection robbed women of all freedom of thought and action, and all incentive for growth, and they logically became the inane weaklings the world would have them, and their condition strengthened the universal belief in their incapacity. This world taught woman nothing skillful and then said her work was valueless. It permitted her no opinions and said she did not know how to think. It forbade her to speak in public, and said the sex had no orators. It denied her the schools, and said the sex had no genius. It robbed her of every vestige of responsibility, and then called her weak. It taught her that every pleasure must come as a favor from men, and when to gain it she decked herself in paint and fine feathers, as she had been taught to do, it called her vain. . . .

When at last the New Woman came, bearing the torch of truth, and with calm dignity asked a share in the world's education, opportunities and duties, it is no wonder these untrained weaklings should have shrunk away in horror. . . . Nor was it any wonder that man should arise to defend the woman of the past, whom he had learned to love and cherish. Her very weakness and dependence were dear to him and he loved to think of her as the tender clinging vine, while he was the strong and sturdy oak. He had worshiped her ideal through the age of chivalry as though she were a goddess, but he had governed her as though she were an idiot. Without the slightest comprehension of the inconsistency of his position, he believed this relation to be in accordance with God's command. . . .

The whole aim of the woman movement has been to destroy the idea that obedience is necessary to women; to train women to such self-respect that they would not grant obedience and to train men to such comprehension of equity they would not exact it. . . . As John Stuart Mill said in speaking of the conditions which preceded the enfranchisement of men: "The noble has been gradually going down on the social ladder and the commoner has been gradually going up. Every half century has brought them nearer to each other"; so we may say, for the past hundred years, man as the dominant power in the world has been going down the ladder and woman has been climbing up. Every decade has brought them nearer together. The opposition to the enfranchisement of women is the last defense of the old theory that obedience is necessary for women, because man alone is the creator of the race.

The whole effort of the woman movement has been to destroy obedience of woman in the home. That end has been very generally attained, and the average civilized woman enjoys the right of individual liberty in the home of her father, her husband, and her son. The individual woman no longer obeys the individual man. She enjoys self-government in the home and in society. The question now is, shall all women as a body obey all men as a body? Shall the woman who enjoys the right of self-government in every other department of life be permitted the right of self-government in the State? It is no more right for all men to govern all women than it was for one man to govern one woman. It is no more right for men to govern women than it was for one man to govern other men.

# 15

## THE SOCIALIST ATTACK

Industrialization brought, among other things, the factory system: big machines in large buildings where thousands of workers did specialized tasks under strict supervision. The factory system vastly increased America's output of such products as glass, machinery, newspapers, soap, cigarettes, beef, and beer. Factories thus provided innumerable new goods and millions of new jobs for Americans. But factories also reduced workers' control over their place of work, made the conditions of labor more dangerous, and played no small part in destroying the dignity of that labor. The first part of the following excerpt from Upton Sinclair's novel *The Jungle* offers a glimpse into the factory system as it operated in a Chicago meatpacking plant around 1905.

Industrialization produced not only big factories but also big cities, particularly in the Northeast and Midwest. Sinclair therefore took pains to show the role of industry and new production techniques in creating urban transportation and other services. The second part of the excerpt suggests a few of the links between industrial growth and Chicago's leaders—the so-called gray wolves who controlled the city's government and businesses. Here again, Sinclair indicates the high toll in human life exacted by unrestrained development.

*The Jungle* caused a sensation when it was first published. The pages describing conditions in Chicago's meatpacking plants aroused horror, disgust, and fury, and sales of meat dropped precipitously. "I aimed at the public's heart," said Sinclair ruefully, "and hit it in the stomach." President Theodore Roosevelt ordered a congressional investigation of meatpacking plants in the nation, and Congress subsequently passed the Meat Inspection Act. But Sinclair, a socialist, did not seek to inspire reform legislation. He was concerned mainly with dramatizing the misery of workers under the capitalist mode of production and with winning recruits to socialism.

Upton Sinclair was born in Baltimore, Maryland, in 1878. After attending college in New York City, he began to write essays and fiction, experiencing his first real success with the publication of *The Jungle* in 1906. Dozens of novels on similar subjects—the coal and oil industries, newspapers, the liquor business, the persecution of radicals, the threat of dictatorship—poured from his pen in the following years, though none had the immediate impact of *The Jungle.* Sinclair's style, with its emphasis on the details of everyday life, resembles the realism of other writers of the time. But he also wrote as a "muckraker" (as Theodore Roosevelt called journalists who wrote exposés), trying to alert readers to the deceit and corruption then prevalent in American life. Unlike most muckrakers, however, Sinclair was politically active, running in California in the 1920s as a socialist candidate for the U.S. Congress. In 1934 he won the Democratic nomination for governor with the slogan "End Poverty in California"(EPIC), but he lost the election. During World War II he was a warm supporter of President Franklin D. Roosevelt and wrote novels about the war, one of which won a Pulitzer Prize. Not long before Sinclair's death in 1968 in Bound Brook, New Jersey, President Lyndon Johnson invited him to the White House to be present at the signing of the Wholesome Meat Act.

**Questions to Consider.** *The Jungle* has been regarded as propaganda, not literature, and has been placed second only to Harriet Beecher Stowe's *Uncle Tom's Cabin* in its effectiveness as a propagandistic novel. Why do you think the novel caused demands for reform rather than converts to socialism? What seems more shocking in the passages from the novel reprinted below, the life of immigrant workers in Chicago in the early twentieth century or the filthy conditions under which meat was prepared for America's dining tables? What did Sinclair reveal about the organization of the work force in Chicago's meatpacking plants? Sinclair centered his story on a Lithuanian worker named Jurgis Rudkus and his wife, Ona. In what ways did he make Jurgis's plight seem typical of urban workers of his time? Why did Jurgis deny that he had ever worked in Chicago before? What did Sinclair reveal about the attitude of employers toward labor unions at that time?

★━━━★━━━★

# The Jungle (1906)

### UPTON SINCLAIR

There was another interesting set of statistics that a person might have gathered in Packingtown—those of the various afflictions of the workers. When Jurgis had first inspected the packing plants with Szedvilas, he had marveled while he listened to the tale of all the things that were made out of the carcasses of animals and of all the lesser industries that were maintained there; now he

Upton Sinclair, *The Jungle* (Doubleday, Page and Co., New York, 1906), 116–117, 265–269.

**A meatpacking house.** Trimmers wielding razor-sharp knives in a Chicago packing house in 1892, more than a decade before the publication of *The Jungle.* (Chicago Historical Society)

found that each one of these lesser industries was a separate little inferno, in its way as horrible as the killing-beds, the source and fountain of them all. The workers in each of them had their own peculiar diseases. And the wandering visitor might be skeptical about all the swindles, but he could not be skeptical about these, for the worker bore the evidence of them about on his own person—generally he had only to hold out his hand.

There were the men in the pickle rooms, for instance, where old Antanas had gotten his death; scarce a one of these had not some spot of horror on his person. Let a man so much as scrape his finger pushing a truck in the pickle rooms, and he might have a sore that would put him out of the world; all the joints in his fingers might be eaten by the acid, one by one. Of the butchers and floormen, the beef boners and trimmers, and all those who used knives, you could scarcely find a person who had the use of his thumb; time and time again the base of it had been slashed, till it was a mere lump of flesh against which the man pressed the knife to hold it. The hands of these men would be criss-crossed with cuts, until you could no longer pretend to count them or to trace them. They would have no nails—they had worn them off pulling hides; their knuckles were swollen so that their fingers spread out like a fan. There were men who worked in the cooking rooms, in the midst of steam and sickening odors, by artificial light; in these rooms the germs of tuberculosis might live for two years, but the supply was renewed every hour. There were the beef luggers, who carried two-hundred-pound quarters into the refrigerator cars, a fearful kind of work, that began at four o'clock in the morning, and that wore out the most powerful man in a few years. There were those who worked in the chilling rooms, and whose special disease was rheumatism; the time limit that a man could work in the chilling rooms was said to be five years. There were the wool pluckers, whose hands went to pieces even sooner than the hands of the pickle men; for the pelts of the sheep had to be painted with acid to loosen the wool, and then the pluckers had to pull out this wool with their bare hands, till the acid had eaten their fingers off. There were those who made the tins for the canned meat, and their hands, too, were a maze of cuts, and each cut represented a chance for blood poisoning. Some worked at the stamping machines, and it was very seldom that one could work long there at the pace that was set, and not give out and forget himself, and have a part of his hand chopped off. There were the "hoisters," as they were called, whose task it was to press the lever which lifted the dead cattle off the floor. They ran along upon a rafter, peering down through the damp and the steam, and as old Durham's architects had not built the killing room for the convenience of the hoisters, at every few feet they would have to stoop under a beam, say four feet above the one they ran on, which got them into the habit of stooping, so that in a few years they would be walking like chimpanzees. Worst of any, however, were the fertilizer men, and those who served in the cooking rooms. These people could not be shown to the visitor—for the odor of a fertilizer man would scare any ordinary visitor at a hundred yards, and as for the other men, who worked in tank rooms full of steam and in some of which there were open vats near the level of the floor, their peculiar trouble was that they fell into the vats; and when they were fished out, there was never enough of them left to be worth exhibiting—sometimes they would be overlooked for days, till all but the bones of them had gone out to the world as Durham's Pure Leaf Lard! . . .

Early in the fall Jurgis set out for Chicago again. All the joy went out of tramping as soon as a man could not keep warm in the hay; and, like many thousands of others, he deluded himself with the hope that by coming early he could avoid the rush. He brought fifteen dollars with him, hidden away in one of his shoes, a sum which had been saved from the saloon keepers, not so much by his conscience, as by the fear which filled him at the thought of being out of work in the city in the wintertime.

He traveled upon the railroad with several other men, hiding in freight cars at night, and liable to be thrown off at any time, regardless of the speed of the train. When he reached the city he left the rest, for he had money and they did not, and he meant to save himself in this fight. He would bring to it all the skill that practice had brought him, and he would stand, whoever fell. On fair nights he would sleep in the park or on a truck or an empty barrel or box, and when it was rainy or cold he would stow himself upon a shelf in a ten-cent lodging-house, or pay three cents for the privileges of a "squatter" in a tenement hallway. He would eat at free lunches, five cents a meal, and never a cent more—so he might keep alive for two months and more, and in that time he would surely find a job. He would have to bid farewell to his summer cleanliness, of course, for he would come out of the first night's lodging with his clothes alive with vermin. There was no place in the city where he could wash even his face, unless he went down to the lake front—and there it would soon be all ice.

First he went to the steel mill and the harvester works, and found that his places there had been filled long ago. He was careful to keep away from the stockyards—he was a single man now, he told himself, and he meant to stay one, to have his wages for his own when he got a job. He began the long, weary round of factories and warehouses, tramping all day, from one end of the city to the other, finding everywhere from ten to a hundred men ahead of him. He watched the newspapers, too—but no longer was he to be taken in by the smooth-spoken agents. He had been told of all those tricks while "on the road."

In the end it was through a newspaper that he got a job, after nearly a month of seeking. It was a call for a hundred laborers, and though he thought it was a "fake," he went because the place was near by. He found a line of men a block long, but as a wagon chanced to come out of an alley and break the line, he saw his chance and sprang to seize a place. Men threatened him and tried to throw him out, but he cursed and made a disturbance to attract a policeman, upon which they subsided, knowing that if the latter interfered it would be to "fire" them all.

An hour or two later he entered a room and confronted a big Irishman behind a desk.

"Ever worked in Chicago before?" the man inquired; and whether it was a good angel that put it into Jurgis's mind, or an intuition of his sharpened wits, he was moved to answer, "no, sir."

"Where do you come from?"

"Kansas City, sir."

"Any references?"

"No sir. I'm just an unskilled man, I've got good arms."

"I want men for hard work—it's all underground, digging tunnels for telephones. Maybe it won't suit you."

"I'm willing, sir—anything for me. What's the pay?"

"Fifteen cents an hour."

"I'm willing, sir."

"All right; go back there and give your name."

So within half an hour he was at work, far underneath the streets of the city. The tunnel was a peculiar one for telephone wires; it was about eight feet high, and with a level floor nearly as wide. It had innumerable branches—a perfect spider-web beneath the city; Jurgis walked over half a mile with his gang to the place where they were to work. Stranger yet, the tunnel was lighted by electricity, and upon it was laid a double-tracked, narrow gauge railroad!

But Jurgis was not there to ask questions, and he did not give the matter a thought. It was nearly a year afterward that he finally learned the meaning of this whole affair. The City Council had passed a quiet and innocent little bill allowing a company to construct telephone conduits under the city streets; and upon the strength of this, a great corporation had proceeded to tunnel all Chicago with a system of railway freight subways. In the city there was a combination of employers, representing hundreds of millions of capital, and formed for the purpose of crushing the labor unions. The chief union which troubled it was the teamsters'; and when these freight tunnels were completed, connecting all the big factories and stores with the railroad depots, they would have the teamsters' union by the throat. Now and then there were rumors and murmurs in the Board of Aldermen, and once there was a committee to investigate—but each time another small fortune was paid over, and the rumors died away; until at last the city woke up with a start to find the work completed. There was a tremendous scandal, of course; it was found that the city records had been falsified and other crimes committed, and some of Chicago's big capitalists got into jail—figuratively speaking. The aldermen declared that they had had no idea of it all, in spite of the fact that the main entrance to the work had been in the rear of the saloon of one of them. . . .

In a work thus carried out, not much thought was given to the welfare of the laborers. On an average, the tunneling cost a life a day and several manglings; it was seldom, however, that more than a dozen or two men heard of any one accident. The work was all done by the new boring-machinery, with as little blasting as possible; but there would be falling rocks and crushed supports and premature explosions—and in addition all the dangers of railroading. So it was that one night, as Jurgis was on his way out with his gang, an engine and a loaded car dashed round one of the innumerable right-angle branches and struck him upon the shoulder, hurling him against the concrete wall and knocking him senseless.

When he opened his eyes again it was to the clanging of the bell of an ambulance. He was lying in it, covered by a blanket, and it was heading its way slowly through the holiday-shopping crowds. They took him to the county hospital, where a young surgeon set his arm, then he was washed and laid upon a bed in a ward with a score or two more of maimed and mangled men.

# 16

# THE REORGANIZATION OF WORK

The railroad was the engine of economic growth in the nineteenth century. The automobile was the engine of growth in the twentieth century. The country produced fewer than a million cars in 1910; by 1920 it produced 8 million, and by 1929, 26 million. In 1929, one out of four-teen manufacturing workers made cars, and the production of cars created huge new markets for petroleum, steel, glass, rubber, and copper. Governments built roads and highways; along those highways appeared tens of thousands of gasoline stations. Single-family housing became the norm for homes outside the East. Because of the car, most newer cities—Des Moines, Dallas, Denver, Los Angeles, Seattle—built out as well as up, extending their reach into newly fashionable suburban developments at the expense of traditional "downtowns."

The key to this phenomenal growth was the Ford Motor Company's decision shortly before World War I to introduce assembly line methods to auto production. The document below, from a leading engineering periodical, provides an excellent description of this revolutionary system. Previously, machine shops made one car at a time, with workers doing several tasks and moving from place to place to work on the vehicle. Ford changed that. By the mid-1920s, Ford turned out a car every ten seconds. And it sold them. As early as 1916, Ford charged just $300 for its durable little high-volume "Model T," a sum within reach of millions of consumers. When the "Model A" appeared in the late 1920s, it too was affordable. Other manufacturers began to apply "Fordism" in their own industries, boosting productivity throughout the economy.

Born in Michigan in 1863, the young Henry Ford was a classic tinkerer. He worked in Detroit machine shops, built his first prototype automobile in 1896, and formed his own company soon after. Although assembly line manufacturing made Ford's reputation and fortune, he gained further renown by doubling his workers' pay to $5 a day and cutting the work week from 48 to 40 hours, stunning innovations in the industrial world of the time. Yet Ford workers were known, despite their pay, as habitual complainers, especially with regard to the company's autocratic management and exhausting work pace. Ford's response was to hire company spies and anti-union police. Henry Ford was also one of America's best-known nativists and anti-Semites; Adoph Hitler quoted him favorably. *The Engineering Magazine,* which published the Arnold and Faurote study below, was the era's leading journal for engineers, just now in the process of establishing themselves as a formal profession.

**Questions to Consider.** What specific features in chassis assembling produced the most gains in labor productivity? Why did Ford use labor time per chassis as the key measure of productivity? How did Ford methods affect a worker's ability to move his feet and body? How did plant managers settle on the precise speed of the chain drive? How would all this have affected worker attitudes? Critics of the system sometimes used the term "alienation" in discussing Ford assembly work. What did they mean by that?

★▬▬★▬▬★

# Ford Methods and the Ford Shops (1915)

### HORACE ARNOLD AND FAY FAUROTE

The Ford motor and chassis assembling methods are believed to show the very first example of minutely dividing the assembling operations of so large and heavy a unit assembly as an automobile. These Ford motor and chassis assembling lines are believed also to show the very first examples of chain-driving an assembly in progress of assembling. . . .

The Ford shops assembling practice is to place the most suitable component on elevated ways or rails, and to carry it past successive stationary sources of component supply, and past successive groups of workmen who fix the various components to the principal component, until the assembly is completed and ready to leave the assembling line.

In some cases, where the shape of the component is unsuited to travel on rails, the principal component is pushed along on a finished iron table from one man or group of men to another man or group of men, past sources of component supply, each workman or group of workmen completing the placing, or the placing and fixing, of one component before moving the assembly in progress to its next station.

In case the assembly in progress moves on elevated rails or ways, it is common Ford practice to drive the assembly in progress by means of a slow-moving chain, and if the components are perfectly to gauge, so that

Horace Lucien Arnold and Fay Leone Faurote, *Ford Methods and the Ford Shops* (New York: The Engineering Magazine Company, 1915), pp. 102–5, 109, 111–112, 114–116, 135–140, 142.

all operations can be performed in predetermined times, it is better to drive the assembly in progress at a fixed suitable speed by chain, at a uniform rate, than to move it on the ways by pushing.

This Ford method of moving the assembly in progress has effected remarkable labor-saving gains over stationary assembling with all components brought to the one point for each assembly, the labor-saving gains being in all cases accompanied by great reductions in floor space required for the assembling operations.

Thus, up to September, 1913, the Ford car chassis assembling occupied 600 feet length of floor space, and required 14 hours of one man's time to assemble one chassis, standing still in one place while being assembled.

April 29, 1914, with the chassis chain-driven while assembling, 1,212 Ford chassis were assembled on three parallel elevated-rail assembling lines, by 2,080 hours of labor, giving one chassis assembled for each 93 minutes of labor. . . . The assembling lines were only 300 feet long. . . .

Besides these almost unbelievable reductions in assembling time, the Ford shops are now making equally surprising gains by the installation of component-carrying slides, or ways, on which components in process of finishing slide by gravity from the hand of one operation-performing workman to the hand of the next operator, this use of work slides being in some instances combined with operation divisions.

All of this Ford practice is of great importance to manufacturers at large, because the Ford engineers assert that these improved methods of handling work by slides, of moving assemblies in progress, and in minutely dividing assembling operations, can be applied to any and all small-machine manufacturing, with very large reductions of labor-cost. . . .

To show what may be done by simply dividing an operation seemingly already reduced to its lowest terms, and placing a short work-slide lengthwise of the assembling bench[,] the first example of the improved Ford practice . . . is the piston and connecting-rod assembling, changed within the last two months, so that now 14 men assemble 4,000 pistons and connecting-rods in one 8-hour day, instead of the 28 men employed to do exactly the same work less than two months ago, and with no change whatever in the tools used, nor in the ultimate operations performed. . . .

This piston-assembling job teaches two lessons of first importance. The first is that there are great savings in labor to be made by splitting operations to such an extent that the workman does not need to change the position of his feet, and the second lesson is that a work-slide so located that the workman can drop his completed operation out of his hand in a certain place, without any search for a place of deposit, and also can reach to a certain place and there find his next job under his hand, is also a very important time-saver. . . .

It was in this same assembling department that the first moving assembly line, that for assembling the Ford fly-wheel magneto, was installed. Of course, every one had everything to learn, and this first Ford assembling rail-line was

built 8 inches lower than it should have been. The correct height for the magneto assembling . . . is 35 inches above the floor for this job. There were the
same uncertainties as to the best height in the case of the chassis-assembing
ways. In all instances it is of first importance that the workman should stand
upright. A stooping posture very soon tires the workman, and greatly reduces
his efficiency. . . .

The chain-drive speed was a matter of trial; it was first made 5 feet per
minute, which was much too fast; then 18 inches per minute was tried, and
found much too slow; the third trial was 44 inches per minute (3 feet 8
inches), and is yet in use, though the foreman believes it could now be increased to advantage. The chain drive proved to be a very great improvement, hurrying the slow men, holding the fast men back from pushing work
on to those in advance, and acting as an all-round adjuster and equalizer. . . .

The Ford chassis assembling in moving lines affords a highly impressive
spectacle to beholders of every class, technical or non-technical. Long lines of
slowly moving assemblies in progress, busy groups of successive operators,
the rapid growth of the chassis as component after component is added from
the overhead sources of supply, and, finally the instant start into self-moving
power—these excite the liveliest interest and admiration in all who witness
for the first time this operation of bringing together the varied elements of
the new and seemingly vivified creation, on the three Ford chassis assembling lines where over 1,200 have been put together and driven out of doors
into John R Street in one single 8-hour day.

**The return of the Great White Fleet** after a victorious Spanish-American War. This painting by Fred Pansing shows Admiral Sampson's Flagship New York in the foreground. (Museum of the City of New York)

CHAPTER FOUR

# Expansion and War

# 17

## THE LURE OF THE EAST

★━━━★━━━★

The United States went to war with Spain over Cuba in 1898. But the U.S. victory in the brief war brought acquisitions in the Pacific (the Philippines and Guam) as well as in the Caribbean (Puerto Rico); at this time the United States also got control of the Hawaiian Islands and Wake Island. In part these acquisitions represented the resumption of a long tradition of westward territorial expansion that had been abandoned since the purchase of Alaska in 1867. In part they represented America's desire for "great power" status at a time when the European nations were winning colonies in Asia and Africa. But powerful economic forces were at work, too, as they had been in the formulation of the recent Open Door policy on access to Chinese markets or, for that matter, in President James Monroe's assertion of his famous Doctrine in 1823.

At the beginning of the war, President William McKinley was unsure himself whether or not the United States should take over the Philippines, and if it did, whether its forces would take only Manila, or the whole island of Luzon, or the entire archipelago. Not until December 1898 did the president finally announce that the United States would pursue a policy of "benevolent assimilation" toward the whole territory. This decision gave rise to a small but vocal anti-imperialist movement at home and, more important, a strong Filipino resistance struggle against the American occupation.

At this point, however, forceful advocates of imperialism rose to defend the president in the most vigorous terms. Of these none was more forceful or more important than Senator Albert J. Beveridge. His Senate speech of January 1900 in support of a (successful) resolution urging colonial status for the Philippines, excerpted below, provided the broadest possible grounds for the president's policy. With the fight thus in hand at home, McKinley turned to winning the fight abroad. Having made his decision, moreover, he stuck doggedly with it. In fact, the Americans overcame the insurgents only after another year's hard fighting and the death of more than a hundred thousand Filipinos.

President McKinley's ally and fellow Ohioan, Albert Beveridge, was only thirty-seven at the time of his imperialist speech of 1900, but he was already known as a proponent of military strength and Anglo-Saxon supremacy. This speech further enhanced his standing in Republican circles. Beveridge left the Senate in 1912 to devote himself to writing. In 1919, eight years before his death in Indiana, his *Life of John Marshall* was awarded the Pulitzer Prize for historical biography.

**Questions to Consider.** Beveridge's speech makes enormous claims for the strategic importance of the Philippines. On what grounds did Beveridge make these claims? Has history borne out Beveridge's predictions about the Pacific Ocean and world commerce? Did Beveridge think acquiring the Philippines would increase or reduce the chances of war? How did he seem to view the Declaration of Independence and the Constitution? Was Beveridge's main concern economics or race?

☒═══☒═══☒

# America's Destiny (1900)

### ALBERT BEVERIDGE

Mr. President, the times call for candor. The Philippines are ours forever, "territory belonging to the United States," as the Constitution calls them. And just beyond the Philippines are China's illimitable markets. We will not retreat from either. We will not repudiate our duty in the archipelago. We will not abandon our opportunity in the Orient. We will not renounce our part in the mission of our race, trustee, under God, of the civilization of the world. And we will move forward to our work, not howling out regrets like slaves whipped to their burdens, but with gratitude for a task worthy of our strength, and thanksgiving to Almighty God that He has marked us as His chosen people, henceforth to lead in the regeneration of the world.

This island empire is the last land left in all the oceans. If it should prove a mistake to abandon it, the blunder once made would be irretrievable. If it proves a mistake to hold it, the error can be corrected when we will. Every other progressive nation stands ready to relieve us.

But to hold it will be no mistake. Our largest trade henceforth must be with Asia. The Pacific is our ocean. More and more Europe will manufacture the most it needs, secure from its colonies the most it consumes. Where shall we turn for consumers of our surplus? Geography answers the question. China is our natural customer. She is nearer to us than to England, Germany, or Russia, the commercial powers of the present and the future. They have moved nearer to China by securing permanent bases on her borders. The Philippines give us a base at the door of all the East.

*Congressional Record,* 56th Congress, 1st session, 704–712.

Lines of navigation from our ports to the Orient and Australia; from the Isthmian Canal to Asia; from all Oriental ports to Australia, converge at and separate from the Philippines. They are a self-supporting, dividend-paying fleet, permanently anchored at a spot selected by the strategy of Providence, commanding the Pacific. And the Pacific is the ocean of the commerce of the future. Most future wars will be conflicts for commerce. The power that rules the Pacific, therefore, is the power that rules the world. And, with the Philippines, that power is and will forever be the American Republic. . . .

Nothing is so natural as trade with one's neighbors. The Philippines make us the nearest neighbors of all the East. Nothing is more natural than to trade with those you know. This is the philosophy of all advertising. The Philippines bring us permanently face to face with the most sought-for customers of the world. National prestige, national propinquity, these and commercial activity are the elements of commercial success. The Philippines give the first; the character of the American people supply the last. It is a providential conjunction of all the elements of trade, of duty, and of power. If we are willing to go to war rather than let England have a few feet of frozen Alaska, which affords no market and commands none, what should we not do rather than let England, Germany, Russia, or Japan have all the Philippines? And no man on the spot can fail to see that this would be their fate if we retired. . . .

Here, then, Senators, is the situation. Two years ago there was no land in all the world which we could occupy for any purpose. Our commerce was daily turning toward the Orient, and geography and trade developments made necessary our commercial empire over the Pacific. And in that ocean we had no commercial, naval, or military base. Today we have one of the three great ocean possessions of the globe, located at the most commanding commercial, naval, and military points in the eastern seas, within hail of India, shoulder to shoulder with China, richer in its own resources than any equal body of land on the entire globe, and peopled by a race which civilization demands shall be improved. Shall we abandon it? That man little knows the common people of the Republic, little understands the instincts of our race, who thinks we will not hold it fast and hold it forever, administering just government by simplest methods. We may trick up devices to shift our burden and lessen our opportunity; they will avail us nothing but delay. We may tangle conditions by applying academic arrangements of self-government to a crude situation; their failure will drive us to our duty in the end. . . .

But, Senators, it would be better to abandon this combined garden and Gibraltar of the Pacific, and count our blood and treasure already spent a profitable loss, than to apply any academic arrangement of self-government to these children. They are not capable of self-government. How could they be? They are not of a self-governing race. They are Orientals, Malays, instructed by Spaniards in the latter's worst estate.

They know nothing of practical government except as they have witnessed the weak, corrupt, cruel, and capricious rule of Spain. What magic will anyone employ to dissolve in their minds and characters those impressions of governors and governed which three centuries of misrule have created? What alchemy will change the oriental quality of their blood and set the self-governing currents of the American pouring through their Malay veins? How shall they, in the twinkling of an eye, be exalted to the heights of self-governing peoples which required a thousand years for us to reach, Anglo-Saxon though we are . . . ?

The Declaration of Independence does not forbid us to do our part in the regeneration of the world. If it did, the Declaration would be wrong, just as the Articles of Confederation, drafted by the very same men who signed the Declaration, was found to be wrong. The Declaration has no application to the present situation. It was written by self-governing men for self-governing men. . . .

Senators in opposition are stopped from denying our constitutional power to govern the Philippines as circumstances may demand, for such power is admitted in the case of Florida, Louisiana, Alaska. How, then, is it denied in the Philippines? Is there a geographical interpretation to the Constitution? Do degrees of longitude fix constitutional limitations? Does a thousand miles of ocean diminish constitutional power more than a thousand miles of land . . . ?

No; the oceans are not limitations of the power which the Constitution expressly gives Congress to govern all territory the nation may acquire. The Constitution declares that "Congress shall have power to dispose of and make all needful rules and regulations respecting the territory belonging to the United States." . . .

Mr. President, this question is deeper than any question of party politics; deeper than any question of the isolated policy of our country even; deeper even than any question of constitutional power. It is elemental. It is racial. God has not been preparing the English-speaking and Teutonic peoples for a thousand years for nothing but vain and idle self-contemplation and self-admiration. No! He has made us the master organizers of the world to establish system where chaos reigns. He has given us the spirit of progress to overwhelm the forces of reaction throughout the earth. He has made us adepts in government that we may administer government among savage and senile peoples. Were it not for such a force as this the world would relapse into barbarism and night. And of all our race He has marked the American people as His chosen nation to finally lead in the regeneration of the world. This is the divine mission of America, and it holds for us all the profit, all the glory, all the happiness possible to man. We are trustees of the world's progress, guardians of its righteous peace. The judgment of the Master is upon us: "Ye have been faithful over a few things; I will make you ruler over many things."

What shall history say of us? Shall it say that we renounced that holy trust, left the savage to his base condition, the wilderness to the reign of waste, deserted duty, abandoned glory, forgot our sordid profit even, because we feared our strength and read the charter of our powers with the doubter's eye and the quibbler's mind? Shall it say that, called by events to captain and command the proudest, ablest, purest race of history in history's noblest work, we declined that great commission? Our fathers would not have had it so. No! They founded no paralytic government, incapable of the simplest acts of administration. They planted no sluggard people, passive while the world's work calls them. They established no reactionary nation. They unfurled no retreating flag. . . .

Mr. President and Senators, adopt the resolution offered, that peace may quickly come and that we may begin our saving, regenerating, and uplifting work. . . . Reject it, and the world, history, and the American people will know where to forever fix the awful responsibility for the consequences that will surely follow such failure to do our manifest duty. . . .

# 18

## THE BIG STICK

★══★══★

Although the Monroe Doctrine of 1823 had proclaimed a special interest in Latin American affairs, it was neither militaristic nor especially interventionist in spirit. But the Spanish-American War signaled a new military and economic aggressiveness in Washington and a new determination to assert the country's ambitions. It was probably inevitable, therefore, that President Theodore Roosevelt should modify the Monroe Doctrine to provide a rationale for direct intervention by armed force on behalf of "progress" and "responsible government." A hero of the U.S. Army's recent Cuban campaign against Spain and an admirer of Admiral George Dewey, Roosevelt, who had succeeded the slain William McKinley as president, urged a policy of expanding the country's military might. Advising the United States to "speak softly and carry a big stick," Roosevelt believed the United States should act as the policeman of Central America and the Caribbean. Between Roosevelt's and Coolidge's administrations the United States sent warships and soldiers to several Caribbean countries, usually to protect U.S. investments, and in some cases left them there for decades.

Theodore Roosevelt, who inaugurated this era of gunboat diplomacy, was born to well-to-do parents in New York City in 1858. After college he juggled politics, writing, and ranching and hunting, until McKinley appointed him assistant secretary of the navy in 1897. He resigned in 1898 to lead a cavalry unit called the Rough Riders in Cuba, but returned to win the governorship of New York in 1899 and 1900. He moved on to the vice presidency in 1901, and in that same year to the presidency when McKinley was killed. Over the next ten years Roosevelt promised a "square deal" and a "new nationalism," both embodying his notions of social and military progress. In 1912 he bolted the Republican Party to head a Progressive ticket that lost to Woodrow Wilson, a Democrat, whose internationalism Roosevelt relentlessly castigated until his death in 1919.

**Questions to Consider.** The Monroe Doctrine had asserted the right of the United States to prevent foreign intervention in the affairs of the Western Hemisphere. Did Roosevelt's "corollary" seem to be concerned mainly with external threats or with internal ones? According to the corollary, under what circumstances would the United States feel justified in interfering in Caribbean and Central American countries? Do you find Roosevelt's insistence on a U.S. right to intervene in this area to insure "reasonable efficiency and decency in social and political matters" valid and persuasive? Why did he describe unilateral U.S. intervention as the exercise of an "international police power"? Roosevelt argued that the interests of the United States and the Caribbean and Central American countries were in fact identical. Do you find this argument persuasive?

★══★══★

# Monroe Doctrine Corollary (1904)

### THEODORE ROOSEVELT

It is not true that the United States feels any land hunger or entertains any projects as regards the other nations of the Western Hemisphere save such as are for their welfare. All that this country desires is to see the neighboring countries stable, orderly, and prosperous. Any country whose people conduct themselves well can count upon our hearty friendship. If a nation shows that it knows how to act with reasonable efficiency and decency in social and political matters, if it keeps order and pays its obligations, it need fear no interference from the United States. Chronic wrongdoing, or an impotence which results in a general loosening of the ties of civilized society, may in America, as elsewhere, ultimately require intervention by some civilized nation, and in the Western Hemisphere the adherence of the United States to the Monroe Doctrine may lead the United States, however reluctantly, in flagrant cases of such wrongdoing or impotence, to the exercise of an international police power. If every country washed by the Caribbean Sea would show the progress in stable and just civilization which with the aid of the Platt amendment Cuba has shown since our troops left the island, and which so many of the republics in both Americas are constantly and brilliantly showing, all question of interference by this Nation with their affairs would be at an end. Our interests and those of our southern neighbors are in reality identical. They have great natural riches, and if within their borders the reign of law and justice obtains, prosperity is sure to come to them. While they thus obey the primary laws of civilized society they may rest assured that they will be treated by us in a spirit of cordial and helpful sympathy. We would interfere with them only in the last resort, and then only if it became evident

James D. Richardson, ed., *A Compilation of the Messages and Papers of the Presidents* (Government Printing Office, Washington, D.C., 1897–1907), XVI: 7371–7377.

that their inability or unwillingness to do justice at home and abroad had violated the rights of the United States or had invited foreign aggression to the detriment of the entire body of American nations. It is a mere truism to say that every nation, whether in America or anywhere else, which desires to maintain its freedom, its independence, must ultimately realize that the right of such independence can not be separated from the responsibility of making good use of it.

In asserting the Monroe Doctrine, in taking such steps as we have taken in regard to Cuba, Venezuela, and Panama, and in endeavoring to circumscribe the theater of war in the Far East, and to secure the open door in China, we have acted in our own interest as well as in the interest of humanity at large. There are, however, cases in which, while our own interests are not greatly involved, strong appeal is made to our sympathies. . . . In extreme cases action may be justifiable and proper. What form the action shall take must depend upon the circumstances of the case; that is, upon the degree of the atrocity and upon our power to remedy it.

# 19

## THE RETURN TO EUROPE

Woodrow Wilson won the presidency in 1912 on behalf of a "new freedom," a program involving lower tariffs, banking reform, antitrust legislation, and, in foreign policy, the repudiation of Theodore Roosevelt's gunboat diplomacy. Even after sending troops to various Caribbean countries and to Mexico, Wilson claimed that his main concern was to promote peace and democracy in the world. When World War I erupted in Europe, Wilson saw the war as the result of imperialistic rivalries ("a war with which we have nothing to do") and urged, despite personal sympathy with Great Britain, that the United States stay neutral so as to influence the peace negotiations.

Wilson won reelection in 1916 largely on a promise to keep the country out of war, a policy that would continue the long-standing trend of American expansion west toward the Pacific rather than eastward toward Europe. But a combination of pro-British propaganda in American newspapers and German submarine attacks on American ships proved formidable, and in April 1917, Wilson finally requested a declaration of war in the following address to Congress. The sweeping, visionary arguments of this remarkable speech shaped not only America's expectations about the war itself but also attitudes about the proper U.S. role in international affairs for years to come.

Born in 1856 in Virginia, Woodrow Wilson grew up in the South; his father was a Presbyterian minister. He attended Princeton and Johns Hopkins, where he earned a doctorate, and began to write and teach in the field of constitutional government and politics. He gained national stature while president of Princeton from 1902 until 1910; he became the Democratic governor of New Jersey in 1911 and, two years later, president of the United States. Wilson's main objective at the peace conference after World War I was to create a League of Nations to help keep the peace. In 1919 during an intensive speechmaking campaign to arouse public support for the League, Wilson suffered a debilitating stroke. He died in Washington, D.C., in 1924.

**Questions to Consider.** Note, in reading the following message, that although Woodrow Wilson believed in the unique and superior

character of American institutions, he was willing to enter into alliances with European powers. What were the four principal grounds
on which Wilson was willing to reverse the American diplomatic tradition? Which of these did he seem to take most seriously? Were there
other American interests that he might have stressed but did not? What
reasons might Wilson have had for stressing so strongly America's at-
tachment to Germany's people as opposed to its government? Might
Wilson's arguments and rhetoric have served to prolong rather than to
shorten the war?

★═══★═══★

# Address to Congress (1917)

## WOODROW WILSON

I have called the Congress into extraordinary session because there are serious, very serious choices of policy to be made, and made immediately, which
it was neither right nor constitutionally permissible that I should assume the
responsibility of making.

On the third of February last I officially laid before you the extraordinary
announcement of the Imperial German Government that on and after the
first day of February it was its purpose to put aside all restraints of law or of
humanity and use its submarines to sink every vessel that sought to approach either the ports of Great Britain and Ireland or the western coasts of
Europe or any of the ports controlled by the enemies of Germany within the
Mediterranean. . . .

I was for a little while unable to believe that such things would in fact be
done by any government that had hitherto subscribed to the humane practices of civilized nations. International law had its origin in the attempt to set
up some law which would be respected and observed upon the seas, where
no nation had right of dominion and where lay the free highways of the
world. . . . This minimum of right the German Government has swept aside
under the plea of retaliation and necessity and because it had no weapons
which it could use at sea except these which it is impossible to employ as it is
employing them without throwing to the winds all scruples of humanity or
of respect for all understandings that were supposed to underlie the inter-
course of the world. I am not now thinking of the loss of property involved,
immense and serious as that is, but only of the wanton and wholesale destruction of the lives of noncombatants, men, women, and children, engaged
in pursuits which have always, even in the darkest periods of modern history, been deemed innocent and legitimate. Property can be paid for; the lives

*The New York Times,* April 3, 1917.

of peaceful and innocent people cannot be. The present German submarine warfare against commerce is a warfare against mankind.

It is a war against all nations. American ships have been sunk, American lives taken, in ways which it has stirred us very deeply to learn of, but the ships and people of other neutral and friendly nations have been sunk and overwhelmed in the waters in the way. There has been no discrimination. The challenge is to all mankind. Each nation must decide for itself how it will meet it. The choice we make for ourselves must be made with a moderation of counsel and a temperateness of judgement befitting our character and our motives as a nation. We must put excited feeling away. Our motive will not be revenge or the victorious assertion of the physical might of the nation, but only the vindication of right, of human right, of which we are only a single champion. . . .

With a profound sense of the solemn and even tragical character of the step I am taking and of the grave responsibilities which it involves, but in unhesitating obedience to what I deem my constitutional duty, I advise that the Congress declare the recent course of the Imperial German Government to be in fact nothing less than war against the government and people of the United States; that it formally accept the status of belligerent which has thus been thrust upon it; and that it take immediate steps not only to put the country in a more thorough state of defense but also to exert all its power and employ all its resources to bring the Government of the German Empire to terms and end the war. . . .

We have no quarrel with the German people. We have no feeling towards them but one of sympathy and friendship. It was not upon their impulse that their government acted in entering this war. It was not with their previous knowledge or approval. It was a war determined upon as wars used to be determined upon in the old, unhappy days when peoples were nowhere consulted by their rulers and wars were provoked and waged in the interest of dynasties or of little groups of ambitious men who were accustomed to use their fellow men as pawns and tools. . . .

We are accepting this challenge of hostile purpose because we know that in such a Government, following such methods, we can never have a friend; and that in the presence of its organized power, always lying in wait to accomplish we know not what purpose, there can be no assured security for the democratic Governments of the world. We are now about to accept gauge of battle with this natural foe to liberty and shall, if necessary, spend the whole force of the nation to check and nullify its pretensions and its power. We are glad, now that we see the facts with no veil of false pretense about them, to fight thus for the ultimate peace of the world and for the liberation of its peoples, the German peoples included: for the rights of nations great and small and the privilege of men everywhere to choose their way of life and of obedience. The world must be made safe for democracy. Its peace must be planted upon the tested foundations of political liberty. We have no selfish ends to serve. We desire no conquest, no dominion. We seek no indemnities for ourselves, no material compensation for the sacrifices we shall freely make. We are but one of the champions of the rights of mankind. We shall be satisfied when those rights have been made as secure as the faith and the freedom of nations can make them. . . .

It will be all the easier for us to conduct ourselves as belligerents in a high spirit of right and fairness because we act without animus, not in enmity towards a people or with the desire to bring any injury or disadvantage upon them, but only in armed opposition to an irresponsible government which has thrown aside all considerations of humanity and of right and is running amuck. We are, let me say again, the sincere friends of the German people, and shall desire nothing so much as the early reestablishment of intimate relations of mutual advantage between us,—however hard it may be for them, for the time being, to believe that this is spoken from our hearts. We have borne with their present Government through all these bitter months because of that friendship,—exercising a patience and forbearance which would otherwise have been impossible. We shall, happily, still have an opportunity to prove that friendship in our daily attitude and actions towards the millions of men and women of German birth and native sympathy who live amongst us and share our life, and we shall be proud to prove it towards all who are in fact loyal to their neighbors and to the Government in the hour of test. They are, most of them, as true and loyal Americans as if they had never known any other fealty of allegiance. They will be prompt to stand with us in rebuking and restraining the few who may be of a different mind and purpose. If there should be disloyalty, it will be dealt with with a firm hand of stern repression; but, if it lifts its head at all, it will lift it only here and there and without countenance except from a lawless and malignant few.

It is a distressing and oppressive duty, Gentlemen of the Congress, which I have performed in thus addressing you. There are, it may be, many months of fiery trial and sacrifice ahead of us. It is a fearful thing to lead this great peaceful people into war, into the most terrible and disastrous of all wars, civilization itself seeming to be in the balance. But the right is more precious than peace, and we shall fight for the things which we have always carried nearest our hearts,—for democracy, for the right of those who submit to authority to have a voice in their own Governments, for the rights and liberties of small nations, for a universal dominion of right by such a concert of free peoples as shall bring peace and safety to all nations and make the world itself at last free. To such a task we can dedicate our lives and our fortunes, everything that we have, with the pride of those who know that the day has come when America is privileged to spend her blood and her might for the principles that gave her birth and happiness and the peace which she has treasured. God helping her, she can do no other.

# 20

## THE DIPLOMACY OF ISOLATION

Many Americans found great glory in World War I. After all, the dough-
boys, as the American infantrymen were called, had turned the tide
against Germany, and John ("Black Jack") Pershing, commander of the
U.S. forces, emerged from the conflict a national hero. But the human
price had been stiff: 100,000 Americans dead and 200,000 wounded.
American casualties in World War I were low compared with European casualties (almost 2 million Germans and 1 million British died)
or with U.S. losses in the Civil War (600,000) or in World War II
(400,000). But the American losses were hardly insignificant, particularly since the country was in the war for only eighteen months and
mobilized only about 4 million men. Much of the dying occurred in
the appalling conditions of the Argonne Forest, where years of trench-
ing and shelling had created a veritable wasteland of death.

Justifying such remarkable carnage would have taken remarkable
results—something similar to the new international order that Woodrow
Wilson had promised. But the physically weakened president was not
able to deliver on this. So the skepticism that had attended U.S. entry
into the war persisted, engendering a somber, even cynical mood beneath the boisterous patriotic surface. Extended into the 1930s, this
mood would make it difficult for the country to strengthen itself for the
looming conflict with the Axis powers. Some historians argue that it
actually played a role in the unraveling of European collective security
measures, since the absence of an American commitment made Great
Britain reluctant to ally itself formally with France, thereby weakening
the common front against a resurgent Germany.

A major reason for the failure of the Senate to ratify the Treaty of
Versailles, and therefore U.S. membership in the League of Nations,
was the opposition of Republican Senator Henry Cabot Lodge of
Massachusetts, the chairman of the Senate Foreign Relations Committee. Wealthy, elderly, conservative, and nationalistic, Lodge opposed
virtually every reform of the era, including women's suffrage, the direct
election of senators, prohibition, and compulsory international arbitra-
tion. A "strong navy" man who had endorsed the imperialist policies of
William McKinley and Teddy Roosevelt, he was vituperatively critical

of Wilson for not entering the war on the side of England right away, and once threw (and landed) a punch at a young American of Swiss-German descent who came to his office to agitate for peace; Lodge's staff then jumped the hapless man and beat him badly. When the war ended Lodge urged harsh peace terms. When Wilson submitted the treaty for Senate confirmation, Lodge's committee reported it out with so many amendments to safeguard U.S. sovereignty that Wilson urged even Senate Democrats to oppose it, thus dooming the measure, and with it the hopes of Wilsonian internationalists. Lodge's victory in the struggle over ratification increased his popularity, which he used to defeat a proposal by President Warren G. Harding to have the United States join the World Court. Lodge remained a senator until his death in Boston in 1924, but his influence endured, as may be seen in the charter of the United Nations, founded in 1945, which gave the Great Powers veto authority over measures they disapproved.

**Questions to Consider.** On what main grounds did Lodge rest his arguments for opposing the Treaty of Versailles as submitted? What two groups did Lodge characterize as the chief "internationalists" of his time? Was this a fair way to deal with the Wilsonians? What was Lodge's attitude toward Europe? Did he want the United States to become part of a broader transatlantic community? What role did Lodge wish to see America play in world affairs? Do you find his arguments for American distinctiveness and exceptionalism compelling? Would they carry the day in the early twentieth-first century as they did in 1919?

★═══★═══★

# Speech to the Senate  (1919)

### HENRY CABOT LODGE

I am anxious as any human being can be to have the United States render every possible service to the civilization and peace of mankind, but I am certain we can do it best by not putting ourselves in leading strings or subjecting our policies and our sovereignty to other nations. The independence of the United States is not only more precious to ourselves but to the world than any single possession.

Look at the United States today. We have made mistakes in the past. We have had shortcomings. We shall make mistakes in the future and fall short of our own best hopes. But nonetheless is there any country today on the face of the earth which can compare with this in ordered liberty, in peace, and in

*The New York Times,* August 13, 1919.

the largest freedom? I feel that I can say this without being accused of undue boastfulness, for it is the simple fact, and in making this treaty and taking on these obligations all that we do is in a spirit of unselfishness and in a desire for the good of mankind. But it is well to remember that we are dealing with nations every one of which has a direct individual interest to serve, and there is grave danger in an unshared idealism.

Contrast the United States with any country on the face of the earth today and ask yourself whether the situation of the United States is not the best to be found. I will go as far as anyone in world service, but the first step to world service is the maintenance of the United States. You may call me self-ish if you will, conservative or reactionary, or use any other harsh adjective you see fit to apply, but an American I was born, an American I have re-mained all my life. I can never be anything else but an American, and I must think of the United States first, and when I think of the United States first in an arrangement like this I am thinking of what is best for the world, for if the United States fails, the best hopes of mankind fail with it. I have never had but one allegiance—I cannot divide it now. I have loved but one flag and I cannot share that devotion and give affection to the mongrel banner invented for a league.

Internationalism, illustrated by the Bolshevik and by the men to whom all countries are alike provided they can make money out of them, is to me re-pulsive. National I must remain, and in that way I like all other Americans can render the amplest service to the world. The United States is the world's best hope, but if you fetter her in the interests and quarrels of other nations, if you tangle her in the intrigues of Europe, you will destroy her power for good and endanger her very existence. Leave her to march freely through the centuries to come as in the years that have gone. Strong, generous, and con-fident, she has nobly served mankind. Beware how you trifle with your mar-velous inheritance, this great land of ordered liberty, for if we stumble and fall freedom and civilization everywhere will go down in ruin.

We are told that we shall "break the heart of the world" if we do not take this league just as it stands. I fear that the hearts of the vast majority of mankind would beat on strongly and steadily and without any quickening if the league were to perish altogether. If it should be effectively and benefi-cently changed the people who would lie awake in sorrow for a single night could be easily gathered in one not very large room but those who would draw a long breath of relief would reach to millions.

We hear much of visions and I trust we shall continue to have visions and dream dreams of a fairer future for the race. But visions are one thing and visionaries are another, and the mechanical appliances of the rhetorician designed to give a picture of a present which does not exist and of a future which no man can predict are as unreal and shortlived as the steam or canvas clouds, the angels suspended on wires and the artificial lights of the stage. They pass with the moment of effect and are shabby and tawdry in the day-light. Let us at least be real. Washington's entire honesty of mind and his fearless look into the face of all facts are qualities which can never go out of fashion and which we should all do well to imitate.

Ideals have been thrust upon us as an argument for the league until the healthy mind which rejects cant revolts from them. Are ideals confined to this deformed experiment upon a noble purpose, tainted, as it is, with bargains and tied to a peace treaty which might have been disposed of long ago to the great benefit of the world if it had not been compelled to carry this rider on its back? . . . No doubt many excellent and patriotic people see a coming fulfillment of nobler ideals in the words "league for peace." We all respect and share these aspirations and desires, but some of us see no hope, but rather defeat, for them in this murky covenant. For we, too, have our ideals, even if we differ from those who have tried to establish a monopoly of idealism. Our first ideal is our country, and we see her in the future, as in the past, giving service to all her people and to the world. Our ideal of the future is that she should continue to render that service of her own free will. She has great problems of her own to solve, very grim and perilous problems, and a right solution, if we can attain to it, would largely benefit mankind. We would have our country strong to resist a peril from the West, as she has flung back the German menace from the East. We would not have our politics distracted and embittered by the dissensions of other lands. We would not have our country's vigor exhausted or her moral force abated, by everlasting meddling and muddling in every quarrel, great and small, which afflicts the world. Our ideal is to make her ever stronger and better and finer, because in that way alone, as we believe, can she be of the greatest service to the world's peace and to the welfare of mankind.

**Jessie Fauset, Langston Hughes, and Zora Neale Hurston,** prominent young writers associated with the Harlem Renaissance, stand before a statue of Booker T. Washington, the most famous African American educator of the era. (Beinecke Library, Yale University)

CHAPTER FIVE

# Interlude

# 21

## HARLEM RENAISSANCE

✪━━✪━━✪

Pushed by racial violence and poverty, pulled by war employment, more than 500,000 African Americans left the South in the years before 1920. Most headed for the big cities of the North, where there was much discrimination but also better schools and wages and more personal freedom. And more dignity. An ex-Southerner wrote from Chicago that here "I don't have to humble to no one," another that "this is a real place for Negroes." Harlem, in uptown New York City, went in a single generation from all white to heavily black, absorbing waves of migrants from the Caribbean and the South and offering them the best housing Americans of color had ever enjoyed. Harlem became the largest African American community in the world, a virtual capital of black America, a host to the most prominent organizations in black America—and its most promising writers, musicians, artists and scholars, whose collective output would constitute what became known as the Harlem Renaissance.

The definitive text of the Renaissance, the publication that announced it to the broader world, was *The New Negro,* an anthology edited by Alain Locke. *The New Negro* offered readers poetry, fiction, and drama; essays on black music, black institutions, and Negro folk literature; and artwork highlighting African origins and imagery. Locke wrote the introduction and essays on spirituals, ancestral arts, and youth (excerpted below). Six women were represented, three whites, and older as well as younger figures. The emphasis, however, was on youth, as indicated by Locke's essay, the prominence given to youthful poet Langston Hughes and fledgling writer Zora Neale Hurston, and the "new" of the anthology's title. Locke did not cover everything—there was nothing on black nationalist Marcus Garvey or the blues—but he nevertheless chose well. Although the Harlem Renaissance itself lasted only a short while, nearly everyone in the anthology eventually gained a significant measure of fame.

Locke's book, besides presenting black writers and artists, served two other interesting purposes. First, "newness" was a crucial concept and slogan in the early twentieth century, as in New Nationalism, New Democracy, New Woman, New Freedom, *New Republic*. *The New Negro* situated Harlem's literary flowering within this wholesale infatuation with bold new departures—black, to be sure, but also quintessentially contemporary American. Second, a wave of racist and nativist literature had recently flooded the country: *The Klansman*, *Essays on the Inequality of Races*, *America's Racial Heritage*, *The Passing of the Great Race*. Many of these targeted Eastern and Southern Europeans, but they all advanced the notion of black inferiority. Locke's book was a counterblast to this literature of racism.

Forty years old in 1925, Alain Locke attended Harvard and Oxford and universities in Germany and France. Having studied philosophy, Greek, modern literature, and German culture, Locke joined the faculty of historically black Howard University in Washington (which would not at that time allow him to offer courses on his new interest, race and the African diaspora). A frequent visitor to Harlem, he made the acquaintance of nearly every important black scholar and artist. Although he had published little so far, he was a logical choice to edit *The New Negro*. In politics, Locke was a Republican, the party of Lincoln; in religion, an Episcopalian, though with an interest in Ba'hai; in social goals, a pluralist, though urging room for a distinctive black voice. He published extensively in the 1930s, including a biography of Frederick Douglass, and taught at Howard until 1953, a year before he died.

**Questions to Consider.** Why did Locke refer to young black writers as the "talented few"? Why did he think young writers could speak best on behalf of what he called the "folk-art" of "the masses," "the streets," and the "racy peasant undersoil"? How likely was it in reality that well-educated, young, urban writers would articulate peasant folk art? Why did Locke think it was necessary? Is this what Locke meant when he called on young writers to speak "as Negroes" rather than "for Negroes"? Why did he call "love of Africa" a spiritual compensation for "the present lack of America"? What evidence is there in the essay that Locke shared some of the "racialist" assumptions of his adversaries? Who constituted the main audience that Locke hoped to reach with this essay and, by implication, the entire anthology?

# Negro Youth Speaks (1925)

## ALAIN LOCKE

The Younger Generation comes, bringing its gifts. They are the first fruits of the Negro Renaissance. Youth speaks, and the voice of the New Negro is heard. What stirs inarticulately in the masses is already vocal upon the lips of the talented few, and the future listens, however the present may shut its ears. Here we have Negro youth, with arresting visions and vibrant prophecies; forecasting in the mirror of art what we must see and recognize in the streets of reality tomorrow, foretelling in new notes and accents the maturing speech of full racial utterance. . . .

Primarily, of course, it is youth that speaks in the voice of Negro youth, but the overtones are distinctive; Negro youth speaks out of an unique experience and with a particular representativeness. . . .

Negro genius to-day relies upon the race-gift as a vast spiritual endowment from which our best developments have come and must come. Racial expression as a conscious motive, it is true, is fading out of our latest art, but just as surely the age of truer, finer group expression is coming in—for race expression does not need to be deliberate to be vital. Indeed at its best it never is. This was the case with our instinctive and quite matchless folk-art, and begins to be the same again as we approach cultural maturity in a phase of art that promises now to be fully representative. The interval between has been an awkward age, where from the anxious desire and attempt to be representative much that was really unrepresentative has come; we have lately had an art that was stiltedly self-conscious, and racially rhetorical rather than racially expressive. Our poets have now stopped speaking for the Negro— they speak as Negroes. Where formerly they spoke to others and tried to interpret, they now speak to their own and try to express. They have stopped posing, being nearer the attainment of poise.

The younger generation has thus achieved an objective attitude toward life. Race for them is but an idiom of experience, a sort of added enriching adventure and discipline, giving subtler overtones to life, making it more beautiful and interesting, even if more poignantly so. So experienced, it affords a deepening rather than a narrowing of social vision. The artistic problem of the Young Negro has not been so much that of acquiring the outer mastery of form and technique as that of achieving an inner mastery of mood and spirit. That accomplished, there has come the happy release from self-consciousness, rhetoric, bombast, and the hampering habit of setting artistic values with primary regard for moral effect—all those pathetic over-compensations of a group inferiority complex which our social dilemmas inflicted upon several

Alain Locke, ed., *The New Negro* (New York: Albert & Charles Boni, 1925), 47–56.

unhappy generations. Our poets no longer have the hard choice between an over-assertive and an appealing attitude. By the same effort they have shaken themselves free from the minstrel tradition and the fowling-nets of dialect, and through acquiring ease and simplicity in serious expression, have carried the folk-gift to the altitudes of art. There they seek and find art's intrinsic values and satisfactions—and if America were deaf, they would still sing.

But America listens—perhaps in curiosity at first; later, we may be sure, in understanding. But—a moment of patience. The generation now in the artistic vanguard inherits the fine and dearly bought achievement of another generation of creative workmen who have been pioneers and path-breakers in the cultural development and recognition of the Negro in the arts. Though still in their prime, as veterans of a hard struggle, they must have the praise and gratitude that is due them. . . . Richer still, I think, in their own endowment of talent, comes the youngest generation of our Afro-American culture: in music Diton, Dett, Grant Still, and Roland Hayes; in fiction, Jessie Fauset, Walter White, Claude McKay (a forthcoming book); in drama, Willis Richardson; in the field of the short story, Jean Toomer, Eric Walrond, Rudolph Fisher; and finally a vivid galaxy of young Negro poets, McKay, Jean Toomer, Langston Hughes and Countée Cullen.

We can say without disparagement of the past that in that short space of time they have gained collectively from publishers, editors, critics and the general public more recognition than has ever before come to Negro creative artists in an entire working lifetime. First novels of unquestioned distinction, first acceptances by premier journals whose pages are the ambition of veteran craftsmen, international acclaim, the conquest for us of new provinces of art, the development for the first time among us of literary coteries and channels for the contact of creative minds, and most important of all, a spiritual quickening and racial leavening such as no generation has yet felt and known. It has been their achievement also to bring the artistic advance of the Negro sharply into stepping alignment with contemporary artistic thought, mood and style. They are thoroughly modern, some of them ultra-modern, and Negro thoughts now wear the uniform of the age.

Through their work, these younger artists have declared for a lusty vigorous realism; the same that is molding contemporary American letters, but their achievement of it, as it has been doubly difficult, is doubly significant. Not merely for modernity of style, but for vital originality of substance, the young Negro writers dig deep into the racy peasant undersoil of the race life.

The newer motive, then, in being racial is to be so purely for the sake of art. Nowhere is this more apparent, or more justified than in the increasing tendency to evolve from the racial substance something technically distinctive, something that as an idiom of style may become a contribution to the general resources of art. In flavor of language, flow of phrase, accent of rhythm in prose, verse and music, color and tone of imagery, idiom and timbre of emotion and symbolism, it is the ambition and promise of Negro artists to make a distinctive contribution. In music such transfusions of racial idioms with the modernistic styles of expression has already taken place; in the other arts it is just as possible and likely. Thus under the sophistications of modern style may be detected in almost all our artists a fresh distinctive note that the majority of them admit as the instinctive gift of the folk-spirit. . . .

Not all the new art is in the field of pure art values. There is poetry of sturdy social protest, and fiction of calm, dispassionate social analysis. But reason and realism have cured us of sentimentality: instead of the wail and appeal, there is challenge and indictment. Satire is just beneath the surface of our latest prose, and tonic irony has come into our poetic wells. These are good medicines for the common mind, for us they are necessary antidotes against social poison. Their influence means that at least for us the worst symptoms of the social distemper are passing. And so the social promise of our recent art is as great as the artistic. . . . They have instinctive love and pride of race, and, spiritually compensating for the present lacks of America, ardent respect and love for Africa, the motherland. Gradually too, under some spiritualizing reaction, the brands and wounds of social persecution are becoming the proud stigmata of spiritual immunity and moral victory.

# 22

## FUNDAMENTALISM AT BAY

The right to read the word of God directly from the Bible was central to the Protestant Reformation and remained central to the various strands of American Protestantism that still constituted the faith of most Americans. This kind of Bible focus tended to encourage (sometimes required) believers to accept the literal accuracy of the scriptural narratives, of, for example, the Creation, the parting of the Red Sea, and Christ's miracles. Science—astronomy, geology, archaeology—had long called Bible literalism into question. But this was mainly among educated Christians who interpreted scripture in accordance with modern science, as suggestive and symbolic rather than absolutely accurate. In the South, swaths of the Midwest and far West, and pockets of the East, "fundamentalist" literalism persisted, as did suspicion of its urban critics.

Darwinian evolutionary theory represented a particularly grave challenge because it argued that, contrary to Genesis, earth was formed over millions of years rather than seven days, and that its vast variety of species (including humans) resulted from mutation and adaptation of prior species rather than God's simultaneous creation. And if the Creation story was wrong, then why not the accounts of the Garden of Eden, Adam and Eve, man as the image of God—much of Christian faith as most congregations lived and understood it—and therefore the social order and sense of security that it sustained? Fundamentalists fought back with a crusade against evolutionary theory that in some ways paralleled the struggle against saloons and immigration. Evangelical preachers attacked Darwin. Several Southern and border states banned the teaching of evolution in the schools. The Southern Baptist Convention condemned "every theory, evolutionary or other, which teaches that man originated or came by way of lower animal ancestry."

In 1925, after Tennessee outlawed teaching about human evolution, John T. Scopes, a young science teacher, did precisely that. Local officials arrested him, and a jury trial ensued. William Jennings Bryan, a three-time Democratic presidential candidate from Nebraska, volunteered to assist in the prosecution of Scopes. Clarence Darrow, a famous Democratic trial lawyer from Chicago, led the defense team. After an eight-day trial, the jury convicted Scopes. The judge fined him a hundred dollars (which was never collected), but reporters covering the trial thought Darrow had won a larger battle by demonstrating the inconsistency and foolishness of fundamentalism. Excerpts of the trial transcript appear below. Fundamentalists gradually retreated from this issue, which, however, surged to the fore again at the end of the twentieth century.

William Jennings Bryan was a great orator, a defender of the "common people" against big business, and a pacifist. Bryan was also a Bible literalist and an advocate of traditional values who took up the anti-evolution cause in part because Social Darwinists were using its "survival of the fittest" principles to excuse appalling industrial and class inequalities. He died shortly after the Scopes trial. Clarence Darrow was a labor lawyer who had defended unpopular militants such as Eugene Debs and Bill Haywood. A rationalist, a liberal, and a civil libertarian who enjoyed the spotlight, Darrow tried to use his cases to educate the public about issues such as labor rights, free speech, and the evils of capital punishment. He died in 1938, heartedly disliked by conservatives of all stripes.

**Questions to Consider.** Who was Bryan's target audience in these trial exchanges? Who was Darrow's audience? What does this suggest about their overall intentions in this trial? Darrow seemed at the time to win the public relations battle by putting Bryan and Bible literalism on trial rather than evolution. Does this seem an accurate reading of the transcript? Was Darrow's tactic fair? Bryan's answers helped convict Scopes. Was there a way he could have won the public relations battle, too? Are there other Bible stories that Darrow could have used to put Bryan and fundamentalism on the defensive? Would Darrow's tactic have worked with any religion, not just Christianity? Are there passages in the transcript that suggest that Bryan was actually defending not only Bible literalism, but also a way of life? Could the same be said of Darrow?

★═══★═══★

# The Trial of John T. Scopes (1925)

### CLARENCE DARROW AND WILLIAM JENNINGS BRYAN

DARROW: You have given considerable study to the Bible, haven't you, Mr. Bryan?
BRYAN: Yes sir, I have tried to. . . .
DARROW: Then you have made a general study of it?

*The World's Most Famous Court Trial: Tennessee Evolution Case* (Cincinnati, 1925), 303–327.

BRYAN: Yes, I have studied the Bible for about fifty years or some time more than that, but, of course, I have studied it more as I have become older than when I was but a boy.

DARROW: Do you claim that everything in the Bible should be literally interpreted?

BRYAN: I believe everything in the Bible should be accepted as it is given there; some of the Bible is given illustratively. For instance: "Ye are the salt of the earth." I would not insist that man was actually salt, or that he had flesh of salt, but it is used in the sense of salt as saving God's people.

DARROW: But when you read that Jonah swallowed the whale—or that the whale swallowed Jonah—excuse me please—how do you literally interpret that?

BRYAN: When I read that a big fish swallowed Jonah—it does not say whale.

DARROW: Doesn't it? Are you sure?

BRYAN: That is my recollection of it. A big fish, and I believe it; and I believe in a God who can make a whale and can make a man and make both do what He pleases.

DARROW: Mr. Bryan, doesn't the New Testament say whale?

BRYAN: I am not sure. My impression is that it says fish; but it does not make so much difference; I merely called your attention to where it says fish—it does not say whale.

DARROW: But in the New Testament it says whale, doesn't it?

BRYAN: That may be true; I cannot remember in my own mind what I read about it.

DARROW: Now, you say, the big fish swallowed Jonah, and he there remained how long? Three days? And then he spewed him upon the land. You believe that the big fish was made to swallow Jonah?

BRYAN: I am not prepared to say that; the Bible merely says it was done.

DARROW: You don't know whether it was the ordinary run of fish, or made for that purpose?

BRYAN: You may guess; you evolutionists guess.

DARROW: But when we do guess, we have [the] sense to guess right.

BRYAN: But do not do it often.

DARROW: You are not prepared to say whether that fish was made especially to swallow a man or not?

BRYAN: The Bible doesn't say, so I am not prepared to say. . . .

DARROW: But you do believe He made them—that He made such a fish and that it was big enough to swallow Jonah?

BRYAN: Yes, sir. Let me add: one miracle is just as easy to believe as another.

DARROW: It is for me. . . .

BRYAN: It is hard to believe for you, but easy for me. A miracle is a thing performed beyond what man can perform. When you get beyond what man can do, you get within the realm of miracles; and it is just as easy to believe the miracle of Jonah as any other miracle in the Bible.

DARROW: Perfectly easy to believe that the whale swallowed Jonah?

BRYAN: If the Bible said so; the Bible doesn't make as extreme statements as evolutionists do.

DARROW: That may be a question, Mr. Bryan, about some of those you have known.

BRYAN: The only thing is, you have a definition of fact that includes imagination.

DARROW: And you have a definition that excludes everything but imagination. . . . Do you consider the story of Jonah and the whale a miracle?

BRYAN: I think it is.

DARROW: Do you believe Joshua made the sun stand still?

BRYAN: I believe what the Bible says. I suppose you mean that the earth stood still?

DARROW: I don't now. I am talking about the Bible now.

BRYAN: I accept the Bible absolutely.

DARROW: The Bible says Joshua commanded the sun to stand still for the purpose of lengthening the day, doesn't it? And you believe it?

BRYAN: I do.

DARROW: Do you believe at that time the entire sun went around the earth?

BRYAN: No, I believe that the earth does around the sun.

DARROW: Do you believe that men who wrote it thought that the day could be lengthened or that the sun could be stopped?

BRYAN: I don't know what they thought.

DARROW: You don't know?

BRYAN: I think they wrote without expression their own thoughts. . . .

DARROW: Have you an opinion as to whether—whoever wrote the book, I believe it is, Joshua, the Book of Joshua, thought the sun went around the earth or not?

BRYAN: I belie that he was inspired . . . that the Bible is inspired, an inspired author, whether one who wrote as he was directed to write understood the things he was writing about, I don't know. . . . I believe it was inspired by the Almighty, and He may have used language that could be understood at that time. Instead of using language that could not be understood until Mr. Darrow was born.

DARROW: So it might . . . have been subject to construction, might it not? . . .

BRYAN: Well, I think anybody can put his own construction upon it, but I do not mean that necessarily that is a correct construction. I have answered the question.

DARROW: Don't you believe that in order to lengthen the day it would have been construed that the earth stood still?

BRYAN: I would not attempt to say what would have been necessary, but I know this, that I can take a glass of water that would fall to the ground without the strength of my hand and to the extent of the glass of water I can overcome the law of gravitation and lift it up, whereas without my hand it would fall to the ground. If my puny hand can overcome the law of gravitation, the most universally understood, to that extent, I would not set power to the hand of Almighty god that made the universe.

DARROW: Can you answer my question directly? If the day was lengthened by stopping either the earth or the sun, it must have been the earth?

BRYAN: Well, I should say so.

DARROW: Yes? But it was language that was understood at that time, and we now know that the sun stood still as it was with the earth. We know that the sun does not stand still.

BRYAN: Well, it is relatively so, as Mr. Einstein would say. . . .

DARROW: Now, Mr. Bryan, have you ever pondered what would have happened to the earth if it had stood still?

BRYAN: No. . . . the God I believe in could have taken care of that, Mr. Darrow. *[applause in the courtroom]*

DARROW: Great applause from the bleachers.

BRYAN: From those whom you call "yokels".

DARROW: I have never called them yokels.

BRYAN: That is the ignorance of Tennessee, the bigotry.

DARROW: You insult every man of science and learning in the world because he does not believe in your fool religion. . . .

Do you believe the story of the temptation of Eve by the serpent?

BRYAN: I do.

DARROW: Do you believe that after Eve ate the apple, or gave it to Adam, whichever way it was, that God cursed Eve, and at that time decreed that all womankind thenceforth and forever should suffer the pains of childbirth in the reproduction of the earth?

BRYAN: I believe what it says, and I believe the fact as fully—. . .

DARROW: And for that reason, every woman born of woman, who has to carry on the race, the reason they have childbirth pains is because Eve tempted Adam in the Garden of Eden?

BRYAN: I will believe just what the Bible says. I ask to put that in the language of the Bible, for I prefer that to your language. Read the Bible and I will answer.

DARROW: All right, I will do that. *[reads from Genesis]*. . . .

BRYAN: Just as it says.

DARROW: And you believe that is the reason that God made the serpent to go on his belly after he tempted Eve? . . .

BRYAN: I believe that.

DARROW: Have you any idea how the snake went before that time?

BRYAN: No, sir.

DARROW: Do you know whether he walked on his tail or not?

BRYAN: No, sir. I have no way to know. *[laughter in audience]*

DARROW: Now, you refer to the cloud that was put in the heaven after the flood, the rainbow. Do you believe in that? . . .

BRYAN: Your Honor, I think I can shorten this testimony. The only purpose Mr. Darrow has is to slander the Bible, but I will answer his question. I will answer it all at once, and I have no objection in the world, I want the world to know that this man, who does not believe in a God, is trying to use a court in Tennessee—

DARROW: I object to that.

BRYAN: to slur at it, and while it will require time, I am willing to take it.

DARROW: I object to your statement. I am examining you on your fool ideas that no intelligent Christian on earth believes.

# 23

## THE BUSINESS OF AMERICA

The U.S. experienced tremendous economic expansion and unprecedented prosperity during the 1920s. Industrial output doubled, per capita income rose by a third. Inflation was low, and so was unemployment. Refrigerators, vacuum cleaners, and washing machines became widespread; the production of electricity to run them skyrocketed. Automobiles became commonplace, as did electric lights, radios and radio programming, phonographs and records, and cameras and film. Motion pictures became the fifth biggest industry, providing films to 20,000 theaters that sold 100 million tickets a week. The stock market boomed, giving millions of new investors a thrilling and lucrative ride. Big long-lived corporations emerged—General Electric, RCA, Kodak, General Motors, DuPont—as did the first big chain store corporations (A&P and Woolworth's) and advertising agencies (Batten, Barton, Durstine & Osborne). There were problems. Income on hard-scrabble farms declined. Ownership and income became dangerously concentrated at the top of society. Organized crime soared, fed by the thirst for alcohol, and so did debt, fed by consumer credit and Wall Street speculation.

But you couldn't argue with the results, an incredibly long period of incredible growth. Praise rained on the businessmen who engineered it. "This is a business country," it went, and needs "less government in business, more business in government." "America stands for one idea: business." Jesus Christ was at bottom the greatest business entrepreneur of all time. The finest game was "business," and the best road to spiritual fulfillment was to "get rich." It seemed self-evident, as least to the dominant Republican party, that the way to end poverty was through business-friendly policies such as lowering taxes, deregulating business, weakening labor unions, and enacting protective tariffs.

No one was more identified with this "New Era" of business prowess than Calvin Coolidge, who was born in rural Vermont in 1872, worked up the political ladder in Massachusetts, and gained fame as governor for his hard line against a Boston police strike. He won the vice presidency on the Republican ticket in 1920, succeeded to the presidency when President Harding died in 1923, and ran and won himself in 1924. During the four years of his administration, Coolidge was one of the most popular presidents in U.S. history. The following address to a New York group reflects his views on the productive power and organizational efficiency of the business community. He died in 1933, the lowest point of the Great Depression of the 1930s.

Not everyone was enamored of the business civilization of the 1920s. Liberal Protestants such as Reinhold Niebuhr looked askance at the decade's crass materialism and the impact of industry on the lives and spiritual well-being of its workers. Born into a German immigrant family in 1892 in Missouri, Niebuhr followed the steps of his father and became a Lutheran minister at age 21. Study at the Yale Divinity School strengthened and deepened his commitment to a liberal Christianity that saw God as forgiving and compassionate rather than harsh and judgmental, a commitment that he took with him in 1915 when he was called to the ministry of a small German Evangelical Synod church in Detroit. In 1928, he returned to the East to teach ethics at Union Theological Seminary in New York, where he began the intellectual, political, and scholarly journey that would make him, by the time of his death in 1971, the most influential American theologian of the twentieth century. Below are excerpts from a journal he kept during his Detroit ministry at the beginning of this journey.

**Questions to Consider.** What, according to Coolidge, were the greatest contributions of the business community to the making of modern America? Why did he say that this could have happened only in the U.S.? How did he compare and contrast New York City and Washington? Which city did he seem to believe was the more important and astonishing? Was government important to business at all? If so, in what specific ways? How had public opinion about big business changed for the better, in his view?

What aspects of "modern industrial civilization" seem to have bothered Niebuhr the most? What did he think Christianity should, or could, do to make things better? How valid was his comparison of the church to the Red Cross? Why did the celebration of Thanksgiving in 1927 bother him? Why did he call it a "pharisaic" rite, an adherence to right rituals rather than right spirit? What different language and phrases did Niebuhr use to describe workers? Given the obvious desire of Americans for affordable industrial goods (Ford's "Lizzy," the Model A, for example), could industrial society be humanized in a way satisfactory to Niebuhr?

# Address to New York Businessmen (1925)

### CALVIN COOLIDGE

This time and place naturally suggest some consideration of commerce in its relation to Government and society. We are finishing a year which can justly be said to surpass all others in the overwhelming success of general business. We are met not only in the greatest American metropolis, but in the greatest center of population and business that the world has ever known. If any one wishes to gauge the power which is represented by the genius of the American spirit, let him contemplate the wonders which have been wrought in this region in the short space of 200 years. Not only does it stand unequaled by any other place on earth, but it is impossible to conceive of any other place where it could be equaled.

The foundation of this enormous development rests upon commerce. New York is an imperial city, but it is not a seat of government. The empire over which it rules is not political, but commercial. The great cities of the ancient world were the seats of both government and industrial power. The Middle Ages furnished a few exceptions. The great capitals of former times were not only seats of government but they actually governed. In the modern world government is inclined to be merely a tenant of the city. Political life and industrial life flow on side by side, but practically separated from each other. When we contemplate the enormous power, autocratic and uncontrolled, which would have been created by joining the authority of government with the influence of business, we can better appreciate the wisdom of the fathers in their wise dispensation which made Washington the political center of the country and left New York to develop into its business center. They wrought mightily for freedom. . . .

When I have been referring to business, I have used the word in its all-inclusive sense to denote alike the employer and employee, the production of agriculture and industry, the distribution of transportation and commerce, and the service of finance and banking. It is the work of the world. In modern life, with all its intricacies, business has come to hold a very dominant position in the thoughts of all enlightened peoples. Rightly understood, this is not a criticism, but a compliment. In its great economic organization it does not represent, as some have hastily concluded, a mere desire to minister to selfishness. The New York Chamber of Commerce is not made up of men merely animated with a purpose to get the better of each other. It is something far more important than a sordid desire for gain. It could not successively

Calvin Coolidge, "Government and Business," *Foundations of the Republic: Speeches and Addresses* (New York, 1926), pp. 317–332.

succeed on that basis. It is dominated by a more worthy impulse; its rests on a higher law. True business represents the mutual organized effort of society to minister to the economic requirements of civilization. It is an effort by which men provide for the material needs of each other. While it is not an end in itself, it is the important means for the attainment of a supreme end. It rests squarely on the law of service. It has for its main reliance truth and faith and justice. In its larger sense it is one of the greatest contributing forces to the moral and spiritual advancement of the race. . . .

It would be difficult, if not impossible, to estimate the contribution which government makes to business. It is notorious that where the government is bad, business is bad. The mere fundamental precepts of the administration of justice, the providing of order and security, are priceless. The prime element in the value of all property is the knowledge that its peaceful enjoyment will be publicly defended. If disorder should break out in your city, if there should be a conviction extending over any length of time that the rights of persons and property could no longer be protected by law, the value of your tall buildings would shrink to about the price of what are now water fronts of old Carthage or what are now corner lots in ancient Babylon. It is really the extension of these fundamental rights that the Government is constantly attempting to apply to modern business. It wants its rightful possessors to rest in security, it wants any wrongs that they may suffer to have a legal remedy, and it is all the time striving through administrative machinery to prevent in advance the infliction of injustice.

But the present generation of business almost universally throughout its responsible organization and management has shown every disposition to correct its own abuses with as little intervention of the Government as possible. This position is recognized by the public, and due to the appreciation of the needs which the country has for great units of production in time of war, and to the better understanding of the service which they perform in time of peace, resulting very largely from the discussion of our tax problems, a new attitude of the public mind is distinctly discernible toward great aggregations of capital. Their prosperity goes very far to insure the prosperity of all the country. The contending elements have each learned a most profitable lesson. . . .

If our people will but use those resources which have been intrusted to them, whether of command over large numbers of men or of command over large investments of capital, not selfishly but generously, not to exploit others but to serve others, there will be no doubt of an increasing production and distribution of wealth.

■══■══■

# An Evangelical's Notebook (1925–28)

### REINHOLD NIEBUHR

## 1925

We went through one of the big automobile factories today. So artificial is life that these factories are like a strange world to me though I have lived close to them for many years. The foundry interested me particularly. The heat was terrific. The men seemed weary. Here manual labor is a drudgery and toil is slavery. The men cannot possibly find any satisfaction in their work. They simply work to make a living. Their sweat and their dull pain are part of the price paid for the fine cars we all run. And most of us run the cars without knowing what price is being paid for them. . . .

We are all responsible. We all want the things which the factory produces and none of us is sensitive enough to care how much in human values the efficiency of the modern factory costs. Beside the brutal facts of modern industrial life, how futile are all our homiletical spoutings! The church is undoubtedly cultivating graces and preserving spiritual amenities in the more protected areas of society. But it isn't changing the essential facts of modern industrial civilization by a hair's breadth. It isn't even thinking about them.

The morality of the church is anachronistic. Will it ever develop a moral insight and courage sufficient to cope with the real problems of modern society? If it does it will require generations of effort and not a few martyrdoms. We ministers maintain our pride and self-respect and our sense of importance only through a vast and inclusive ignorance. If we knew the world in which we live a little better we would perish in shame or be overcome by a sense of futility.

## 1926

The excitement about the Federation of Labor convention in Detroit subsided, but there are echoes of the event in various magazines. Several ministers have been commended for "courage" because they permitted labor leaders to speak in their churches who represented pretty much their own convictions and said pretty much what they had been saying for years.

It does seem pretty bad to have the churches lined up so solidly against labor and for the open shop policy of the town. The ministers are hardly to blame, except if they are to be condemned for not bringing out the meaning of Christianity for industrial relations more clearly in their ministry previous

Reinhold Niebuhr, *Leaves from the Notebook of a Tamed Cynic* (Chicago and New York, 1929), pp. 78–79, 82–84, 111–113, 116–117, 141–144, 147–150, 195–198.

to the moment of crisis. As it was, few of the churches were sufficiently liberal to be able to risk an heretical voice in their pulpits. The idea that these A. F. of L. leaders are dangerous heretics is itself a rather illuminating clue to the mind of Detroit. I attended several sessions of the convention and the men impressed me as having about the same amount of daring and imagination as a group of village bankers.

The ministers of the country are by various methods dissociating themselves from the Detroit churches and are implying that they would have acted more generously in a like situation. Perhaps so. There are few cities in which wealth, suddenly acquired and proud of the mechanical efficiency which produced it, is so little mellowed by social intelligence. Detroit produces automobiles and is not yet willing to admit that the poor automata who are geared in on the production lines have any human problems. . . .

The church is like the Red Cross service in war time. It keeps life from degenerating into a consistent inhumanity, but it does not materially alter the fact of the struggle itself. The Red Cross neither wins the war nor abolishes it. Since the struggle between those who have and those who have not is a never-ending one, society will always be, in a sense, a battleground. It is therefore of some importance that human loveliness be preserved outside of the battle lines. But those who are engaged in this task ought to realize that the brutalities of the conflict may easily negate the most painstaking humanizing efforts behind the lines, and that these efforts may become a method for evading the dangers and risks of the battlefield.

## 1927

I wonder if it is really possible to have an honest Thanksgiving celebration in an industrial civilization. Harvest festivals were natural enough in peasant communities. The agrarian feels himself dependent upon nature's beneficence and anxious about nature's caprices. When the autumnal harvest is finally safe in the barns there arise, with the sigh of relief, natural emotions of gratitude that must express themselves religiously, since the bounty is actually created by the mysterious forces of nature which man may guide but never quite control.

All that is different in an industrial civilization in which so much wealth is piled up by the ingenuity of the machine, and, at least seemingly, by the diligence of man. Thanksgiving becomes increasingly the business of congratulating the Almighty upon his most excellent coworkers, ourselves. I have had that feeling about the Thanksgiving proclamations of our Presidents for some years. An individual, living in an industrial community might still celebrate a Thanksgiving day uncorrupted by pride, because he does benefit from processes and forces which he does not create or even guide. But a national Thanksgiving, particularly if it is meant to express gratitude for material bounty, becomes increasingly a pharisaic rite. . . .

## 1927

Mother and I visited at the home of—today where the husband is sick and was out of employment before he became sick. The folks have few connections in the city. They belong to no church. What a miserable existence it is to be friendless in a large city. And to be dependent upon a heartless industry. The man is about 55 or 57 I should judge, and he is going to have a desperate time securing employment after he gets well. These modern factories are not meant for old men. They want young men and they use them up pretty quickly. Your modern worker, with no skill but what is in the machine, is a sorry individual. After he loses the stamina of youth, he has nothing to sell.

I promised—I would try to find him a job. I did it to relieve the despair of that family, but I will have a hard time making good on my promise. According to the ethics of our modern industrialism men over fifty, without special training, are so much junk. It is a pleasure to see how such an ethic is qualified as soon as the industrial unit is smaller and the owner has a personal interest in his men. I could mention quite a few such instances. But unfortunately the units are getting larger and larger and more inhuman.

I think I had better get in contact with more of these victims of our modern industrialism and not leave that end of our work to mother alone. A little such personal experience will help much to save you from sentimentality. . . .

What a civilization this is! Naïve gentlemen with a genius for mechanics suddenly become the arbiters over the lives and fortunes of hundreds of thousands. Their moral pretentions are credulously accepted at full value. No one bothers to ask whether an industry which can maintain a cash reserve of a quarter of a billion ought not make some provision for its unemployed. It is enough that the new car is a good one. Here is a work of art in the only realm of art which we can understand. We will therefore refrain from making undue ethical demands upon the artist. Artists of all the ages have been notoriously unamenable to moral discipline. The cry of the hungry is drowned in the song, "Henry has made a lady out of Lizzy." . . .

## 1928

Modern industry, particularly American industry, is not Christian. The economic forces which move it are hardly qualified at a single point by really ethical considerations. If, while it is in the flush of its early triumphs, it may seem impossible to bring it under the restraint of moral law, it may strengthen faith to know that life without law destroys itself. If the church can do nothing else, it can bear witness to the truth until such a day as bitter experience will force a recalcitrant civilization to a humility which it does not now possess.

**The "White Angel Breadline" in San Francisco, 1933.** (Copyright the Dorothea Lange Collection, Oakland Museum of California, City of Oakland. Gift of Paul S. Taylor)

CHAPTER SIX

# Crisis and Hope

# 24

## AMERICAN EARTHQUAKE

American industrialization meant not only surging production but also periodic business "busts"—in the 1870s, the 1890s, 1907, and 1919–21. In each of these cases, prices, profits, and employment all plunged and remained low until the economy's basic strength pushed them again to higher levels. But no previous bust matched the Great Depression, which descended on the nation in the early 1930s. From 1929, when Herbert Hoover became the third consecutive Republican president since World War I, until 1933, when Franklin D. Roosevelt, a Democrat, succeeded him, the economy all but collapsed. Stocks and bonds lost three-fourths of their value, bank failures increased from five hundred to four thousand a year, farm income fell by half, and unemployment rose from 4 percent to almost 25 percent.

It was this last figure that most stunned and terrified ordinary Americans. There had been unemployment before, but never so much or for so long. And this joblessness was not limited to minorities or factory workers, as so often had been the case. The ranks of the destitute now included hundreds of thousands of white-collar workers, small businesspeople, and sharecroppers. Most disturbing of all, millions of women were now jobless and impoverished; many were homeless, with nowhere to turn. The country found it disquieting in the extreme.

People were aware of the massive human suffering of the Great Depression both because it was so widespread and because it was reported with such immediacy and attention to stark detail. Great fiction appeared, from Jack Conroy's *The Disinherited* at the beginning of the period to *The Grapes of Wrath,* John Steinbeck's epic of displaced Okies, at its end. Gripping photography and murals and innovative drama and poetry, glittering with unprecedented concreteness of detail, all depicted facets of the American ordeal. Journalism followed a similar path. Meridel LeSueur's article on Minnesota women, excerpted below, appeared in *New Masses,* a lively, irreverent Communist party literary journal that attracted and published much excellent social writing. In this case, the editors—staunch Stalinists—praised LeSueur's writing but also reproached her for defeatism and lack of "true revolutionary spirit."

Meridel LeSueur was born in 1900 in Iowa. Her grandfather was a Protestant fundamentalist temperance zealot; her father helped found the Industrial Workers of the World. After high school LeSueur attended the American Academy of Dramatic Art and worked in Hollywood as an actress and stuntwoman in the 1920s. During the 1930s she lived with her two children in Minneapolis while writing what a critic called "luminous short stories" as well as articles on farmers and the unemployed, especially women. Hailed in the 1930s as a major writer, she was blacklisted during the 1940s as a Communist sympathizer and lived by writing children's books and women's articles under a pseudonym. One of the first writers to examine the lives of poor women, her literary career revived during the 1970s with the emergence of feminism. Between 1971 and 1985 twelve of her books, new and old, appeared.

**Questions to Consider.** Who were the poor women LeSueur described in "Women on the Breadlines"? What did they have in common besides their poverty? Were they equally poor? Were their aspirations the same? How did their gender affect their condition and behavior during the Great Depression? How did they relate to one another, to authority figures, and to men? In later years conservatives would attack LeSueur for her radicalism. Can the reasons for these attacks be seen in this article? When Stalinists of the 1930s attacked her for being too negative and defeatist, were the attacks justified?

★▬▬★▬▬★

# Women on the Breadlines (1932)

## MERIDEL LESUEUR

I am sitting in the city free employment bureau. It's the woman's section. We have been sitting here now for four hours. We sit here every day, waiting for a job. There are no jobs. Most of us have had no breakfast. Some have had scant rations for over a year. Hunger makes a human being lapse into a state of lethargy, especially city hunger. Is there any place else in the world where a human being is supposed to go hungry amidst plenty without an outcry, without protest, where only the boldest steal or kill for bread, and the timid crawl the streets, hunger like the beak of a terrible bird at the vitals?

We sit looking at the floor. No one dares think of the coming winter. There are only a few more days of summer. Everyone is anxious to get work to lay up something for that long siege of bitter cold. But there is no work. Sitting

*New Masses* (January 1932), 5–7.

in the room we all know it. That is why we don't talk much. We look at the floor dreading to see that knowledge in each other's eyes. There is a kind of humiliation in it. We look away from each other. We look at the floor. It's too terrible to see this animal terror in each other's eyes.

So we sit hour after hour, day after day, waiting for a job to come in. There are many women for a single job. A thin sharp woman sits inside the wire cage looking at a book. For four hours we have watched her looking at that book. She has a hard little eye. In the small bare room there are half a dozen women sitting on the benches waiting. Many come and go. Our faces are all familiar to each other, for we wait here everyday.

This is a domestic employment bureau. Most of the women who come here are middle-aged, some have families, some have raised their families and are now alone, some have men who are out of work. Hard times and the man leaves to hunt for work. He doesn't find it. He drifts on. The woman probably doesn't hear from him for a long time. She expects it. She isn't surprised. She struggles alone to feed the many mouths. Sometimes she gets help from the charities. If she's clever she can get herself a good living from the charities, if she's naturally a lick-spittle, naturally a little docile and cunning. If she's proud then she starves silently, leaving her children to find work, coming home after a day's searching to wrestle with her house, her children.

Some such story is written on the faces of all these women. There are young girls too, fresh from the country. Some are made brazen too soon by the city. There is a great exodus of girls from the farms into the city now. Thousands of farms have been vacated completely in Minnesota. The girls are trying to get work. The prettier ones can get jobs in the stores when there are any, or waiting on table, but these jobs are only for the attractive and the adroit; the others, the real peasants, have a more difficult time. . . .

A young girl who went around with Ellen [a poor, attractive young woman] tells about seeing her last evening back of a cafe downtown outside the kitchen door, kicking, showing her legs so that the cook came out and gave her some food and some men gathered in the alley and threw small coin on the ground for a look at her legs. And the girl says enviously that Ellen had a swell breakfast and treated her to one too, that cost two dollars.

A scrub woman whose hips are bent forward from stooping with hands gnarled like water soaked branches clicks her tongue in disgust. No one saves their money, she says, a little money and these foolish young things buy a hat, a dollar for breakfast, a bright scarf. And they do. If you've ever been without money, or food, something very strange happens when you get a bit of money, a kind of madness. You don't care. You can't remember that you had no money before, that the money will be gone. You can remember nothing but that there is the money for which you have been suffering. Now here it is. A lust takes hold of you. You see food in the windows. In imagination you eat hugely; you taste a thousand meals. You look in windows. Colours are brighter; you buy something to dress up in. An excitement takes hold of you. You know it is suicide but you can't help it. You must have food, dainty, splendid food and a bright hat so once again you feel blithe, rid of that ratty gnawing shame.

"I guess she'll go on the street now," a thin woman says faintly and no one takes the trouble to comment further. Like every commodity now the body is difficult to sell and the girls say you're lucky if you get fifty cents. . . .

It's one of the great mysteries of the city where women go when they are out of work and hungry. There are not many women in the bread line. There are no flop houses for women as there are for men, where a bed can be had for a quarter or less. You don't see women lying on the floor at the mission in the free flops. They obviously don't sleep in the jungle or under newspapers in the park. There is no law I suppose against their being in these places but the fact is they rarely are.

Yet there must be as many women out of jobs in cities and suffering extreme poverty as there are men. What happens to them? Where do they go? Try to get into the Y.W. without any money or looking down at heel. Charities take care of very few and only those that are called "deserving." The lone girl is under suspicion by the virgin women who dispense charity.

I've lived in cities for many months broke, without help, too timid to get in bread lines. I've known many women to live like this until they simply faint on the street from privations, without saying a word to anyone. A woman will shut herself up in a room until it is taken away from her, and eat a cracker a day and be as quiet as a mouse so there are no social statistics concerning her. . . .

Sometimes a girl facing the night without shelter will approach a man for lodging. A woman always asks a man for help. Rarely another woman. I have known girls to sleep in men's rooms for the night, on a pallet without molestation, and given breakfast in the morning. . . .

Mrs. Gray, sitting across from me is a living spokesman for the futility of labour. She is a warning. Her hands are scarred with labour. Her body is a great puckered scar. She has given birth to six children, buried three, supported them all alive and dead, bearing them, burying them, feeding them. Bred in hunger they have been spare, susceptible to disease. For seven years she tried to save her boy's arm from amputation, diseased from tuberculosis of the bone. It is almost too suffocating to think of that long close horror of years of child bearing, child feeding, rearing, with the bare suffering of providing a meal and shelter.

Now she is fifty. Her children, economically insecure, are drifters. She never hears of them. She doesn't know if they are alive. She doesn't know if she is alive. Such subtleties of suffering are not for her. For her the brutality of hunger and cold, the bare bone of life. That is enough. These will occupy a life. Not until these are done away with can those subtle feelings that make a human being be indulged.

She is lucky to have five dollars ahead of her. That is her security. She has a tumour that she will die of. She is thin as a worn dime with her tumour sticking out of her side. She is brittle and bitter. Her face is not the face of a human being. She has borne more than it is possible for a human being to bear. She is reduced to the least possible denominator of human feelings.

It is terrible to see her little bloodshot eyes like a beaten hound's, fearful in terror.

We cannot meet her eyes. When she looks at any of us we look away. She is like a woman drowning and we turn away. . . .

The young ones know though. I don't want to marry. I don't want any children. So they all say. No children. No marriage. They arm themselves alone, keep up alone. The man is helpless now. He cannot provide. If he propagates he cannot take care of his young. The means are not in his hands. So they live alone. Get what fun they can. The life risk is too horrible now. Defeat is too clearly written on it.

It is appalling to think that these women sitting so listless in the room may work as hard as it is possible for a human being to work, may labour night and day, like Mrs. Gray, wash street cars from midnight to dawn and offices in the early evening, scrubbing for fourteen and fifteen hours a day, sleeping only five hours or so, doing this their whole lives, and never earn one day of security, having always before them the pit of the future. The endless labour, the bending back, the water soaked hands, earning never more than a week's wages, never having in their hands more life than that.

# 25

# THE POLITICS OF UPHEAVAL

★━━★━━★

There are cycles in American presidential politics. Of the first nine presidential elections, for instance, Jefferson's Democratic Republicans won seven, the Federalists two. The Democrats also won six of the next nine elections. Then a new cycle began in which the Republicans won seven of nine elections from 1860 to 1892 (versus just two for the once-mighty Democrats) and also won seven of the next nine, with their only setbacks coming at the hands of Woodrow Wilson in 1912 and 1916. At this point, the cataclysm of the Great Depression and the charisma of Franklin D. Roosevelt returned the Democrats to dominance. They won, often by landslide margins, every election from 1932 to 1964, except for two losses to Dwight Eisenhower in the 1950s. After that, however, they reverted to their post–Civil War form, enabling the Nixon-Reagan-Bush-Bush GOP to post a six-to-three score through 2000.

Given the magnitude of the Great Depression and Franklin D. Roosevelt's role in triggering so massive a political realignment, his inaugural address in 1933 might appear moderate. It calls for confidence, honest labor, the protection of agriculture and land, organized relief, and a bit of economic planning. Only Roosevelt's castigation of the "money changers" and his plea for executive authority to meet the crisis seemed to prefigure the sweeping liberalism that many observers instinctively associate with the Roosevelt years. Nevertheless, the address was charged with emotion and a sense of mission. Its moderation reflected both the confusion of the times, when few people understood the nation's problems and still fewer had solutions, and the personal conservatism of the speaker, who was ultimately American capitalism's savior as well as its reformer.

Franklin Delano Roosevelt, a distant cousin of Theodore Roosevelt, was born in 1882 to a wealthy New York family. He attended exclusive schools and colleges and practiced law in New York City. He married his cousin Eleanor in 1905, entered Democratic politics—serving in the state senate from 1910 to 1913—and became assistant secretary of the navy in 1913. After running (and losing) as the Democrats' vice-presidential candidate in 1920, he contracted polio, which left him permanently crippled. Remaining active in politics, he served as governor of New York from 1928 to 1932, when he defeated Hoover for the presidency. During the 1932 campaign Roosevelt criticized Hoover for excessive government spending and an unbalanced budget. Nevertheless, after entering the White House, Roosevelt also was obliged to adopt a spending policy to help those who were starving, put people to work, and revive the economy. His New Deal stressed economic recovery as well as relief and reform. Roosevelt's programs, backed by the great Democratic majorities that he forged, mitigated many of the effects of the Great Depression, though the slump never actually ended until the advent of World War II. Roosevelt achieved reelection in 1936, 1940, and 1944, a record unequaled then and unconstitutional since 1951. He died in office in Warm Springs, Georgia, in 1945.

**Questions to Consider.** Why, in his first inaugural address, did Roosevelt place great emphasis on candor, honesty, and truth? Did he display these qualities himself in discussing the crisis? In what ways did he try to reassure the American people? What reasons did he give for the Great Depression? What values did he think were important for sustaining the nation in a time of trouble? What solutions did he propose for meeting the economic crisis? How did he regard his authority to act under the Constitution? How would you have reacted to his address if you had been an unemployed worker, a hard-pressed farmer, or a middle-class citizen who had lost a home through foreclosure?

★═══★═══★

# First Inaugural Address (1933)

## FRANKLIN D. ROOSEVELT

This is a day of national consecration, and I am certain that my fellow-Americans expect that on my induction into the Presidency I will address them with a candor and a decision which the present situation of our nation impels. This is pre-eminently the time to speak the truth, the whole truth, frankly and boldly. Nor need we shrink from honestly facing conditions in our country today. This great nation will endure as it has endured, will revive and will prosper.

So first of all let me assert my firm belief that the only thing we have to fear is fear itself—nameless, unreasoning, unjustified terror which paralyzes needed efforts to convert retreat into advance. In every dark hour of our national life a leadership of frankness and vigor has met with that understanding and support

*The New York Times,* March 5, 1933.

**F.D.R.** Franklin D. Roosevelt, the "happy warrior," with his wife, Eleanor, and their daughter Anna, en route from the railroad to the family cottage in Warm Springs, Georgia, a favorite spot for rest and recreation. (Franklin D. Roosevelt Library)

of the people themselves which is essential to victory. I am convinced that you will again give that support to leadership in these critical days.

In such a spirit on my part and on yours we face our common difficulties. They concern, thank God, only material things. Values have shrunken to fantastic levels; taxes have risen; our ability to pay has fallen; government of all kinds is faced by serious curtailment of income; the means of exchange are frozen in the currents of trade; the withered leaves of industrial enterprise lie on every side; farmers find no markets for their produce; the savings of many years in thousands of families are gone.

More important, a host of unemployed citizens face the grim problem of existence, and an equally great number toil with little return. Only a foolish optimist can deny the dark realities of the moment.

Yet our distress comes from no failure of substance. We are stricken by no plague of locusts. Compared with the perils which our forefathers conquered because they believed and were not afraid, we have still much to be thankful for. Nature still offers her bounty and human efforts have multiplied it. Plenty is at our doorstep, but a generous use of it languishes in the very sight of the supply. Primarily, this is because the rulers of the exchange of mankind's goods have failed through their own stubbornness and their own incompetence, have admitted their failure and abdicated. Practices of the unscrupulous money changers stand indicted in the court of public opinion, rejected by the hearts and minds of men.

True, they have tried, but their efforts have been cast in the pattern of an outworn tradition. Faced by failure of credit, they have proposed only the lending of more money. Stripped of the lure of profit by which to induce our people to follow their false leadership, they have resorted to exhortations, pleading tearfully for restored confidence. They know only the rules of a generation of self-seekers. They have no vision, and when there is no vision the people perish.

The money changers have fled from their high seats in the temple of our civilization. We may now restore that temple to the ancient truths. The measure of the restoration lies in the extent to which we apply social values more noble than mere monetary profit.

Happiness lies not in the mere possession of money; it lies in the joy of achievement, in the thrill of creative effort. The joy and moral stimulation of work no longer must be forgotten in the mad chase of evanescent profits. These dark days will be worth all they cost us if they teach us that our true destiny is not to be ministered unto but to minister to ourselves and to our fellow-men.

Recognition of the falsity of material wealth as the standard of success goes hand in hand with the abandonment of the false belief that public office and high political position are to be valued only by the standards of pride of place and personal profit; and there must be an end to a conduct in banking and in business which too often has given to a sacred trust the likeness of callous and selfish wrongdoing. Small wonder that confidence languishes, for it thrives only on honesty, on honor, on the sacredness of obligations, on faithful protection, on unselfish performance. Without them it cannot live.

Restoration calls, however, not for changes in ethics alone. This nation asks for action, and action now.

Our greatest primary task is to put people to work. This is no unsolvable problem if we face it wisely and courageously. It can be accomplished in part by direct recruiting by the Government itself, treating the task as we would treat the emergency of war, but at the same time, through this employment, accomplishing greatly needed projects to stimulate and reorganize the use of our natural resources.

Hand in hand with this, we must frankly recognize the overbalance of population in our industrial centers and, by engaging on a national scale in the redistribution, endeavor to provide a better use of the land for those best fitted for the land. The task can be helped by definite efforts to raise the values of agricultural products and with this the power to purchase the output of our cities. It can be helped by preventing realistically the tragedy of the growing loss, through foreclosure, of our small homes and our farms. It can be helped by insistence that the Federal, State and local governments act forthwith on the demand that their cost be drastically reduced. It can be helped by the unifying of relief activities which today are often scattered, uneconomical and unequal. It can be helped by national planning for a supervision of all forms of transportation and of communications and other utilities which have a definitely public character. There are many ways in which it can be helped, but it can never be helped merely by talking about it. We must act, and act quickly. . . .

This I propose to offer, pledging that the larger purposes will bind upon us all as a sacred obligation with a unity of duty hitherto evoked only in the time of armed strife.

With this pledge taken, I assume unhesitatingly the leadership of this great army of our people, dedicated to a disciplined attack upon our common problems.

Action in this image and to this end is feasible under the form of government which we have inherited from our ancestors. Our Constitution is so simple and practical that it is possible always to meet extraordinary needs by changes in emphasis and arrangement without loss of essential form. That is why our constitutional system has proved itself the most superbly enduring political mechanism the modern world has produced. It has met every stress of vast expansion of territory, of foreign wars, of bitter internal strife, of world relations.

It is to be hoped that the normal balance of executive and legislative authority may be wholly adequate to meet the unprecedented task before us. But it may be that an unprecedented demand and need for undelayed action may call for temporary departure from that normal balance of public procedure.

I am prepared under my constitutional duty to recommend the measures that a stricken nation in the midst of a stricken world may require. These measures, or such other measures as the Congress may build out of its experience and wisdom, I shall seek, within my constitutional authority, to bring to speedy adoption.

But in the event that the Congress shall fail to take one of these two courses, and in the event that the national emergency is still critical, I shall not evade the clear course of duty that will then confront me. I shall ask the Congress for the one remaining instrument to meet the crisis—broad Executive power to wage a war against the emergency as great as the power that would be given me if we were in fact invaded by a foreign foe.

For the trust reposed in me I will return the courage and the devotion that befit the time. I can do no less.

# 26

## A NEW DEAL

In 1933, Franklin D. Roosevelt promised the country a "New Deal" to combat the Great Depression and over the next several years oversaw the passage of legislation to fulfill that promise. The result was not particularly systematic. "It is common sense to take a method and try it," Roosevelt said. "If it fails, admit it frankly and try another. But above all try something." The New Deal was therefore a grab bag of programs intended to cope with the immediate collapse, to ward off future collapses, and if possible to forge a fairer, more stable society through banking and utility reform, low-cost housing loans, and electric power generation. A Public Works Administration built airports, dams, and other large facilities. The Social Security Act provided old-age pensions, unemployment compensation, and aid to the disabled. Other acts raised taxes on corporations and the wealthy, regulated wages and hours, and made it easier to organize unions.

But most of these programs would have an effect only in the long run. The immediate problem was massive unemployment. Emergency relief to the states helped. The Civilian Conservation Corps, which hired 2 million people to do conservation work, helped. But the biggest initiative to provide jobs came with the establishment in 1935 of the Works Progress Administration (WPA), a program that dwarfed prior efforts and eventually employed one-third of all jobless Americans—8.5 million overall. The goal of the WPA was to replace make-work relief programs with employment on projects of real value: roads and post offices, parks, recreational facilities, day nurseries, theaters, tourist guides, bookbinding, and scholarly research. By late 1941, with war looming, nearly 40 percent of WPA employees worked in the defense industry. Roosevelt disbanded the program in 1943.

Roosevelt saw human as well as practical significance in the WPA. "We have a human problem as well as an economic problem," he said in January 1935. "To dole out relief is to administer a narcotic, a subtle destroyer of the human spirit." The following speech by Harry Hopkins, whom the president chose to administer the new program, laid out the administration's thinking. Harry Hopkins, a professional social worker from Sioux City, Iowa, had helped direct relief work in

New York when Roosevelt was governor and went to Washington in 1933 to administer emergency federal relief. He soon became the president's closest advisor and confidant, a role he continued to play with the coming of World War II. He died in 1946.

**Questions to Consider.** What different arguments did Harry Hopkins use in support of establishing the Works Progress Administration? Which of these seems to have been most important to him? Who was to blame, in Hopkins's view, for Depression unemployment? Why did he think meaningful work, as provided through the WPA, would strengthen families, and why was this important? Do his arguments about avoiding a permanent class of unemployed seem to have been valid for the time? Why did he call this possibility an "ominous" threat? How would the WPA help prevent this?

★═══★═══★

# The Works Progress Administration  (1935)

### HARRY HOPKINS

There are now around 5,000,000 American families on relief. That is to say that there are 5,000,000 families receiving public assistance because the head of the family has no job. This figure, of course, does not take into account that other extremely important fraction of the American population, the unemployed who have so far stayed off going on relief rolls, often by means dangerous to the health of their children.

Our wage-paying habits are such that it frequently takes the pooled earnings of every available member to keep the family going even at a subsistence level. In 1,000,000 of the relief families there is no employable member. But after we have taken into consideration the large numbers who are temporarily on relief because they are victims of the drought, there remain about 3,500,000 relief families containing slightly over 5,000,000 jobless workers, employable in the sense that they are between 16 and 65 years of age, able and willing to work. . . .

However, let us suppose that for lack of an employable member one-fifth of our relief households are to become quasi-permanent charges upon straight public assistance and that they will have to be given old age pensions, mothers' aid, straight relief or institutional care. Are we going to make no differentiation between these incapable dependents and the five million workers who are on relief solely because they have no job? Are we going to pursue a course which can have no other end in view than to turn the relief population into a permanent charge upon the public treasury? Can we afford this course financially even if we have no particular interest in the fulfillment of life for as many persons as are physically capable of achieving it?

This last objective is sometimes attributed to the alleged sentimentalism of the social worker, though it has long been the accepted objective of that most realistic of all professions, medicine. Often those economists and financiers who most shy away from the humane objectives of better living for larger numbers and retreat behind what sometimes seem to be irrefutable columns of mounting costs are the very ones to complain that straight relief creates dependency by corroding character. They deplore that once upstanding citizens now accept public money without a murmur and come back for more. It sometimes would appear that the classical economist is a very slipshod social thinker when he faces the human realities of unemployment. . . .

Straight relief, direct relief, the dole, or whatever you want to call it, maintains life not at a subsistence level, but at a level of deterioration.

The loss of skill, the loss of work habits, muscle and resolve are only the half of it. The complete loss of any sense of importance to their job, to their families, to society and to themselves is the loss which is being sustained by millions of our workers. By their enforced idleness we are laying by a store of social problems.

Because of these three different enmities which the unemployed have incurred through no fault of their own—that of business, of their recent fellow-workers and in a sense of the forces which sustain and elevate the family as a unit of social life—the unemployed are in danger of being perpetuated as a class. They will have to seek and are already seeking through protest groups social protection as a class.

The most ominous threat which the unemployed can hold over the present structure is that they should as a class be perpetuated, unwillingly unproductive, and held in a straitjacket of idleness.

# 27

## THE RIGHTS OF LABOR

Until the late 1930s the federal judiciary was largely unsympathetic to the American trade union movement. Between 1880 and 1930 judges issued 4,300 injunctions against workers attempting to strike for better wages, hours, and working conditions. In many cases federal or National Guard troops enforced the injunctions at gunpoint, leading to a practice that union leaders called "Gatling gun injunctions." The courts also prohibited "secondary boycotts" that tried to pressure employers to settle strikes or face organized consumer retaliation.

The Great Depression witnessed a shift in the political climate as the reputation and standing of both corporations and the Republican party declined, and the Supreme Court shifted accordingly. In 1935, for example, the Court struck down the National Industrial Recovery Act (NIRA), a key piece of New Deal legislation, as an infringement on states' rights and the right of contract. But in 1937 it upheld not only the constitutionality of the National Labor Relations Act, which Congress had passed in 1935 to enhance the organizing efforts of labor, but specific rulings of the National Labor Relations Board, the federal agency established by the 1935 act.

*National Labor Relations Board* v. *Jones & Laughlin Steel* (excerpted below) has been called the Magna Carta and even the Emancipation Proclamation of the American labor movement because it seemed to guarantee the union organizing rights that generations of workers had sought. It was in practice nothing of the kind, since its protections and guarantees were gradually whittled down by more conservative Court decisions and acts of Congress, beginning in the 1940s. But it was important at the time. Moreover, by construing "interstate commerce" in a very broad way, the decision gave Congress unprecedented authority to regulate the American economy, a view that has largely endured. In this sense, *NLRB* v. *Jones & Laughlin* marked perhaps the most dramatic about-face in the history of the Supreme Court.

Charles Evans Hughes, the author of the 1937 decision, was born in 1862 in upstate New York. He attended Brown University, practiced law in New York City, and won fame for exposing abusive insurance company practices. A lifelong Republican, he had served two terms as governor when President William Howard Taft appointed him to the Supreme Court in 1910. In 1916 Hughes resigned from the Court in order to run for president against Woodrow Wilson. Defeated, he returned to the law until 1921, when he became Warren G. Harding's secretary of state. In 1930 Herbert Hoover appointed him chief justice of the Supreme Court, where he was moderately supportive of civil liberties, civil rights, and (despite voting in 1935 to strike down the NIRA) expansive federal economic powers, as in his *NLRB* v. *Jones & Laughlin* opinion. Hughes resigned from the Court for the last time in 1941. He died in Massachusetts in 1948.

**Questions to Consider.** What led Charles Evans Hughes to devote more space to a description of the operations of the Jones & Laughlin Steel Corporation than to any other part of his opinion? Hughes argued here that workers needed the right to form labor unions because an individual worker, dependent on his daily wage to survive, had no power to bargain with a big business except collectively with other workers. Was this a reasonable argument given the conditions of the American economy in the 1930s? Do you find it still persuasive today? Hughes defended his position in defense of union organizing rights in part by arguing (next to last paragraph below) that collective bargaining agreements would promote industrial peace. Some constitutional lawyers have detected a fundamental contradiction between support for union rights and the goal of industrial peace. Are they right? If this is a contradiction, is it an important one?

★━━★━━★

# National Labor Relations Board v. Jones & Laughlin Steel (1937)

### CHARLES EVANS HUGHES

In a proceeding under the National Labor Relations Act of 1935, the National Labor Relations Board found that the petitioner, Jones & Laughlin Steel Corporation, had violated the Act by engaging in unfair labor practices affecting commerce. . . .

The National Labor Relations Board . . . ordered the corporation to cease and desist from such discrimination and coercion, to offer reinstatement to ten of the employees named, to make good their losses in pay, and to post for thirty days notices that the corporation would not discharge or discriminate against members, or those desiring to become members, of the labor union. . . .

*NLRB* v. *Jones & Laughlin Steel,* 301 U.S. 1 (1937).

**Strike pickets.** During the winter of 1936–1937 the Congress of Industrial Organizations climaxed its drive to unionize America's basic industries with a series of strikes that caused conflict in some communities and tensions in most of the rest. Here, workers picket a New York City radio station for bargaining rights and higher wages in December 1937. By the following Christmas total union membership had zoomed to almost 8 million. Workers were responding to CIO organizers who sang, "You'll win. What I mean . . . Take it easy . . . but take it!" (Library of Congress)

The facts as to the nature and scope of the business of the Jones & Laughlin Steel Corporation have been found by the Labor Board and, so far as they are essential to the determination of this controversy, they are not in dispute. The Labor Board has found: The corporation is organized under the laws of Pennsylvania and has its principal office at Pittsburgh. It is engaged in the business of manufacturing iron and steel in plants situated in Pittsburgh and nearby Aliquippa, Pennsylvania. It manufactures and distributes a widely diversified line of steel and pig iron, being the fourth largest producer of steel in the United States. With its subsidiaries—nineteen in number—it is a completely integrated enterprise, owning and operating ore, coal and limestone properties, lake and river transportation facilities and terminal railroads located at its manufacturing plants. It owns or controls mines in Michigan and Minnesota. It operates four ore steamships on the Great Lakes, used in the transportation of ore to its factories. It owns coal mines in Pennsylvania. It operates towboats and steam barges used in carrying coal to its factories. It owns limestone properties in various places in Pennsylvania and West Virginia. It owns the Monongahela connecting railroad which connects the plants of the Pittsburgh works and forms an interconnection with the Pennsylvania, New York Central and Baltimore and Ohio Railroad systems. It owns the Aliquippa and Southern Railroad Company which connects the Aliquippa works with the Pittsburgh and Lake Erie, part of the New York Central system. Much of its product is shipped to its warehouses in Chicago, Detroit, Cincinnati and Memphis,—to the last two places by means of its own barges and transportation equipment. In Long Island City, New York, and in New Orleans it operates structural steel fabricating shops in connection with the warehousing of semi-finished materials sent from its works. Through one of its wholly-owned subsidiaries it owns, leases and operates stores, warehouses and yards for the distribution of equipment and supplies for drilling and operating oil and gas mills and for pipe lines, refineries and pumping stations. It has sales offices in twenty cities in the United States and a wholly-owned subsidiary which is devoted exclusively to distributing its product in Canada. Approximately 75 per cent of its product is shipped out of Pennsylvania.

Summarizing these operations, the Labor Board concluded that the works in Pittsburgh and Aliquippa "might be likened to the heart of a self-contained, highly integrated body. They draw in the raw materials from Michigan, Minnesota, West Virginia, Pennsylvania in part through arteries and by means controlled by the respondent; they transform the materials and then pump them out to all parts of the nation through the vast mechanism which the respondent has elaborated."

To carry on the activities of the entire steel industry, 33,000 men mine ore, 44,000 men mine coal, 4,000 men quarry limestone, 16,000 men manufacture coke, 343,000 men manufacture steel, and 83,000 men transport its product. Respondent has about 10,000 employees in its Aliquippa plant, which is located in a community of about 30,000 persons.

Practically all the factual evidence in the case, except that which dealt with the nature of respondent's business, concerned its relations with the employees in the Aliquippa plant whose discharge was the subject of the complaint. These employees were active leaders in the labor union. . . .

The right of employees to self-organization and to select representatives of their own choosing for collective bargaining or other mutual protection without restraint or coercion by their employer . . . is a fundamental right. Employees have as clear a right to organize and select their representatives for lawful purposes as the respondent has to organize its business and select its own officers and agents. Discrimination and coercion to prevent the free exercise of the right of employees to self-organization and representation is a proper subject for condemnation by competent legislative authority. Long ago we stated the reason for labor organizations. We said that they were organized out of the necessities of the situation; that a single employee was helpless in dealing with an employer; that he was dependent ordinarily on his daily wage for the maintenance of himself and family; that if the employer refused to pay him the wages that he thought fair, he was nevertheless unable to leave the employ and resist arbitrary and unfair treatment; that union was essential to give laborers opportunity to deal on an equality with their employer. . . . Fully recognizing the legality of collective action on the part of employees in order to safeguard their proper interests, we said that Congress was not required to ignore this right but could safeguard it. Congress could seek to make appropriate collective action of employees an instrument of peace rather than of strife. We said that such collective action would be a mockery if representation were made futile by interference with freedom of choice. . . .

Experience has abundantly demonstrated that the recognition of the right of employees to self-organization and to have representatives of their own choosing for the purpose of collective bargaining is often an essential condition of industrial peace. Refusal to confer and negotiate has been one of the most prolific causes of strife. This is such an outstanding fact in the history of labor disturbances that it is a proper subject of judicial notice and requires no citation of instances. But with respect to the appropriateness of the recognition of self-organization and representation in the promotion of peace, the question is not essentially different in the case of employees in industries of such a character that interstate commerce is put in jeopardy from the case of employees of transportation companies. And of what avail is it to protect the facility of transportation, if interstate commerce is throttled with respect to the commodities to be transported!

Our conclusion is that the order of the Board was within its competency and that the Act is valid as here applied.

# 28

## WAR AIMS

★━━★━━★

Circumstances change, said Franklin D. Roosevelt, and so did he as president, from (in other words) "Mr. New Deal" facing the dangers of the Great Depression in the 1930s to "Mr. Win-the-War" facing the dangers of the Axis Powers in the 1940s. Historians have sometimes seen the coming of war as a discontinuity in his administration.

But the break was not so sharp as it might have been. One thread providing continuity was that Roosevelt was never disinterested in world affairs, even during the most urgent days of the Depression. As the Nazi threat to France and England and the Japanese threat to China grew in the late 1930s, so did Roosevelt's determination to help—if he could do so without declaring war. Another thread was that Roosevelt perceived the looming conflict partly in ideological terms—as a struggle, with the forces of authoritarianism and social reaction pitted against the forces of democracy and social progress. To some extent, Roosevelt's view of the conflict resembled Woodrow Wilson's goal in World War I of making the world "safe for democracy." It also followed logically from the nature of the enemy, which most people regarded as nothing but a coalition of racist, militaristic tyrants. Opposing such an enemy meant, by extension, opposing what the enemy stood for.

In his "Four Freedoms" address, delivered to Congress and broadcast to the public in January 1941—prior to America's formal entry into the war—Roosevelt went beyond Woodrow Wilson in his statement of war goals. In this speech, as in others he delivered over the next four years, the president made it clear that he considered this war to be not just about freedom of speech, press, and religion, as his predecessors might have it. This was also a war about freedom from want, the philosophy underlying many of the New Deal programs. And it was about freedom from fear, a sentiment that had filled his first inaugural address eight years before. At least in this 1941 statement, "Mr. Win-the-War" continued to be "Mr. New Deal."

**Questions to Consider.** Isolationist, antiwar feelings were still very strong in the country in early 1941. How did Roosevelt try at the beginning of his speech to neutralize antiwar sentiment? At what point in the address did he introduce what might be considered progressive political ideas of the kind that characterized the New Deal? According to Roosevelt, what were the foundations of "a healthy and strong democracy"? Would all Americans have agreed with his list of democratic "foundations"? Why did the president demand individual sacrifice and warn people not to try to get rich from his programs? Of the "four freedoms" Roosevelt eventually enumerated, which do you think would have been most popular in the 1940s?

★═══★═══★

# The Four Freedoms (1941)

### FRANKLIN D. ROOSEVELT

I address you, the Members of the Seventy-seventh Congress, at a moment unprecedented in the history of the Union. I use the word "unprecedented," because at no previous time has American security been as seriously threatened from without as it is today. . . .

Every realist knows that the democratic way of life is at this moment being directly assailed in every part of the world—assailed either by arms, or by secret spreading of poisonous propaganda by those who seek to destroy unity and promote discord in nations still at peace.

During sixteen months this assault has blotted out the whole pattern of democratic life in an appalling number of independent nations, great and small. The assailants are still on the march, threatening other nations, great and small.

Therefore, as your President, performing my constitutional duty to "give to the Congress information on the state of the Union," I find it necessary to report that the future and the safety of our country and of our democracy are overwhelmingly involved in events far beyond our borders.

Armed defense of democratic existence is now being gallantly waged in four continents. If that defense fails, all the population and all the resources of Europe, Asia, Africa, and Australasia will be dominated by the conquerors. The total of those populations and their resources greatly exceeds the sum total of the population and resources of the whole of the Western Hemisphere—many times over. . . .

No realistic American can expect from a dictator's peace international generosity, or return of true independence, or world disarmament, or freedom of expression, or freedom of religion—or even good business.

Such a peace would bring no security for us or for our neighbors. Those who would give up essential liberty to purchase a little temporary safety deserve neither liberty nor safety. . . .

*The New York Times,* January 7, 1941.

There is much loose talk of our immunity from immediate and direct invasion from across the seas. Obviously, as long as the British Navy retains its power, no such danger exists. Even if there were no British Navy, it is not probable that any enemy would be stupid enough to attack us by landing troops in the United States from across thousands of miles of ocean, until it had acquired strategic bases from which to operate.

But we learn much from the lessons of the past years in Europe—particularly the lesson of Norway, whose essential seaports were captured by treachery and surprise built up over a series of years. . . .

As long as the aggressor nations maintain the offensive, they, not we, will choose the time and the place and the method of their attack. . . .

Let us say to the democracies, "We Americans are vitally concerned in your defense of freedom. We are putting forth our energies, our resources, and our organizing powers to give you the strength to regain and maintain a free world. We shall send you, in ever-increasing numbers, ships, planes, tanks, guns. This is our purpose and our pledge."

In fulfillment of this purpose we will not be intimidated by the threats of dictators that they will regard as a breach of international law and as an act of war our aid to the democracies which dare to resist their aggression. Such aid is not an act of war, even if a dictator should unilaterally proclaim it so to be.

When the dictators are ready to make war upon us, they will not wait for an act of war on our part. They did not wait for Norway or Belgium or The Netherlands to commit an act of war.

Their only interest is in a new one-way international law, which lacks mutuality in its observance and, therefore, becomes an instrument of oppression. . . .

As men do not live by bread alone, they do not fight by armaments alone. Those who man our defenses, and those behind them who build our defenses, must have the stamina and courage which come from an unshakable belief in the manner of life which they are defending. The mighty action which we are calling for cannot be based on a disregard of all things worth fighting for.

There is nothing mysterious about the foundations of a healthy and strong democracy. The basic things expected by our people of their political and economic systems are simple.

They are:

Equality of opportunity for youth and for others.
Jobs for those who can work.
Security for those who need it.
The ending of special privilege for the few.
The preservation of civil liberties for all.
The enjoyment of the fruits of scientific progress in a wider and constantly rising standard of living.

These are the simple and basic things that must never be lost sight of in the turmoil and unbelievable complexity of our modern world. The inner and abiding strength of our economic and political systems is dependent upon the degree to which they fulfill these expectations. . . .

I have called for personal sacrifice. I am assured of the willingness of almost all Americans to respond to that call.

A part of the sacrifice means the payment of more money in taxes. . . .

No person should try, or be allowed to get rich out of this program. . . .

In the future days, which we seek to make secure, we look forward to a world founded upon four essential human freedoms.

The first is freedom of speech and expression, everywhere in the world.

The second is freedom of every person to worship God in his own way, everywhere in the world.

The third is freedom from want, which, translated into world terms, means economic understandings which will secure to every nation a healthy peacetime life for its inhabitants, everywhere in the world.

The fourth is freedom from fear—which, translated into world terms, means a worldwide reduction of armaments to such a point and in such a thorough fashion that no nation will be in a position to commit an act of physical aggression against any neighbor—anywhere in the world.

That is no vision of a distant millennium. It is a definite basis for a kind of world attainable in our own time and not the so-called new order of tyranny which the dictators seek to impose. That kind of world is the very antithesis of the kind created with the crash of a bomb.

To that new order we oppose the greater conception—the moral order. A good society is able to face schemes of world domination and foreign revolutions alike without fear.

Since the beginning of our American history we have been engaged in change—in a perpetual peaceful revolution—a revolution which goes on steadily, quietly adjusting itself to changing conditions—without the concentration camp or the quicklime in the ditch. The world order which we seek is the cooperation of free countries, working together in a friendly, civilized society.

This Nation has placed its destiny in the hands and heads and hearts of its millions of free men and women; and its faith in freedom under the guidance of God. Freedom means the supremacy of human rights everywhere. Our support goes to those who struggle to gain those rights or keep them. Our strength is in our unity of purpose.

To that high concept there can be no end save victory.

# 29

## ENVISIONING POSTWAR AMERICA

★━━★━━★

People who thought seriously about the postwar world generally followed one of two paths. One involved efforts to prevent another monstrous war. For Franklin Roosevelt, that meant, besides smashing Nazism and militarism, a sustained level of international cooperation—to which end his administration planned as early as 1943 for the creation of an international peacekeeping body, the United Nations Organization. Congress endorsed the idea, and the U.S. became a full member of both the UN and its specialized agencies, including the World Health Organization, the International Children's Emergency Fund (UNICEF), and the Educational, Scientific, and Cultural Organization (UNESCO). The administration also sponsored and immersed itself in the World Bank, the International Monetary Fund, and the General Agreement on Tariffs and Trade, all created or planned during the Roosevelt years.

A second path involved consideration of the nature of postwar America if and when the Allies subdued the Axis. The following speech by Secretary of Labor Frances Perkins is an example. Perkins gave this particular address at a forum of women leaders, a sign that nontraditional constituencies were hoping to shape the postwar era. Perkins was not a close confidant of Roosevelt. But she worked closely with him on several important initiatives, including Social Security and labor laws, and became a shrewd observer of his political inclinations and style. Moreover, this early in the war, long before the Normandy invasion and the reconquest of the Philippines, Perkins would certainly have cleared her remarks with the White House.

Frances Perkins was born in Boston in 1882. A college graduate and one-time school teacher and church worker, Perkins took advanced degrees in economics and worked from 1911 to 1933 in various New York agencies related to consumer protection and industrial safety. One of Roosevelt's first and most important cabinet appointees, she became the first woman cabinet member in American history. A strong advocate and defender of innovative welfare and labor measures throughout her life, Perkins died in New York City in 1965.

**Questions to Consider.**  Why did Perkins place the extension of the social security system at the center of her remarks? Was it her experience, the nature of her audience for this speech, the ideals of her boss, or her overall understanding of how societies function that seem to have driven this speech? What specific troubles did she anticipate when the war ended? What international role did she urge the U.S. to play, and why? How did she think about the concept of freedom? Would a conservative Republican have agreed?

★━━━★━━━★

# What Kind of World Do We Want? (1943)

## FRANCES PERKINS

To secure a free world and to give some reality to the hope that it be a better world we must build upon foundations which already exist and which we understand. And so when you ask me tonight to say what kind of a world do I want, I say boldly that I want and believe we can have a world in which individuals have both liberty and security on the basis of the extension of already known patterns and habits of social cooperation. . . .

Certain types of public activity will need to be extended usefully in most countries, certainly in our own.

The extension of special provisions for child welfare—assuring all children a freedom from oppressive child labor, access to suitable educational opportunity and vocational preparation, health assistance, and whatever assistance in conserving home life or providing special protection their needs may require, will clearly be part of useful public activity.

A large measure of public responsibility for the establishment of steady employment is undoubtedly to be expected. It should be possible to reduce the suffering due to unemployment, which might follow industrial and military demobilization (1) by extension of the Social Security program, (2) previously planned public works (such as bridges, roads, housing, etc.), and (3) the retraining of men and women for peacetime occupations.

Adoption of an expanded Social Security program in the near future so as to provide enlarged benefits covering all major hazards of wage earners would give the United States a curb on inflation now and a brake on deflation later. It would also mitigate many demobilization difficulties in the postwar period.

If wise and practical extension is undertaken now the Social Security program will be able correspondingly to provide to all wage-earners and to such self-employed people as care to buy into the system, unemployment benefits, retirement, or old age benefits, a retraining benefit, a benefit in periods of disability due to illness or accidents, and maternity benefits to wives in insured families, funeral benefits, and a survivor's benefit to the widows and dependents of those who do not live to collect their old-age benefit and a modest hospitalization benefit.

In addition a strong and developed Employment Placement Service for use not only in wartime but in the period of demobilization and thereafter can be of inestimable value. The sense of security which returning soldiers and sailors will have because their families are protected as well as themselves, if such a system is put into its beginning operations now, will do much to stabilize our political and social development in the future.

Such extensions should include appropriations of Federal funds to aid States in public assistance to the aged not covered, to dependent children, to the handicapped, etc., in inverse proportion to the taxable income of the States.

The demobilization of those now employed in the wartime industries and their reassignment to peacetime production would be cushioned against the doubt and uncertainty with which today many persons view that period.

There can be no question of our ability to pay for an adequate system of Social Security at this time. Indeed, we can hardly envisage an equally propitious time to introduce a plan of postponed spending. The funds paid into Social Security contributions now will flow back in the future to those who pay them to the social improvement of the whole of society. . . .

The carrying out of such a program as I have outlined would certainly go far toward achieving for the American people the freedom from want which from the economic and social standpoint is one of the most important elements in our common aspiration for the future.

In this connection we should realize that public responsibility must express itself both in the national and in the international sphere. All nations must stand ready at the conclusion of this war to make many resources available in the reconstruction of the world. How those resources are to be made available must still be determined. Temporary grants on the basis of need, in cases of suffering with future adjustment, may be necessary.

Stable economic society exists not on the basis of free grants of assistance but rather on the basis of mutually advantageous exchanges of goods and services. The world is rich, but every nation that must depend upon its own resources alone is poor. Economic as well as personal and social cooperation of the many for the welfare of all may be the key to a dynamic and orderly world in the next fifty years.

The free world which we want to emerge from the war needs to be a world designed to produce security and minimum comfort for the ordinary man, the wage earner, the farmer, the merchant, the teacher. He must have opportunity to earn his livelihood in useful contributory pursuits. He needs to live in a world which makes provision for the disadvantaged groups of the community: the young, the old, the sick, those without adequate bargaining power, those whose family resources make it impossible for them to develop fully their innate capacities. In a free world the resources of science, of management, of organizing capacity and of statesmanship can be harnessed to produce a constantly rising level of living.

**The Berlin Wall.**  A West German greets friends and family in East Germany across the Berlin Wall. Constructed in 1961, the Berlin Wall was built by East Germany to keep its inhabitants from escaping to the West. The construction of the Wall added fuel to the Cold War and heightened tensions between the United States and the Soviet Union. (© Rene Burri/Magnum Photos)

CHAPTER SEVEN

# Protracted Conflict

# 30

## CONTAINMENT

When Germany invaded Poland in September 1939, Britain and France came to Poland's aid, and World War II began. But the surrender of Germany in May 1945 did not mean a free and independent Poland. Instead, when the war ended, the Soviet Union took over most of eastern Europe, including Poland, and installed regimes of its own choosing, backed by military force. The Russians had suffered severely in both World War I and World War II from invasions from the West and were determined to surround themselves with a ring of friendly states after the war. But American policy makers, shocked by the ruthlessness with which the Russians had accomplished their purpose, interpreted Soviet policy as expansionist rather than defensive in nature and began to fear that the Soviet Union had designs on western Europe as well. The United States therefore sponsored economic aid (the Marshall Plan) as well as military aid (the Truman Doctrine) to nations in Europe that seemed threatened by Soviet aggression; it also persuaded the nations of western Europe to organize the North Atlantic Treaty Organization (NATO). Thus was born the cold war between the Soviet Union and the United States.

In July 1947 an article entitled "The Sources of Soviet Conduct" appeared in *Foreign Affairs,* an influential journal published in New York. The author, identified only as "X," was later revealed to be George F. Kennan, head of the policy-planning staff of the State Department, so the article may have reflected official American views on Soviet foreign policy. Pointing out that the Soviet Union based its policies on a firm belief in the "innate antagonism between capitalism and socialism," Kennan warned that the Russians were going to be difficult to deal with for a long time. He added that the Kremlin was "under no ideological compulsion to accomplish its purposes in a hurry" and that the only wise course for the United States to follow was that of "a long-term, patient but firm and vigilant containment of Russian expansionist tendencies." Kennan's article, which is excerpted below, shaped as well as reflected American policy.

George F. Kennan was born in Milwaukee, Wisconsin, in 1904. After graduating from Princeton University in 1925, he joined the foreign service, in which he specialized in Russian affairs while serving in minor European posts. In 1933, he went to Moscow when the United States extended diplomatic recognition to the Soviet Union and opened an embassy there. Kennan served elsewhere in the late 1930s, but he returned to the Soviet Union during World War II and was appointed U.S. ambassador there in 1952. Kennan continued to write extensively on Russian and American diplomacy even after leaving the foreign service in the late 1950s. He came to deplore the excessively military application of the containment doctrine he had outlined in 1947, and in his later books and articles he made various proposals for demilitarization and disengagement that might diminish cold war tensions and lessen the chances of nuclear war.

**Questions to Consider.** In assigning responsibility for the cold war to a combination of Marxist ideology, the Kremlin's desire for power, and the world Communist movement, Kennan was also arguing, of course, that the West was largely defensive and even innocent. What evidence from twentieth-century history might be introduced to counter this argument? Kennan argued, similarly, that the Soviet threat was likely to last, practically speaking, forever. Given his views on Soviet objectives, were social or political changes conceivable that might alter these objectives or the Soviet capacity to pursue them? Did changes of this type in fact occur? Again, Kennan's article outlined his notions of Soviet society clearly enough. What assumptions, according to the evidence of the article, was Kennan making about American society? Finally, Kennan wrote his essay to mold American policy. One can imagine, however, various policies flowing from this analysis: an effort to roll back Russian power in Europe, an armed "garrison" state in the United States, intense economic or propaganda competition, and even a pre-emptive nuclear strike. Which of these did Kennan himself hope to see?

★━━★━━★

# The Sources of Soviet Conduct (1947)

### GEORGE F. KENNAN

The political personality of Soviet power as we know it today is the product of ideology and circumstances: ideology inherited by the present Soviet leaders from the movement in which they had their political origin, and

Reprinted by permission of Foreign Affairs, July 25, 1947. Copyright 1947 by the Council on Foreign Relations, Inc. www.ForeignAffairs.org

circumstances of the power which they now have exercised for nearly three decades in Russia. . . .

Marxian ideology, in its Russian-Communist projection, has always been in process of subtle evolution. The materials on which it bases itself are extensive and complex. But the outstanding features of Communist thought as it existed in 1916 may perhaps be summarized as follows: (a) that the central factor in the life of man, the fact which determines the character of public life . . . is the system by which material goods are produced and exchanged; (b) that the capitalist system of production is a nefarious one which inevitably leads to the exploitation of the working class. . . ; (c) that capitalism contains the seeds of its own destruction . . . ; and the final phase of capitalism leads directly to war.

It must be noted that there was no assumption that capitalism would perish without proletarian revolution. A final push was needed from a revolutionary proletariat movement in order to tip over the tottering structure. But it was regarded as inevitable that sooner or later that push be given. . . .

Now the outstanding circumstance concerning the Soviet regime is that down to the present day the process of political consolidation has never been completed and the men in the Kremlin have continued to be predominantly absorbed with the struggle to secure and make absolute the power which they seized in November 1917. They have endeavored to secure it primarily against forces at home, within Soviet society itself. But they have also endeavored to secure it against the outside world. For ideology, as we have seen, taught them that the outside world was hostile and that it was their duty eventually to overthrow the political forces beyond their borders. The powerful hands of Russian history and tradition reached up to sustain them in this feeling. . . .

As things stand today, the rulers can no longer dream of parting with these organs and suppression. The quest for absolute power, pursued now for nearly three decades with a ruthlessness unparalleled (in scope at least) in modern times, has again produced internally as it did externally, its own reaction. The excesses of the police apparatus have fanned the potential opposition to the regime into something far greater and more dangerous than it could have been before those excesses began. . . .

So much for the historical background. What does it spell in terms of the political personality of Soviet power as we know it today?

Of the original ideology, nothing has been officially junked. Belief is maintained in the basic badness of capitalism, in the inevitability of its destruction, in the obligation of the proletariat to assist in that destruction and to take power into its own hands. But stress has come to be laid primarily on those concepts which relate most specifically to the Soviet regime itself: to its position as the sole truly Socialist regime in a dark and misguided world, and to the relationships of power within it.

The first of these concepts is that of the innate antagonism between capitalism and Socialism. . . . It means that there can never be on Moscow's side any sincere assumption of a community of aims between the Soviet Union and powers which are regarded as capitalism. It must invariably be assumed in Moscow that the aims of the capitalist world are antagonistic to the Soviet regime and, therefore, to the interests of the peoples it controls. If the Soviet Government occasionally sets its signature to documents which would indicate the contrary, this is to be regarded as a tactical maneuver permissible in dealing with the enemy (who is without honor) and should be taken in the spirit of *caveat emptor* [let the buyer beware]. Basically, the antagonism remains. . . .

This means that we are going to continue for a long time to find the Russians difficult to deal with. It does not mean that they should be considered as embarked upon a do-or-die program to overthrow our society by a given date. The theory of the inevitability of the eventual fall of capitalism has the fortunate connotation that there is no hurry about it. The forces of progress can take their time in preparing the final *coup de grace.* Meanwhile, what is vital is that the "Socialist fatherland"—that oasis of power which has been already won for Socialism in the person of the Soviet Union—should be cherished and defended by all good Communists at home and abroad, its fortunes promoted, its enemies badgered and confounded. The promotion of premature, "adventuristic" revolutionary projects abroad which might embarrass Soviet power in any way would be an inexcusable, even a counter-revolutionary act. The cause of Socialism is the support and promotion of Soviet power, as defined in Moscow.

This brings us to the second of the concepts important to contemporary Soviet outlook. This is the infallibility of the Kremlin. The Soviet concept of power, which permits no focal points of organization outside the Party itself, requires that the Party leadership remain in theory the sole repository of truth. For if truth were to be found elsewhere, there would be justification for its expression in organized activity. But it is precisely that which the Kremlin cannot and will not permit.

The leadership of the Communist Party is therefore always right, and has been always right ever since in 1929 Stalin formalized his personal power by announcing that decisions of the Politburo were being taken unanimously. . . .

We have seen that the Kremlin is under no ideological compulsion to accomplish its purposes in a hurry. Like the Church, it is dealing in ideological concepts which are of long-term validity, and it can afford to be patient. It has no right to risk the existing achievements of the revolution for the sake of vain baubles of the future. The very teachings of Lenin himself require great caution and flexibility in the pursuit of Communist purposes. Again, these precepts are fortified by the lessons of Russian history: of centuries of obscure battles between nomadic forces over the stretches of a vast unfortified plain. Here caution, circumspection, flexibility and deception are the valuable qualities; and their value finds natural appreciation in the Russian or the oriental mind. . . .

These considerations make Soviet diplomacy at once easier and more difficult to deal with than the diplomacy of individual aggressive leaders like Napoleon and Hitler. On the one hand it is more sensitive to contrary force, more ready to yield on individual sectors of the diplomatic front when that force is felt to be too strong, and thus more rational in the logic and rhetoric of power. On the other hand it cannot be easily defeated or discouraged by a single victory on the part of its opponents. And the patient persistence by which it is animated means that it can be effectively countered not by sporadic acts which represent the momentary whims of democratic opinion but only by intelligent long-range policies on the part of Russia's adversaries—policies no less steady in their purpose, and no less variegated and resourceful in their application, than those of the Soviet Union itself.

In these circumstances it is clear that the main element of any United States policy toward the Soviet Union must be that of a long-term, patient but firm and vigilant containment of Russian expansive tendencies. It is important to note, however, that such a policy has nothing to do with outward histrionics: with threats or blustering or superfluous gestures of outward "toughness." While the Kremlin is basically flexible in its reaction to political realities, it is by no means unamenable to considerations of prestige. Like almost any other government, it can be placed by tactless and threatening gestures in a position where it cannot afford to yield even though this might be dictated by its sense of realism. The Russian leaders are keen judges of human psychology, and as such they are highly conscious that loss of temper and of self-control is never a source of strength in political affairs. They are quick to exploit such evidence of weakness. For these reasons, it is a *sine qua non* of successful dealing with Russia that the foreign government in question should remain at all times cool and collected and that its demands on Russian policy should be put forward in such a manner as to leave the way open for a compliance not too detrimental to Russian prestige. . . .

It is clear that the United States cannot expect in the foreseeable future to enjoy political intimacy with the Soviet regime. It must continue to regard the Soviet Union as a rival, not a partner, in the political arena. It must continue to expect that Soviet policies will reflect no abstract love of peace and stability, no real faith in the possibility of a permanent happy coexistence of the Socialist and capitalist worlds, but rather a cautious, persistent pressure toward the disruption and weakening of all rival influence and rival power.

Balanced against this are the fact that Russia, as opposed to the Western world in general, is still by far the weaker party, that Soviet policy is highly flexible, and that Soviet society may well contain deficiencies which will eventually weaken its own total potential. This would of itself warrant the United States entering with reasonable confidence upon a policy of firm containment, designed to confront the Russians with unalterable counterforce at every point where they show signs of encroaching upon the interests of a peaceful and stable world. . . .

It would be an exaggeration to say that American behavior unassisted and alone could exercise a power of life and death over the Communist movement and bring about the early fall of Soviet power in Russia. But the United States has it in its power to increase enormously the strains under which Soviet policy must operate, to force upon the Kremlin a far greater degree of moderation and circumspection than it has had to observe in recent years, and in this way to promote tendencies which must eventually find their outlet in either the breakup or the gradual mellowing of Soviet power. . . .

Thus the decision will really fall in large measure in this country itself. The issue of Soviet-American relations is in essence a test of the overall worth of the United States as a nation among nations. To avoid destruction the United States need only measure up to its own best traditions and prove itself worthy of preservation as a great nation.

Surely, there was never a fairer test of national quality than this. In the light of these circumstances, the thoughtful observer of Russian-American relations will find no cause for complaint in the Kremlin's challenge to American society. He will rather experience a certain gratitude to a Providence which, by providing the American people with this implacable challenge, has made their entire security as a nation dependent on their pulling themselves together and accepting the responsibilities of moral and political leadership that history plainly intended them to bear.

# 31

## SEEING REDS

★══★══★

In 1946 Joseph R. McCarthy defeated progressive Senator Robert M. La Follette, Jr., in the Republican primary in Wisconsin and went on to win election to the U.S. Senate that fall. During the primary contest he was supported by Wisconsin Communists who were infuriated by La Follette's pre–Pearl Harbor anti-interventionism and by his criticisms of Soviet dictator Joseph Stalin. Asked about the support the Communists were giving him against La Follette, McCarthy said airily, "The Communists have votes, too, don't they?" Four years later he became the leader of an impassioned crusade against Communism, and the word "McCarthyism" came to mean a reckless and demagogic assault on domestic dissent.

McCarthyism did not operate in a vacuum. Revelations of Communist spy activity in Canada, England, and the United States after World War II produced demands for counterespionage measures, and in 1947 President Truman inaugurated a loyalty program to ferret out Communists in government. Meanwhile, a series of "spy" cases hit the headlines: the trial and conviction of eleven Communist leaders under the Smith Act for conspiring to advocate the violent overthrow of the government; the conviction of former State Department official Alger Hiss, denounced as a Communist spy, for perjury; and the trial and execution of Julius and Ethel Rosenberg, government workers charged with passing atomic secrets to the Russians. For many Americans, the distinction between the expression of unpopular ideas and deliberate conspiratorial activity on behalf of a foreign power became increasingly blurred. In 1950, Senator McCarthy obliterated the distinction.

In a radio speech (excerpted below) given in Wheeling, West Virginia, in February 1950, McCarthy announced that he had in his hand a list of Communists in the State Department "known to the Secretary of State" and "still working and making policy." Overnight McCarthy became a national figure. Although he never showed anyone his famous "list" and was increasingly vague about the precise number of names it contained (205 or 81 or 57 or "a lot"), he came to exercise great influence in the U.S. Senate and in the nation. In July 1950, a Senate subcommittee headed by Maryland's Millard Tydings dismissed McCarthy's charges as "a fraud and a hoax." But when Tydings, a conservative Democrat, ran for reelection that fall, McCarthy's insinuations that he was pro-Communist helped defeat him. Similar accusations helped defeat Connecticut Democrat William Benton in 1952.

Not every Republican admired Senator McCarthy or approved his tactics, even when they benefited Republican candidates. Margaret Chase Smith of Maine, the only woman in the U.S. Senate in 1950, had served with McCarthy on the Permanent Investigations Subcommittee of the Senate and had become perturbed by his lack of concern for the unfair damage the subcommittee might do to individuals' reputations. Smith became still more perturbed following McCarthy's West Virginia speech in February 1950 about Communists in the State Department. When the Democrats failed to rebut McCarthy's charges effectively, she determined to speak out. Six other Republican senators endorsed Smith's "Declaration of Conscience."

It would take more than a statement by a handful of Senate Republicans to halt Joe McCarthy. In 1951 McCarthy charged that George C. Marshall, President Truman's former secretary of state and of defense, was part of "a conspiracy so immense and infamy so black as to dwarf any previous venture in the history of man." During the 1952 presidential campaign McCarthy talked ominously of "twenty years of treason" under the Democrats. His followers identified Roosevelt's New Deal, Truman's Fair Deal, and, indeed, all efforts for social reform since the Great Depression as Communist inspired. In 1953, as chairman of the Senate Committee on Government Operations, McCarthy launched a series of investigations of federal agencies, including the Voice of America, the International Information Agency, and the Army Signal Corps installation at Fort Monmouth, New Jersey. When the army decided to fight back, McCarthyism reached its climax in a series of televised Senate hearings in the spring of 1954. During these hearings, the Wisconsin senator's accusations and defamations of character gradually alienated all but his most devoted followers. On July 30, Republican Senator Ralph Flanders of Vermont, who had not endorsed Margaret Chase Smith's 1950 Declaration, introduced a resolution of censure. In December, the Senate voted, 67 to 32, to censure McCarthy for his behavior.

Joseph R. McCarthy was born in Grand Chute, Wisconsin, in 1908 to middle-class Roman Catholic parents. He graduated from Marquette University and entered the legal profession in Wisconsin in 1935. Originally a Democrat, he won his first political race (for a local judgeship) as a Republican in 1939. After serving as a Marine from 1942 to 1944, he became a state Republican power with his defeat of La Follette in the 1946 senatorial race. McCarthy's strongest bases of support were Wisconsin's small business owners and voters of German heritage; they reelected him in 1952 and largely continued their support even after his fall from national popularity. He died at the Bethesda Naval Hospital in Maryland in 1957.

**Questions to Consider.** Why did McCarthy launch his attack in 1950 rather than in 1949 or 1951? What area of the world most concerned him and what had happened there to give his message impact? Why did he attack from an out-of-the-way place (Wheeling, West Virginia) rather than from Washington or even his home state, Wisconsin, and why, moreover, on the radio? What reasons might McCarthy have had for singling out the State Department for attack, rather than, for example, the Department of Defense or the Department of Justice? In view of the fact that seven twentieth-century presidents and even more secretaries of state had attended just four private colleges (Yale, Harvard, Princeton, and Amherst), was there a certain logic in men such as McCarthy trying to link a Communist conspiracy with a conspiracy of "those who have had all the benefits"?

★═══★═══★

# Lincoln Day Address (1950)

## JOSEPH R. MCCARTHY

Ladies and gentlemen, tonight as we celebrate the one hundred and forty-first birthday of one of the greatest men in American history, I would like to be able to talk about what a glorious day today is in the history of the world. As we celebrate the birth of this man who with his whole heart and soul hated war, I would like to be able to speak of peace in our time, of war being outlawed, and of worldwide disarmament. These would be truly appropriate things to be able to mention as we celebrate the birthday of Abraham Lincoln.

Five years after a world war has been won, men's hearts should anticipate a long peace, and men's minds should be free from the heavy weight that comes with war. But this is not such a period—for this is not a period of peace. This is a time of the "cold war." This is a time when all the world is split into two vast, increasingly hostile armed camps—a time of a great armaments race.

Today we are engaged in a final, all-out battle between Communistic atheism and Christianity. The modern champions of Communism have selected this as the time. And, ladies and gentlemen, the chips are down—they are truly down.

Six years ago, at the time of the first conference to map out the peace— Dumbarton Oaks—there was within the Soviet orbit 180 million people.

*The Congressional Record,* 81st Congress, v. 96, part 2 (February 20, 1950).

Lined up on the antitotalitarian side there were in the world roughly 1,625 million people. Today, only six years later, there are 800 million people under the absolute domination of Soviet Russia—an increase of over 400 percent. On our side, the figure has shrunk to around 500 million. In other words, in less than six years the odds have changed from 9 to 1 in our favor to 8 to 5 against us. This indicates the swiftness of the tempo of Communist victories and American defeats in the cold war. As one of our outstanding historical figures once said, "When a great democracy is destroyed, it will not be because of enemies from without, but rather because of enemies from within."

The truth of this statement is becoming terrifyingly clear as we see this country each day losing on every front. . . .

The reason why we find ourselves in a position of impotency is not because our only powerful potential enemy has sent men to invade our shores, but rather because of the traitorous actions of those who have been treated so well by this Nation. It has not been the less fortunate or members of minority groups who have been selling this Nation out, but rather those who have had all the benefits that the wealthiest nation on earth has had to offer—the finest homes, the finest college education, and the finest jobs in Government we can give.

This is glaringly true in the State Department. There the bright young men who are born with silver spoons in their mouths are the ones who have been worst. . . .

When Chiang Kai-shek was fighting our war, the State Department had in China a young man named John S. Service. His task, obviously, was not to work for the Communization of China. Strangely, however, he sent official reports back to the State Department urging that we torpedo our ally Chiang Kai-shek and stating, in effect, that Communism was the best hope for China.

Later, this man—John Service—was picked up by the Federal Bureau of Investigation for turning over to the Communists secret State Department information. Strangely, however, he was never prosecuted. However, Joseph Grew, the Under Secretary of State, who insisted on his prosecution, was forced to resign. Two days after Grew's successor, Dean Acheson, took over as Under Secretary of State, this man—John Service—who had been picked up by the FBI and who had previously urged that Communism was the best hope of China, was not only reinstated in the State Department but promoted. And finally, under Acheson, placed in charge of all placements and promotions.

Today, ladies and gentlemen, this man Service is on his way to represent the State Department and Acheson in Calcutta—by far and away the most important listening post in the Far East. . . .

This, ladies and gentlemen, gives you somewhat of a picture of the type of individuals who have been helping to shape our foreign policy. In my opinion the State Department, which is one of the most important government departments, is thoroughly infested with Communists.

I have in my hand 57 cases of individuals who would appear to be either card carrying members or certainly loyal to the Communist Party, but who nevertheless are still helping to shape our foreign policy.

One thing to remember in discussing the Communists in our Government is that we are not dealing with spies who get 30 pieces of silver to steal the blueprints of a new weapon. We are dealing with a far more sinister type of activity because it permits the enemy to guide and shape our policy. . . .

As you hear this story of high treason, I know that you are saying to yourself, "Well, why doesn't the Congress do something about it?" Actually, ladies and gentlemen, one of the important reasons for the graft, the corruption, the dishonesty, the disloyalty, the treason in high Government positions—one of the most important reasons why this continues is a lack of moral uprising on the part of the 140 million American people. In the light of history, however, this is not hard to explain.

It is the result of an emotional hangover and a temporary moral lapse which follows every war. It is the apathy to evil which people who have been subjected to the tremendous evils of war feel. As the people of the world see mass murder, the destruction of defenseless and innocent people, and all of the crime and lack of morals which go with war, they become numb and apathetic. It has always been thus after war.

However, the morals of our people have not been destroyed. They still exist. This cloak of numbness and apathy has only needed a spark to rekindle them. Happily, this spark has finally been supplied.

As you know, very recently the Secretary of State [Dean Acheson] proclaimed his loyalty to a man [Alger Hiss] guilty of what has always been considered as the most abominable of all crimes—of being a traitor to the people who gave him a position of great trust. The Secretary of State in attempting to justify his continued devotion to the man who sold out the Christian world to the atheistic world, referred to Christ's Sermon on the Mount as a justification and reason therefor, and the reaction of the American people to this would have made the heart of Abraham Lincoln happy.

When this pompous diplomat in striped pants, with a phony British accent, proclaimed to the American people that Christ on the Mount endorsed Communism, high treason, and betrayal of a sacred trust, the blasphemy was so great that it awakened the dormant indignation of the American people.

He has lighted the spark which is resulting in a moral uprising and will end only when the whole sorry mess of twisted, warped thinkers are swept from the national scene so that we may have a new birth of national honesty and decency in Government.

# 32

## A QUESTION OF COMMAND

★━━━★━━━★

In 1950 the cold war between the United States and the Soviet Union turned suddenly hot in Korea, a peninsula abutting China near Japan. Korea had been freed from Japanese rule at the end of World War II, divided at the 38th parallel, and occupied by Russian troops in the north and American troops in the south. The Russians installed a friendly regime in North Korea and then withdrew; the United Nations, at U.S. urging, did the same in South Korea. On June 25, 1950, North Korean armies suddenly crossed the 38th parallel and launched a full-scale invasion of South Korea. President Truman, seeing the hand of China and therefore of the Soviet Union behind this move, promptly committed American troops to the defense of South Korea. He won the backing of the United Nations for his action and announced American determination to support anticommunist governments throughout East Asia. The Korean War lasted from June 1950 until the armistice of July 1953. Under United Nations auspices, sixteen nations participated in the conflict against North Korea. South Korea remained independent, but the Korean War cost the United States $22 billion and 34,000 dead.

The Korean War also prompted a major reassertion of the constitutional primacy of civilian rule in the U.S. government. The United Nations commander in the Korean theater was General Douglas MacArthur, one of the greatest U.S. heroes of World War II and the American proconsul in charge of transforming postwar Japanese society. Against the advice of the American joint chiefs of staff, MacArthur launched a brilliant amphibious landing behind Communist lines. He then recaptured the capital city of Seoul and moved far enough into North Korea to reach the border with China.

MacArthur had gambled that China would not commit troops to the conflict; President Truman's advisers feared it would. MacArthur was wrong. Massive Chinese forces poured across the border, pushing U.N. forces back down the peninsula. Embarrassed, MacArthur publicly called for President Truman to order massive air strikes on China. The president, fearing a long and costly land war with China, refused the general's request and asked him not to argue U.S. policy in the newspapers. MacArthur again called for air attacks on China, took a swipe at the doctrine of limited (non-nuclear, geographically restricted) war, and implied that the administration's support for containment was little more than appeasement. President Truman had had enough. On April 10, 1951, he fired MacArthur for insubordination, thus reasserting the long-established Constitutional subordination of military to civilian authority.

The immediate political outcry was deafening. Newspapers called for Truman's impeachment; crowds burned him in effigy. MacArthur returned home to ticker-tape parades and an invitation to address a joint session of Congress. He spoke for 34 minutes; cheers and ovations interrupted him 30 times. One congressman called him "the voice of God"; some actually feared a coup d'etat. MacArthur angled for the Republican nomination for president but lost to Dwight Eisenhower, a moderate who ended the fighting in Korea with a truce that left the peninsula divided. Conservatives welcomed MacArthur, who had provided them with a one-word definition of containment ("appeasement") and a slogan ("no substitute for victory") that energized hardliners seeking to "roll back" communism, if necessary with nuclear weapons.

Douglas MacArthur was born in 1880 into a wealthy family that at one point governed the US colony of the Philippines. A West Point graduate, MacArthur compiled a distinguished record in World War I and was perhaps the most famous American general of World War II, commanding forces that wrested control of New Guinea and the Philippines from the Japanese. As proconsul of postwar Japan he introduced numerous reforms, including women's suffrage and the dismantling of industrial and financial monopolies. His brilliant performance in Korea enhanced his military reputation even as his flamboyant personality and advocacy of unrestrained force alarmed an increasingly cautious electorate. He died in New York City in 1964.

**Questions to Consider.** In what ways did MacArthur defend his demand for a more aggressive policy in East Asia? Were his reasons mainly strategic or mainly ideological? How might the experience of World War II have shaped his attitudes? What did Americans of MacArthur's generation find so frustrating about the Korean War? In what way would agreeing to MacArthur's demands have undermined the containment policy, and why were policy-makers in Washington reluctant to do this? Was Truman right to fire him? Was the firing unprecedented in American history?

■══■══■

# Farewell Address to Congress  (1951)

## DOUGLAS MACARTHUR

The Communist threat is a global one. Its successful advance in one sector threatens the destruction of every other sector. You cannot appease or otherwise surrender to Communism in Asia without simultaneously undermining our efforts to halt its advance in Europe. . . .

While I was not consulted prior to the President's decision to intervene in support of the Republic of Korea, that decision, from a military standpoint, proved a sound one, as we hurled back the invader and decimated his forces. Our victory was complete and our objectives within reach when Red China intervened with numerically superior ground forces. This created a new war and an entirely new situation—a situation not contemplated when our forces were committed against the North Korean invaders—a situation which called for new decisions in the diplomatic sphere to permit the realistic adjustment of military strategy. Such decisions have not been forthcoming.

While no man in his right mind would advocate sending our ground forces into continental China and such was never given a thought, the new situation did urgently demand a drastic revision of strategic planning if our political aim was to defeat this new enemy as we had defeated the old. . . .

For entertaining these views, all professionally designed to support our forces committed to Korea and bring hostilities to an end with the least possible delay and at a saving of countless American and Allied lives, I have been severely criticized in lay circles, principally abroad, despite my understanding that from a military standpoint the above views have been fully shared in the past by practically every military leader concerned with the Korean campaign, including our own Joint Chiefs of Staff.

I called for reinforcements, but was informed that reinforcements were not available. I made clear that if not permitted to destroy the enemy buildup bases north of the Yalu; if not permitted to utilize the friendly Chinese force of some 600,000 men on Formosa; if not permitted to blockade the China coast to prevent the Chinese Reds from getting succor from without; and if there were to be no hope of major reinforcements, the position of the command from the military standpoint forbade victory. We could hold in Korea . . . but we could hope at best for only an indecisive campaign. . . . I have constantly called for the new political decisions essential to a solution. Efforts have been made to distort my position. It has been said that I was in effect a war monger. Nothing could be further from the truth. I know war as few other men now living know it, and nothing to me is more revolting. . . .

*Congressional Record,* April 19, 1951.

**General Douglas MacArthur.** On June 29, 1950, the American government ordered combat troops into Korea under the command of General MacArthur. Three months later, MacArthur's forces engineered a brilliant landing behind North Korean lines and quickly overran the northern half of the country. This position proved untenable because, contrary to MacArthur's prediction, Chinese troops entered the war and pushed the Americans far into the south—one of the longest retreats in U.S. history. Here MacArthur, left, receives a decoration from President Harry S. Truman—who would soon strip him of his command for insubordination. (National Archives)

But once war is forced upon us, there is no other alternative than to apply every available means to bring it to a swift end. War's very object is victory—not prolonged indecision. In war, indeed, there can be no substitute for victory.

There are some who for varying reasons would appease Red China. They are blind to history's clear lesson. For history teaches with unmistakable emphasis that appeasement but begets new and bloodier war. It points to no single instance where the end has justified that means—where appeasement has led to more than a sham peace. Like blackmail, it lays the basis for new and successively greater demands, until, as in blackmail, violence becomes the only alternative. Why, my soldiers asked of me, surrender military advantages to an enemy in the field? I could not answer. Some may say to avoid spread of the conflict into an all-out war with China; others, to avoid Soviet intervention. Neither explanation seems valid. For China is already engaging with the maximum power it can commit and the Soviet will not necessarily mesh its actions with our moves. Like a cobra, any new enemy will more likely strike whenever it feels that the relativity in military or other potential is in its favor on a world-wide basis. . . .

I am closing my fifty-two years of military service. When I joined the Army even before the turn of the century, it was the fulfillment of all my boyish hopes and dreams. The world has turned over many times since I took the oath on the Plain at West Point, and the hopes and dreams have long since vanished. But I still remember the refrain of one of the most popular barrack ballads of that day which proclaimed most proudly that—

"Old soldiers never die, they just fade away."

And like the old soldier of that ballad, I now close my military career and just fade away—an old soldier who tried to do his duty as God gave him the light to see that duty.

# 33

## THE DEFENSE OF FREEDOM

Although the New Frontier of President John F. Kennedy had a significant domestic component centering on civil rights and social welfare programs, Kennedy's primary emphasis, as his inaugural address, reprinted below, makes clear, was on the development of a vigorous foreign policy. Kennedy perceived the Soviet threat in much the same way that Richard M. Nixon, his Republican opponent, had perceived it during the 1960 presidential campaign: as ubiquitous and unremitting and therefore to be countered at every turn. But Kennedy's views held significant differences from the policy pursued by the Eisenhower administration.

Kennedy was more willing than Eisenhower to increase defense spending; he was also more skeptical about the value of responding to revolutions in the Third World by threatening thermonuclear war. Departing from the policies of his predecessor, Kennedy moved toward a doctrine of "flexible response" that stressed conventional forces over atomic weapons and emphasized international propaganda and public relations over armaments. At once idealistic and demanding, like the 1961 inaugural address itself, Kennedy's views led to the signing of treaties with the Soviet Union that banned atmospheric nuclear testing and to the establishment of emergency communications between the White House and the Kremlin. But these same views also led to the sending of more and more military personnel to South Vietnam, to prevent Ho Chi Minh, the Communist leader of North Vietnam, from unifying Vietnam under his rule.

John F. Kennedy was born in 1917 to a wealthy Irish-American family. After graduating with honors from Harvard in 1940, he served for a time as secretary to his father, who was then U.S. ambassador to Great Britain. *Why England Slept*—his best-selling book on British military policies during the 1930s—was published in 1940. During World War II he served in the U.S. Navy and won the Navy and Marine Corps Medal for his heroism. After the war he entered politics in Massachusetts, winning election to the House of Representatives in 1946 and to the Senate in 1952. His book *Profiles in Courage,* published in 1956, won the Pulitzer Prize, and in 1960 he narrowly bested Richard Nixon in a contest for the presidency. The youngest man and the only Roman

Catholic ever elected president, Kennedy projected an image of intelligence, vitality, and sophistication. The world mourned after he was assassinated in Dallas, Texas, on November 22, 1963.

**Questions to Consider.** Some historians have argued that in this address Kennedy formally shifted the focus of the cold war from Europe to the nonaligned or economically underdeveloped part of the world. Do you agree or disagree? If you agree, do you also believe there was a connection between this shift and Kennedy's emphasis on feeding and clothing the world—on winning by doing good? Was there also a connection between this shift and Kennedy's preference for invoking human rights instead of democracy? Historians have also read the address as an unprecedented fusion of "adversarialism" with "universalism." Again, do you agree or disagree? Was this fusion connected with Kennedy's sense of facing an "hour of maximum danger" in which Americans might have to "pay any price" for liberty?

# Inaugural Address (1961)

### JOHN F. KENNEDY

We observe today not a victory of party but a celebration of freedom—symbolizing an end as well as a beginning—signifying renewal as well as change. For I have sworn before you and Almighty God the same solemn oath our forbears prescribed nearly a century and three-quarters ago.

The world is very different now. For man holds in his mortal hands the power to abolish all forms of human poverty and all forms of human life. And yet the same revolutionary beliefs for which our forbears fought are still at issue around the globe—the belief that the rights of man come not from the generosity of the state but from the hand of God.

We dare not forget today that we are the heirs of that first revolution. Let the word go forth from this time and place, to friend and foe alike, that the torch has been passed to a new generation of Americans—born in this century, tempered by war, disciplined by a hard and bitter peace, proud of our ancient heritage—and unwilling to witness or permit the slow undoing of those human rights to which this nation has always been committed, and to which we are committed today at home and around the world.

Let every nation know, whether it wishes us well or ill, that we shall pay any price, bear any burden, meet any hardship, support any friend, oppose any foe to assure the survival and the success of liberty.

*The New York Times,* January 21, 1961.

**John F. Kennedy.** Kennedy, with his wife, Jacqueline, sitting at his side, during the presidential inauguration, 1961. (Paul Schutzer/TimeLife Picture/Getty Images)

This much we pledge—and more.

To those old allies whose cultural and spiritual origins we share, we pledge the loyalty of faithful friends. United, there is little we cannot do in a host of co-operative ventures. Divided, there is little we can do—for we dare not meet a powerful challenge at odds and split asunder.

To those new states whom we welcome to the ranks of the free, we pledge our word that one form of colonial control shall not have passed away merely to be replaced by a far more iron tyranny. We shall not always expect to find them supporting our view. But we shall always hope to find them strongly supporting their own freedom—and to remember that, in the past, those who foolishly sought power by riding the back of the tiger ended up inside.

To those people in the huts and villages of half the globe struggling to break the bonds of mass misery, we pledge our best efforts to help them help themselves, for whatever period is required—not because the Communists may be doing it, not because we seek their votes, but because it is right. If a free society cannot help the many who are poor, it cannot save the few who are rich.

To our sister republics south of our border, we offer a special pledge—to convert our good words into good deeds—in a new alliance for progress—to assist free men and free governments in casting off the chains of poverty. But this peaceful revolution of hope cannot become the prey of hostile powers. Let all our neighbors know that we shall join with them to oppose aggression or subversion anywhere in the Americas. And let every other power know that this hemisphere intends to remain the master of its own house.

To that world assembly of sovereign states, the United Nations, our last best hope in an age where the instruments of war have far outpaced the instruments of peace, we renew our pledge of support—to prevent it from becoming merely a forum for invective—to strengthen its shield of the new and the weak—and to enlarge the area in which its writ may run.

Finally, to those nations who would make themselves our adversary, we offer not a pledge but a request: that both sides begin anew the quest for peace, before the dark powers of destruction unleashed by science engulf all humanity in planned or accidental self-destruction.

We dare not tempt them with weakness. For only when our arms are sufficient beyond doubt can we be certain beyond doubt that they will never be employed.

But neither can two great and powerful groups of nations take comfort from our present course—both sides overburdened by the cost of modern weapons, both rigidly alarmed by the steady spread of the deadly atom, yet both racing to alter that uncertain balance of terror that stays the hand of mankind's final war.

So let us begin anew—remembering on both sides that civility is not a sign of weakness, and sincerity is always subject to proof. Let us never negotiate out of fear. But let us never fear to negotiate.

Let both sides explore what problems unite us instead of belaboring those problems which divide us.

Let both sides, for the first time, formulate serious and precise proposals for the inspection and control of arms—and bring the absolute power to destroy other nations under the absolute control of all nations.

Let both sides seek to invoke the wonders of science instead of its terror. Together let us explore the stars, conquer the deserts, eradicate disease, tap the ocean depths, and encourage the arts and commerce.

Let both sides unite to heed in all corners of the earth the command of Isaiah—to "undo the heavy burdens . . . [and] let the oppressed go free."

And if a beachhead of co-operation may push back the jungle of suspicion, let both sides join in creating a new endeavor, not a new balance of power, but a new world of law, where the strong are just and the weak secure and the peace preserved.

All this will not be finished in the first one hundred days. Nor will it be finished in the first one thousand days, nor in the life of this administration, nor even perhaps in our lifetime on this planet. But let us begin.

In your hands, my fellow citizens, more than mine, will rest the final success or failure of our course. Since this country was founded, each generation of Americans has been summoned to give testimony to its national loyalty. The graves of young Americans who answered the call to service surround the globe.

Now the trumpet summons us again—not as a call to bear arms, though arms we need—not as a call to battle, though embattled we are—but a call to bear the burden of a long twilight struggle, year in and year out, "rejoicing in hope, patient in tribulation"—a struggle against the common enemies of man: tyranny, poverty, disease, and war itself.

Can we forge against these enemies a grand and global alliance, North and South, East and West, that can assure a more fruitful life for all mankind? Will you join in that historic effort?

In the long history of the world, only a few generations have been granted the role of defending freedom in its hour of maximum danger. I do not shrink from this responsibility—I welcome it. I do not believe that any of us would exchange places with any other people or any other generation. The energy, the faith, the devotion which we bring to this endeavor will light our country and all who serve it—and the glow from that fire can truly light the world.

And so, my fellow Americans: ask not what your country can do for you—ask what you can do for your country.

My fellow citizens of the world: ask not what America will do for you, but what together we can do for the freedom of man.

Finally, whether you are citizens of America or citizens of the world, ask of us here the same high standards of strength and sacrifice which we ask of you. With a good conscience our only sure reward, with history the final judge of deeds, let us go forth to lead the land we love, asking His blessing and His help, but knowing that here on earth God's work must truly be our own.

# 34

## BLANK CHECK

★━━★━━★

American involvement in Vietnam began modestly enough with a promise in 1945 to help France restore colonial rule there. The United States backed France because Ho Chi Minh, the leader of the struggle for Vietnamese independence, was a Communist. American policy makers were more impressed by Ho's Communism than by his nationalism; they viewed him as a tool of the Kremlin, although he had the backing of many non-Communists in Indochina who wanted freedom from French control. In 1954, Ho's forces defeated the French, and the French decided to withdraw from Vietnam. At this point the United States stepped in, backed a partition of Vietnam, and gave aid to the South Vietnamese government in Saigon. American policy continued to be based on the belief that Communism in Vietnam was inspired by China or the Soviet Union, if not both. If Vietnam went Communist, Washington warned, other countries in Asia might topple like so many dominoes, and Communist influence in the world would grow at the expense of America's.

U.S. military personnel entered the Vietnamese conflict between North and South under Presidents Eisenhower and Kennedy. American bombers began raiding North Vietnam in 1965, after the reelection of Kennedy's successor, Lyndon B. Johnson. By 1969, American troops in South Vietnam numbered around 550,000, and American planes had dropped more bombs in Vietnam than had been dropped on Germany and Japan during World War II. Yet the Vietcong (the South Vietnamese insurgents), aided by North Vietnamese military units, seemed stronger than ever. International opinion had now turned against the United States.

A key episode in Lyndon Johnson's escalation came with the so-called Tonkin Gulf incident. On August 2, 1964, the U.S.S. *Maddox,* an American destroyer supporting South Vietnamese commando raids against North Vietnam, came under attack by enemy patrol boats. The attackers suffered heavy damage; the *Maddox* was unharmed. Two days later the *Maddox* and another U.S. destroyer again moved into North Vietnamese waters. Although the weather was bad, sonar equipment indicated enemy torpedoes. When the captain of the *Maddox* later questioned members of his crew, no one could recall any enemy attacks, and subsequent investigations of the incident likewise turned up no evidence of hostile fire. The American destroyers nevertheless reportedly leveled heavy fire against North Vietnamese patrol boats. President Johnson, despite the questionable evidence and without admitting that U.S. ships were supporting raids against the North, ordered air strikes on North Vietnamese naval bases and announced on television that he was retaliating for "unprovoked" attacks. U.S. planes would now, he said, bomb North Vietnam.

On August 5, Johnson, in the address excerpted below, asked Congress to give him authority to repel "any armed attack against the forces of the United States and to prevent further aggression." The resolution passed the House by 435 to 0 and passed the Senate by 88 to 2. The resolution, as Johnson eventually argued, was tantamount to a declaration of war—which Congress has not voted against any country since December 1941. Under its auspices, the president authorized not only the carpet-bombing of North Vietnam but the American buildup to over a half-million combat troops. Its effect in 1964 was to preempt criticism from Republican presidential candidate Barry Goldwater, a hawk on foreign policy, help raise Johnson's approval rating in the polls from 42 percent to 72 percent, and contribute to a major victory in that fall's election.

Born in the poor hill country of central Texas in 1908, Lyndon Johnson worked his way through Southwest Texas State Teachers College in San Marcos and went to Washington as assistant to a local congressman in 1931. An intensely ambitious and ardent New Deal Democrat, Johnson began his political career with his election to fill a congressional vacancy in 1937. He was elected to the U.S. Senate in 1948. Unmatched at arranging the compromises and distributing the favors and money on which congressional politics rested, he became Senate minority leader in 1953 and majority leader in 1955, when the Democrats regained control of the Senate. As the vice-presidential nominee in 1960, he helped John F. Kennedy carry enough Southern states to become president; he became president himself upon Kennedy's assassination in 1963. As president, Johnson helped enact the most sweeping civil rights legislation of the century, but he also dramatically escalated a fundamentally unpopular war. Faced with widespread opposition to his policies, he declined to run for reelection in 1968. He died in San Antonio in 1973.

**Questions to Consider.** On what grounds did Johnson defend the American presence in Vietnam? How did he deal with the problematic nature of the evidence of North Vietnamese attacks on U.S. ships? Johnson wanted authorization not only for limited retaliation over this specific incident but to attack North Vietnam on a large scale over a long period of time. How did he move in this address from the particular incident to the general goal? What parts of the speech might have been especially effective in undercutting Barry Goldwater's criticism of the Democrats as "soft on Communism"? Was Johnson demanding, in effect, a declaration of war? If so, why didn't he ask for that?

# Message on the Gulf of Tonkin (1964)

### LYNDON B. JOHNSON

Last night I announced to the American people that the North Vietnamese regime had conducted further deliberate attacks against U.S. naval vessels operating in international waters, and that I had therefore directed air action against gun boats and supporting facilities used in these hostile operations. This air action has now been carried out with substantial damage to the boats and facilities. Two U.S. aircraft were lost in the action.

After consultation with the leaders of both parties in the Congress, I further announced a decision to ask the Congress for a Resolution expressing the unity and determination of the United States in supporting freedom and in protecting peace in Southeast Asia.

These latest actions of the North Vietnamese regime have given a new and grave turn to the already serious situation in Southeast Asia. Our commitments in that area are well known to the Congress. They were first made in 1954 by President Eisenhower. They were further defined in the Southeast Asia Collective Defense Treaty approved by the Senate in February 1955.

This Treaty with its accompanying protocol obligates the United States and other members to act in accordance with their Constitutional processes to meet Communist aggression against any of the parties or protocol states.

Our policy in Southeast Asia has been consistent and unchanged since 1954. I summarized it on June 2 in four simple propositions:

1. *America keeps her word.* Here as elsewhere, we must and shall honor our commitments.
2. *The issue is the future of Southeast Asia as a whole.* A threat to any nation in that region is a threat to all, and a threat to us.
3. *Our purpose is peace.* We have no military, political or territorial ambitions in the area.
4. *This is not just a jungle war, but a struggle for freedom on every front of human activity.* Our military and economic assistance to South Vietnam and Laos in particular has the purpose of helping these countries to repel aggression and strengthen their independence.

The threat to the free nations of Southeast Asia has long been clear. The North Vietnamese regime has constantly sought to take over South Vietnam and Laos. This Communist regime has violated the Geneva Accords for Vietnam. It has systematically conducted a campaign of subversion, which includes the direction, training, and supply of personnel and arms for the conduct of guerrilla warfare in South Vietnamese territory. In Laos, the North Vietnamese regime has maintained military forces, used Laotian territory

*The New York Times,* August 6, 1964.

for infiltration into South Vietnam, and most recently carried out combat operations—all in direct violation of the Geneva Agreements of 1962.

In recent months, the actions of the North Vietnamese regime have become steadily more threatening. In May, following new acts of Communist aggression in Laos, the United States undertook reconnaissance flights over Laotian territory, at the request of the Government of Laos. These flights had the essential mission of determining the situation in territory where Communist forces were preventing inspection by the International Control Commission. When the Communists attacked these aircraft, I responded by furnishing escort fighters with instructions to fire when fired upon. Thus, these latest North Vietnamese attacks on our naval vessels are not the first direct attack on armed forces of the United States.

As President of the United States I have concluded that I should now ask the Congress, on its part, to join in affirming the national determination that all such attacks will be met, and that the U.S. will continue in its basic policy of assisting the free nations of the area to defend their freedom.

As I have repeatedly made clear, the United States intends no rashness, and seeks no wider war. We must make it clear to all that the United States is united in its determination to bring about the end of Communist subversion and aggression in the area. We seek the full and effective restoration of the international agreements signed in Geneva in 1954, with respect to South Vietnam, and again in Geneva in 1962, with respect to Laos.

I recommend a Resolution expressing the support of the Congress for all necessary action to protect our armed forces and to assist nations covered by the SEATO Treaty. At the same time, I assure the Congress that we shall continue readily to explore any avenues of political solution that will effectively guarantee the removal of Communist subversion and the preservation of the independence of the nations of the area.

The Resolution could well be based upon similar resolutions enacted by the Congress in the past—to meet the threat to Formosa in 1955, to meet the threat to the Middle East in 1957, and to meet the threat in Cuba in 1962. It could state in the simplest terms the resolve and support of the Congress for action to deal appropriately with attacks against our armed forces and to defend freedom and preserve peace in Southeast Asia in accordance with the obligations of the United States under the Southeast Asia Treaty. I urge the Congress to enact such a Resolution promptly and thus to give convincing evidence to the aggressive Communist nations, and to the world as a whole, that our policy in Southeast Asia will be carried forward—and that the peace and security of the area will be preserved.

The events of this week would in any event have made the passage of a Congressional Resolution essential. But there is an additional reason for doing so at a time when we are entering on three months of political campaigning. Hostile nations must understand that in such a period the United States will continue to protect its national interests, and that in these matters there is no division among us.

# 35

## THE COLLAPSE OF CONSENSUS

The escalation of American involvement in Vietnam provoked perhaps the greatest wartime opposition in U.S. history. By the end of 1965, the first draft card burnings occurred. Students in major universities throughout the country organized "teach-ins" (named after the civil rights "sit-ins") to discuss the nature of the war. The first antiwar march converged on Washington. By 1967 protest rallies were drawing hundreds of thousands, and evasion of the draft among middle-class students was widespread.

There was less movement on the political front. Some prominent figures—Senators Wayne Morse and J. William Fulbright, the Reverends Martin Luther King Jr. and William Sloan Coffin—were vehemently criticizing the Johnson administration for its Vietnam policy. But Lyndon Johnson had a hammerlock on the Democratic Party machinery and was not reluctant to use it to coerce support for the administration's hard line on the war. It would take political courage to contest a sitting president in the primaries of his own party, especially at a time when many people still thought of dissent as tantamount to treason.

In November 1967 Senator Eugene McCarthy of Minnesota took the plunge to end the war. McCarthy called for an end to U.S. fighting in Vietnam and announced that he would oppose Johnson in the 1968 New Hampshire primary, the earliest in the country. Asked what made him think he could contest Johnson, McCarthy replied, "This war. When the coffins start coming home to the small towns of Minnesota, people are going to turn against this war." He gave the speech reprinted below in late 1967 to a Conference of Concerned Democrats in Chicago.

McCarthy was an inspiration to thousands of young people who cut their hair, shaved their beards, dressed up, and went "Clean for Gene" to knock on doors for him. Johnson won the New Hampshire primary, but with only 49 percent of the vote. McCarthy got 42 percent, a showing that shook the Democratic establishment. Four days later, Senator Robert Kennedy, the brother of the late John F. Kennedy, entered the race as well. Kennedy's candidacy split the antiwar movement. Johnson announced that he would not seek re-election and endorsed

Vice President Hubert Humphrey, also from Minnesota. Kennedy, running strong, was then assassinated, shocking a nation still struggling to come to grips with the murder of Martin Luther King a few weeks earlier. Having transformed American politics in an almost unprecedented way—"He stood up alone, and something happened"— McCarthy eventually slipped in the polls and gave way to Humphrey, who lost that fall to Richard Nixon.

Eugene J. "Gene" McCarthy was born in 1916 in Watkins, Minnesota, to a devout German mother and a strong-willed Irish father. McCarthy attended Catholic schools, took a graduate degree at the University of Minnesota, and trained briefly to become a Benedictine monk before deciding to teach. A member of the liberal Minnesota Democratic-Farmer-Labor party, he served in Congress for eight years until his election in 1959 to the Senate, where he remained until 1971. Various small parties endorsed him for president over the next 15 years. A leader among Senate liberals and a vocal opponent of the assaults of Joe McCarthy (no relation) on civil liberties, McCarthy was also courtly and sharp-witted, with a taste for poetry, theology, and baseball. Never predictable in politics, he endorsed Ronald Reagan for president in 1980. He died at his farm outside Washington at the age of 89.

**Questions to Consider.** What did McCarthy mean by "the spirit of 1963"? What point was he making by specifically invoking the Peace Corps and the Alliance for Progress, a program of economic aid to Latin America? What types of escalation in Vietnam did he cite in this speech? With what other "wars" of the Johnson years did he contrast the Vietnam War? Why did he attack U.S. leaders for invoking "Munich" as a defense for their Vietnam policy? How did McCarthy craft his speech so that he would seem within the political and historical mainstream? How did he link the Vietnam War to domestic needs?

★━━★━━★

# An Indefensible War (1967)

### EUGENE MCCARTHY

In 1952, in this city of Chicago, the Democratic party nominated as its candidate for the presidency Adlai Stevenson.

His promise to his party and to the people of the country then was that he would talk sense to them. And he did in the clearest tones. He did not speak above the people, as his enemies charged, but he raised the hard and difficult

Eugene J. McCarthy, "An Indefensible War." Reprinted by permission of the Estate of Eugene J. McCarthy.

questions and proposed the difficult answers. His voice became the voice of America. He lifted the spirit of this land. The country, in his language, was purified and given direction.

Before most other men, he recognized the problem of our cities and called for action.

Before other men, he measured the threat of nuclear war and called for a test-ban treaty.

Before other men, he anticipated the problem of conscience which he saw must come with maintaining a peacetime army and a limited draft and urged the political leaders of this country to put their wisdom to the task.

In all of these things he was heard by many but not followed, until under the presidency of John F. Kennedy his ideas were revived in new language and in a new spirit. To the clear sound of the horn was added the beat of a steady and certain drum.

John Kennedy set free the spirit of America. The honest optimism was released. Quiet courage and civility became the mark of American government, and new programs of promise and of dedication were presented: the Peace Corps, the Alliance for Progress, the promise of equal rights for all Americans—and not just the promise, but the beginning of the achievement of that promise.

All the world looked to the United States with new hope, for here was youth and confidence and an openness to the future. Here was a country not being held by the dead hand of the past, nor frightened by the violent hand of the future which was grasping at the world.

This was the spirit of 1963.

What is the spirit of 1967? What is the mood of America and of the world toward America today?

It is a joyless spirit—a mood of frustration, of anxiety, of uncertainty.

In place of the enthusiasm of the Peace Corps among the young people of America, we have protests and demonstrations.

In place of the enthusiasm of the Alliance for Progress, we have distrust and disappointment.

Instead of the language of promise and of hope, we have in politics today a new vocabulary in which the critical word is *war:* war on poverty, war on ignorance, war on crime, war on pollution. None of these problems can be solved by war but only by persistent, dedicated, and thoughtful attention.

But we do have one war which is properly called a war—the war in Vietnam, which is central to all of the problems of America.

A war of questionable legality and questionable constitutionality.

A war which is diplomatically indefensible; the first war in this century in which the United States, which at its founding made an appeal to the decent opinion of mankind in the Declaration of Independence, finds itself without the support of the decent opinion of mankind.

A war which cannot be defended in the context of the judgment of history. It is being presented in the context of an historical judgment of an era which is past. Munich appears to be the starting point of history for the secretary of state and for those who attempt to support his policies. What is necessary is a realization that the United States is a part of the movement of history itself; that it cannot stand apart, attempting to control the world by imposing covenants and treaties and by violent military intervention; that our role is not to police the planet but to use military strength with restraint and within limits, while at the same time we make available to the world the great power of our economy, of our knowledge, and of our good will.

A war which is not defensible even in military terms; which runs contrary to the advice of our greatest generals—Eisenhower, Ridgway, Bradley, and MacArthur—all of whom admonished us against becoming involved in a land war in Asia. Events have proved them right, as estimate after estimate as to the time of success and the military commitment necessary to success has had to be revised—always upward: more troops, more extensive bombing, a widening and intensification of the war. Extension and intensification have been the rule, and projection after projection of success have been proved wrong.

With the escalation of our military commitment has come a parallel of overleaping of objectives: from protecting South Vietnam, to nation building in South Vietnam, to protecting all of Southeast Asia, and ultimately to suggesting that the safety and security of the United States itself is at stake.

Finally, it is a war which is morally wrong. The most recent statement of objectives cannot be accepted as an honest judgment as to why we are in Vietnam. It has become increasingly difficult to justify the methods we are using and the instruments of war which we are using as we have moved from limited targets and somewhat restricted weapons to greater variety and more destructive instruments of war, and also have extended the area of operations almost to the heart of North Vietnam.

Even assuming that both objectives and methods can be defended, the war cannot stand the test of proportion and of prudent judgment. It is no longer possible to prove that the good that may come with what is called victory, or projected as victory, is proportionate to the loss of life and property and to other disorders that follow from this war. . . .

Those of us who are gathered here tonight are not advocating peace at any price. We are willing to pay a high price for peace—for an honorable, rational, and political solution to this war, a solution which will enhance our world position, which will permit us to give the necessary attention to our other commitments abroad, both military and nonmilitary, and leave us with both human and physical resources and with moral energy to deal effectively with the pressing domestic problems of the United States itself.

I see little evidence that the administration has set any limits on the price which it will pay for a military victory which becomes less and less sure and more hollow and empty in promise.

The scriptural promise of the good life is one in which the old men see visions and the young men dream dreams. In the context of this war and all of its implications, the young men of America do not dream dreams, but many live in the nightmare of moral anxiety, of concern and great apprehension; and the old men, instead of visions which they can offer to the young, are projecting, in the language of the secretary of state, a specter of one billion Chinese threatening the peace and safety of the world—a frightening and intimidating future.

The message from the administration today is a message of apprehension, a message of fear, yes—even a message of fear of fear.

This is not the real spirit of America. I do not believe that it is. This is a time to test the mood and spirit:

To offer in place of doubt—trust.

In place of expediency—right judgment.

In place of ghettos, let us have neighborhoods and communities.

In place of incredibility—integrity.

In place of murmuring, let us have clear speech; let us again hear America singing.

In place of disunity, let us have dedication of purpose.

In place of near despair, let us have hope.

This is the promise of greatness which was stated for us by Adlai Stevenson and which was brought to form and positive action in the words and actions of John Kennedy.

Let us pick up again these lost strands and weave them again into the fabric of America.

Let us sort out the music from the sounds and again respond to the trumpet and the steady drum.

# 36

## A COLD WAR BREAKTHROUGH

American diplomacy has centered on China as much as on Russia or Europe. A thriving China trade was a minor goal in America's war for independence and a major motive for acquiring California and its harbors during the Mexican War. China was also the main focus of John Hay's Open Door policy and helped determine America's Pacific strategy in the Spanish-American War. Finally, a prime U.S. concern after the Russian Revolution of 1917 was to avoid "losing China" to communism, either from internal insurrection or from Russian intervention. When the Chinese Communists did seize power in 1949, Washington took it as a major defeat for the United States and therefore a commensurate victory for the Soviets, a view apparently confirmed when the Soviet Union and China jointly supported North Korea and North Vietnam during the wars in Korea and Vietnam. Never did international communism seem more aggressively monolithic than in the years immediately after 1949, when the United States sought to isolate China internationally and backed one dictator after another in South Korea, South Vietnam, and Taiwan (Republic of China), all in the name of "containment."

Yet nationalism eventually reasserted itself, and before long a bitter falling-out between the Russian and the Chinese dictatorships occurred. By the 1960s the Soviet Union and China had resumed their historic national rivalry. Clearly, Communist China was no mere extension of the Kremlin and never had been. During the same decade the Chinese and the Russians competed bitterly for influence in the Third World and among European Communist parties, jockeyed for power in the Far East, and vilified each other. By 1970, more Russian troops guarded the Soviet border against China than against Western Europe. The way was open to rapprochement between the United States and China. In 1972, President Richard M. Nixon, seeking to end the Vietnamese conflict and find a possible counterweight to the Soviet Union, abandoned America's nonrecognition policy by visiting the People's Republic of China and paving the way for the establishment of friendly relations. The results of the trip were modest, as the following communiqué shows. But the trip represented a profound shift toward flexibility in dealing with Communist nations. By the 1980s, American corporations were beginning to invest in China, and the U.S. government was speaking of military aid. The close desire for relations with Beijing (Peking) quickly became an important feature of American diplomacy. One aspect of the cold war of the 1950s appeared to be over.

The new China policy was all the more dramatic because of Richard Nixon's reputation as a militant anticommunist. Born in 1913 to a middle-class California family, Nixon graduated from Whittier College in 1934 and from Duke University School of Law in 1937. He practiced law for several years and served in the U.S. Navy during World War II. In 1946 he defeated a Democratic incumbent for Congress by implying that the Communists secretly supported the man. In the House of Representatives he was zealous in investigating communism in government, and in 1950 he was elected to the Senate from California after again implying that the Communists supported his opponent. Two years later he became Dwight Eisenhower's running mate. He served as vice president for eight years and in 1960 lost the election for the presidency to John Kennedy. Then, in 1968, in an impressive comeback, he captured the Republican presidential nomination and went on to defeat the Democratic candidate in November. In 1971, he initiated U.S. troop withdrawal from Vietnam to de-escalate the war; a cease-fire was signed in 1973. In 1972 he won overwhelmingly in his bid for re-election. Nixon's administration was marked chiefly by bold foreign-policy initiatives, such as the China trip, and efforts to reach agreements with the Soviet Union on strategic arms limitations. In 1974, however, threatened with impeachment for abusing his powers of office, he was forced to resign.

**Questions to Consider.** The United States–China communiqué is illuminating in its efforts to lay out acceptable differences and areas of common ground. What were the most striking differences in the two lists and the language used? Why, for instance, did China's tone on Japan differ so radically from America's? What differences seem to have been most crucial? In the next section, what was the significance of the final sentence concerning "collusion" and "spheres of influence"? What guest, so to speak, threatened to crash the banquet? Taiwan presented perhaps the thorniest problem of all, greater even than Korea or Vietnam. What circumstances of the post-World War II era made Taiwan so delicate an issue? In Washington, many conservatives would attack the language of the communiqué as a "sellout" on the Taiwan question. Was it?

★═══★═══★

# The United States–China Communiqué of 1972

### RICHARD M. NIXON ET AL.

President Richard Nixon of the United States of America visited the People's Republic of China at the invitation of Premier Chou En-lai of the People's Republic of China from Feb. 21 to Feb. 28, 1972. . . .

President Nixon met with Chairman Mao Tse-tung of the Communist party of China on Feb. 21. The two leaders had a serious and frank exchange of views on Sino-U.S. relations and world affairs. . . .

The U.S. side stated:

Peace in Asia and peace in the world require efforts both to reduce immediate tensions and to eliminate the basic causes of conflict. The United States will work for a just and secure peace: just, because it fulfills the aspirations of peoples and nations for freedom and progress; secure, because it removes the danger of foreign aggression. The United States supports individual freedom and social progress for all the peoples of the world, free of outside pressure or intervention.

The United States believes that the effort to reduce tensions is served by improving communications between countries that have different ideologies so as to lessen the risks of confrontation through accident, miscalculation or misunderstanding. Countries should treat each other with mutual respect and be willing to compete peacefully, letting performance be the ultimate judge. No country should claim infallibility and each country should be prepared to reexamine its own attitudes for the common good.

The United States stressed that the peoples of Indochina should be allowed to determine their destiny without outside intervention; its constant primary objective has been a negotiated solution; the eight-point proposal put forward by the Republic of Vietnam and the United States on Jan. 27, 1972, represents the basis for the attainment of that objective; in the absence of a negotiated settlement the United States envisages the ultimate withdrawal of all U.S. forces from the region consistent with the aim of self-determination for each country of Indochina.

The United States will maintain its close ties with and support for the Republic of Korea. The United States will support efforts of the Republic of Korea to seek a relaxation of tension and increase communications in the Korean peninsula. The United States places the highest value on its friendly relations with Japan; it will continue to develop the existing close bonds. . . .

The Chinese side stated:

Wherever there is oppression, there is resistance. Countries want independence, nations want liberation and the people want revolution—this has

Richard Nixon et al, "The United States-China Communique of 1972" *The New York Times,* February 28, 1972.

**Nixon in China.** This photograph shows President Richard M. Nixon (left center) with Chinese Deputy Premier Li Hsien-Nien (gesturing) at the Great Wall during Nixon's historic visit to the People's Republic of China in February 1972. Conceived partly to help end the Vietnam conflict and partly to balance Nixon's forthcoming trip to the Soviet Union, the China visit signaled U.S. acceptance of the Communist government in Peking. It led to Chinese admission to the United Nations, Sino-American economic and cultural exchanges, and the eventual exchange of ambassadors. To the right of Li Hsien-Nien is Secretary of State William P. Rogers; absent is a key architect of the China initiative, National Security Adviser Henry Kissinger. (United Press International photo)

become the irresistible trend of history. All nations, big or small, should be equal; big nations should not bully the small and strong nations should not bully the weak. China will never be a superpower and it opposes hegemony and power politics of any kind.

The Chinese side stated that it firmly supports the struggles of all oppressed people and nations for freedom and liberation and that the people of all countries have the right to choose their social systems according to their own wishes and the right to safeguard the independence, sovereignty and territorial integrity of their own countries and oppose foreign aggression, interference, control and subversion. All foreign troops should be withdrawn to their own countries.

The Chinese side expressed its firm support to the peoples of Vietnam, Laos and Cambodia in their efforts for the attainment of their goals and its firm support to the seven-point proposal of the Provisional Revolutionary Government of the Republic of South Vietnam and the elaboration of February this year on the two key problems in the proposal, and to the Joint Declaration of the Summit Conference of the Indochinese Peoples.

It firmly supports the eight-point program for the peaceful unification of Korea put forward by the Government of the Democratic People's Republic of Korea on April 12, 1971, and the stand for the abolition of the "U.N. Commission for the Unification and Rehabilitation of Korea." It firmly opposes the revival and outward expansion of Japanese militarism and firmly supports the Japanese people's desire to build an independent Japan. . . .

There are essential differences between China and the United States in their social systems and foreign policies. However, the two sides agreed that countries, regardless of their social systems, should conduct their relations on the principles of respect for the sovereignty and territorial integrity of all states, nonaggression against other states, noninterference in the internal affairs of other states, equality and mutual benefit, and peaceful coexistence. International disputes should be settled on this basis, without resorting to the use or threat of force. The United States and the People's Republic of China are prepared to apply these principles to their mutual relations.

With these principles of international relations in mind the two sides stated that:

> Progress toward the normalization of relations between China and the United States is in the interests of all countries.
>
> Both wish to reduce the danger of international military conflict.
>
> Neither should seek hegemony in the Asia-Pacific region and each is opposed to the efforts by any other country or group of countries to establish such hegemony; and
>
> Neither is prepared to negotiate on behalf of any third party or to enter into agreements or understandings with the other directed at other states.

Both sides are of the view that it would be against the interests of the peoples of the world for any major country to collude with another against other countries, or for major countries to divide up the world into spheres of interest.

The sides reviewed the long-standing serious disputes between China and the United States.

The Chinese side reaffirmed its position: The Taiwan question is the crucial question obstructing the normalization of relations between China and the United States; the Government of the People's Republic of China is the sole legal government of China; Taiwan is a province of China which has long been returned to the motherland; the liberation of Taiwan is China's internal affair in which no other country has the right to interfere; and all U.S. forces and military installations must be withdrawn from Taiwan. The Chinese government firmly opposes any activities which aim at the creation of "one China, one Taiwan," "one China, two governments," "two Chinas" and "Independent Taiwan" or advocate that "the status of Taiwan remains to be determined."

The U.S. side declared: The United States acknowledges that all Chinese on either side of the Taiwan Strait maintain there is but one China and that Taiwan is a part of China. The United States Government does not challenge that position. It reaffirms its interest in a peaceful settlement of the Taiwan question by the Chinese themselves. With this prospect in mind, it affirms the ultimate objective of the withdrawal of all U.S. forces and military installations from Taiwan. In the meantime, it will progressively reduce its forces and military installations on Taiwan as the tension in the area diminishes.

The two sides agreed that it is desirable to broaden the understanding between the two peoples. To this end, they discussed specific areas in such fields as science, technology, culture, sports and journalism, in which people-to-people contacts and exchanges would be mutually beneficial. Each side undertakes to facilitate the further development of such contacts and exchanges.

Both sides view bilateral trade as another area from which mutual benefits can be derived, and agree that economic relations based on equality and mutual benefit are in the interest of the peoples of the two countries. They agree to facilitate the progressive development of trade between their two countries.

The two sides agree that they will stay in contact through various channels.

**Elizabeth Eckford approaching Little Rock's Central High School during the integration crisis of 1957.** The crowd began to curse and yell, "Lynch her! Lynch her!" A national guardsman blocked her entrance into the school with his rifle. Faced with this, Eckford retreated back down the street away from the mob. But a week later, under the protection of U.S. Army troops, she finally attended, and integrated, Central High School. (Alfred Eisenstaedt/TimeLife Pictures/Getty Images)

CHAPTER EIGHT

# The Liberal Hour

# 37

## BREAKING THE COLOR LINE

Racial segregation was a fact of life everywhere in the South until the middle of the twentieth century. Organizations such as the National Association for the Advancement of Colored People (NAACP) and the Congress of Racial Equality (CORE) fought hard against segregation and its handmaiden, disfranchisement of blacks. But in 1896 the Supreme Court had ruled in *Plessy* v. *Ferguson* that separate facilities for blacks and whites were legal, and there seemed little recourse from this decree, especially given the unsympathetic racial views of the national government in this period. Only in 1947 did some tentative preliminary change come with the integration of major-league baseball for commercial reasons, the integration of the armed forces by presidential order, and the integration of Southern law schools by a Supreme Court decision that year arguing that such schools were inherently unequal because they denied opportunities to those excluded.

Then, in 1954, in an NAACP lawsuit entitled *Brown* v. *The Board of Education of Topeka,* the Supreme Court extended its reasoning from law schools to the entire segregated school system, thereby reversing the "separate-but-equal" doctrine some sixty years after its adoption. Written by Chief Justice Earl Warren on behalf of a unanimous Court, at first this momentous decision, reprinted below, was met with bitter resentment and resistance from most Southern whites. Yet it marked the beginning of the end for legally segregated schools in the nation. The Court and the massive civil rights movement led by Martin Luther King, Jr., and others, it ended the segregation of all public facilities, whether buses, beaches, lunch counters, voting booths, or schools.

Earl Warren was born in Los Angeles in 1891. After he was graduated from the University of California at Berkeley, he practiced law in the San Francisco area until joining the army during World War I. In the 1920s Warren embarked on a successful political career in California, serving as district attorney, state attorney general, and governor. His only electoral defeat came as Republican vice-presidential candidate in 1948. When President Eisenhower appointed him chief justice in 1953, Warren was considered a rather traditional Republican moderate. His leadership of the Court, however, brought an unexpected burst of judicial activism that strengthened not only minority rights but also the rights of voters, trial defendants, and witnesses before congressional committees. Warren resigned from the Court in 1969 and died in Washington in 1974.

**Questions to Consider.** Note, in this decision, that Warren virtually disregarded what had once seemed so crucial—the actual differences between the races. Note, too, that Warren read very large public purposes into the bountiful commitment of local governments to public education: good citizenship, values, training, and social adjustment. Were these two factors—colorblindness and purposeful public education—enough to account for the Court's 1954 decision? If so, why did Warren introduce psychological studies into his argument? Was it merely a reflection of the findings of modern social science? In what other areas besides education might modern courts attempt to use the equal protection clause of the Fourteenth Amendment as construed by the Warren Court?

★════★════★

# Brown v. The Board of Education of Topeka (1954)

### EARL WARREN

These cases come to us from the States of Kansas, South Carolina, Virginia, and Delaware. They are premised on different facts and different local conditions, but a common legal question justifies their consideration together in this consolidated opinion.

In approaching this problem, we cannot turn the clock back to 1868 when the [14th] Amendment was adopted, or even to 1896 when *Plessy v. Ferguson* was written. We must consider public education in the light of its full development and its present place in American life throughout the Nation. Only in this way can it be determined if segregation in public schools deprives these plaintiffs of the equal protection of the laws.

Today, education is perhaps the most important function of state and local governments. Compulsory school attendance laws and the great expenditures for education both demonstrate our recognition of the importance of education to our democratic society. It is required in the performance of our most basic public responsibilities, even service in the armed forces. It is the very foundation of good citizenship. Today it is a principal instrument in awakening the child to cultural values, in preparing him for later professional training,

*Brown v. The Board of Education of Topeka,* 347 U.S. 483 (1954).

and in helping him to adjust normally to his environment. In these days, it is doubtful that any child may reasonably be expected to succeed in life if he is denied the opportunity of an education. Such an opportunity, where the state has undertaken to provide it, is a right which must be made available to all on equal terms.

We come then to the question presented: Does segregation of children in public schools solely on the basis of race, even though the physical facilities and other "tangible" factors may be equal, deprive the children of the minority group of equal educational opportunities? We believe that it does.

In *Sweatt* v. *Painter*, . . . in finding that a segregated law school for Negroes could not provide them equal educational opportunities, this Court relied in large part on "those qualities which are incapable of objective measurement but which make for greatness in a law school." In *McLaurin* v. *Oklahoma State Regents*, . . . the Court, in requiring that a Negro admitted to a white graduate school be treated like all other students, again resorted to intangible considerations: ". . . his ability to study, to engage in discussions and exchange views with other students, and, in general, to learn his profession." Such considerations apply with added force to children in grade and high schools. To separate them from others of similar age and qualifications solely because of their race generates a feeling of inferiority as to their status in the community that may affect their hearts and minds in a way unlikely ever to be undone. The effect of this separation on their educational opportunities was well stated by a finding in the Kansas case by a court which nevertheless felt compelled to rule against the Negro plaintiffs:

> Segregation of white and colored children in public schools has a detrimental effect upon the colored children. The impact is greater when it has the sanction of the law; for the policy of separating the races is usually interpreted as denoting the inferiority of the Negro group. A sense of inferiority affects the motivation of a child to learn. Segregation with the sanction of the law, therefore, has a tendency to retard the educational and mental development of Negro children and to deprive them of some of the benefits they would receive in a racially integrated school system.

Whatever may have been the extent of psychological knowledge at the time of *Plessy* v. *Ferguson*, this finding is amply supported by modern authority. Any language in *Plessy* v. *Ferguson* contrary to this finding is rejected.

We conclude that in the field of public education the doctrine of "separate but equal" has no place. Separate educational facilities are inherently unequal. Therefore, we hold that the plaintiffs and others similarly situated for whom the actions have been brought are, by reason of the segregation complained of, deprived of the equal protection of the laws guaranteed by the Fourteenth Amendment. . . .

# 38

## WOMEN'S LIBERATION

✪══✪══✪

After its bright triumph of the early 1920s, interest in the movement for women's rights lagged, then gathered new steam in the 1950s. This resurgence resulted partly from a trend in the workforce: 27 percent of adult women worked outside the home in 1940, 33 percent in 1960, and 50 percent in 1980. With so many women in the workforce, they gradually made their concerns heard: equal pay for equal work, managerial positions in heretofore all-male administrations, elimination of sexual and physical harassment. Working wives, it turned out, often strained traditional male-dominant marriages, and both the divorce rate and the need for new child-care arrangements increased. Also, married or not, working women saw their lives focusing less exclusively on children and domesticity. They therefore looked increasingly to modern birth control devices and to abortion. (The Supreme Court declared abortion legal in 1973.) From 1960 to 1980, the birth rate decreased 50 percent.

But if these trends provided the underpinnings for the modern women's movement, true feminism—the struggle for women's liberation—came only with the addition of "consciousness raising" to these socioeconomic tendencies. Here, too, there was a crucial underlying trend: many more women were college-educated than ever before. In 1940 approximately 15 percent of American women had completed at least one year of college, and women earned about one-fourth of all bachelor's degrees given by U.S. colleges. By 1960, about 20 percent of all women had gone to college, and women earned one-third of all bachelor's degrees. By 1990, the percentage of women attending college was over 45 percent and women earned nearly half of all U.S. bachelor's degrees.

In part, Betty Friedan was addressing these millions of educated but underemployed women in her pathbreaking *The Feminine Mystique,* published in 1963 and excerpted below. Friedan attacked the mass media for brainwashing women into models of domesticity. The National Organization for Women (NOW), created in 1966 with Friedan's support, pressed for eliminating all discriminatory legal sexual distinctions. A half-century after the suffrage amendment, politics witnessed major gains for women. They became governors in numerous states, including Texas, one of the three largest. Female senators were elected from several states, including California. Mayors in many of the nation's largest cities, including Chicago and Houston, were women. They held three cabinet positions under Jimmy Carter and one each under Reagan and Bush. Two women were appointed Supreme Court justices. A woman ran as a Democratic Party vice-presidential candidate, another for the Democratic presidential nomination. Women were commonplace in the American military forces in the two Persian Gulf wars, although not initially in official combat roles.

Betty Friedan was born in 1921 in Illinois and attended Smith College and the University of California at Berkeley. In the early 1960s Friedan was a wife and mother who, having lost her job as a newspaper reporter, was contributing to popular magazines. Noticing that editors frequently cut her references to women's careers in favor of more material on homemaking, she began to analyze the housewife fantasy and to interview housewives themselves. The result was *The Feminine Mystique* (1963), an instant best seller that catapulted its author to the forefront of the women's movement and earned her countless offers to lecture and teach. Friedan was the founding president of the National Organization for Women from 1966 to 1970 and also helped found the National Women's Political Caucus and the National Association to Repeal Abortion Laws. None of it was easy. "A lot of people," she recalled, "treated me like a leper."

**Questions to Consider.** Betty Friedan argued in *The Feminine Mystique* that American women suffered from a "problem that has no name." What was that problem? Was she the first to discover it? What were her methods of investigating and reporting it? Why did it have no name? Did Friedan name it? Would all American women have responded to Friedan's arguments? What kinds of women would have been most likely to respond? How revolutionary was her message? What social or political measures would be required to deal effectively with this problem?

★━━★━━★

# The Feminine Mystique (1963)

### BETTY FRIEDAN

The suburban housewife—she was the dream image of the young American women and the envy, it was said, of women all over the world. The American housewife—freed by science and labor-saving appliances from the drudgery,

**A balding Jock Semple of the Boston Athletic Association accosts Karen Switzer of Syracuse in an effort to enforce the BAA's rule barring women from running in the Boston Marathon, 1967.** In the late 1960s there were still few opportunities for women to participate in serious sports at any level, a situation that changed significantly only with the passage of federal antidiscrimination legislation. (© Bettmann/Corbis)

the dangers of childbirth and the illnesses of her grandmother. She was healthy, beautiful, educated, concerned only about her husband, her children, her home. She had found true feminine fulfillment. As a housewife and mother, she was respected as a full and equal partner to man in his world. She was free to choose automobiles, clothes, appliances, supermarkets; she had everything that women ever dreamed of.

In the fifteen years after World War II, this mystique of feminine fulfillment became the cherished and self-perpetuating core of contemporary American culture. Millions of women lived their lives in the image of those pretty pictures of the American suburban housewife, kissing their husbands goodbye in front of the picture window, depositing their stationwagonsful of children at school, and smiling as they ran the new electric waxer over the spotless kitchen floor. They baked their own bread, sewed their own and their children's clothes, kept their new washing machines and dryers running all day. They changed the sheets on the beds twice a week instead of once, took the rug-hooking class in adult education, and pitied their poor frustrated mothers, who had dreamed of having a career. Their only dream was to be perfect wives and mothers; their highest ambition to have five children and a beautiful house, their only fight to get and keep their husbands. They had no thought for the unfeminine problems of the world outside the home; they wanted the men to make the major decisions. They gloried in their role as women, and wrote proudly on the census blank: "Occupation: housewife."

For over fifteen years, the words written for women, and the words women used when they talked to each other, while their husbands sat on the other side of the room and talked shop or politics or septic tanks, were about problems with their children, or how to keep their husbands happy, or improve their children's school, or cook chicken or make slipcovers. Nobody argued whether women were inferior or superior to men; they were simply different. Words like *emancipation* and *career* sounded strange and embarrassing; no one had used them for years. . . .

But on an April morning in 1959, I heard a mother of four, having coffee with four other mothers in a suburban development fifteen miles from New York, say in a tone of quiet desperation, "the problem." And the others knew, without words, that she was not talking about a problem with her husband, or her children, or her home. Suddenly they realized they all shared the same problem, the problem that has no name. They began, hesitantly, to talk about it. Later, after they had picked up their children at nursery school and taken them home to nap, two of the women cried, in sheer relief, just to know they were not alone. . . .

Just what was this problem that has no name? What were the words women used when they tried to express it? Sometimes a woman would say "I feel empty somehow . . . incomplete." Or she would say, "I feel as if I don't exist." Sometimes she blotted out the feeling with a tranquilizer. Sometimes she thought the problem was with her husband, or her children, or that what she really needed was to redecorate her house, or move to a better neighborhood, or have an affair, or another baby. Sometimes, she went to a doctor with symptoms she could hardly describe: "A tired feeling . . . I get so angry with the children it scares me . . . I feel like crying without any reason." (A Cleveland doctor called it "the housewife's syndrome.") A number of women told me about great bleeding blisters that break out on their hands and arms. "I call it the housewife's blight," said a family doctor in Pennsylvania. "I see it so often lately in these young women with four, five and six children who bury themselves in their dishpans. But it isn't caused by detergent and it isn't cured by cortisone." . . .

In 1960, the problem that has no name burst like a boil through the image of the happy American housewife. In the television commercials the pretty housewives still beamed over their foaming dishpans and *Time's* cover story on "The Suburban Wife, an American Phenomenon" protested: "Having too good a time . . . to believe that they should be unhappy." But the actual unhappiness of the American housewife was suddenly being reported—from the *New York Times* and *Newsweek* to *Good Housekeeping* and CBS Television

("The Trapped Housewife"), although almost everybody who talked about it found some superficial reason to dismiss it. . . .

Of the growing thousands of women currently getting private psychiatric help in the United States, the married ones were reported dissatisfied with their marriages, the unmarried ones suffering from anxiety and, finally, depression. Strangely, a number of psychiatrists stated that, in their experience, unmarried women patients were happier than married ones. So the door of all those pretty suburban houses opened a crack to permit a glimpse of uncounted thousands of American housewives who suffered alone from a problem that suddenly everyone was talking about, and beginning to take for granted, as one of those unreal problems in American life that can never be solved—like the hydrogen bomb. . . .

I do not accept the answer that there is no problem because American women have luxuries that women in other times and lands never dreamed of; part of the strange newness of the problem is that it cannot be understood in terms of the age-old material problems of man: poverty, sickness, hunger, cold. The women who suffer this problem have a hunger that food cannot fill. . . .

Are the women who finished college, the women who once had dreams beyond housewifery, the ones who suffer the most? According to the experts they are, but . . . housewives of all educational levels suffer the same feeling of desperation.

The fact is that no one today is muttering angrily about "women's rights," even though more and more women have gone to college. In a recent study of all the classes that have graduated from Barnard College, a significant minority of earlier graduates blamed their education for making them want "rights," later classes blamed their education for giving them career dreams, but recent graduates blamed the college for making them feel it was not enough simply to be a housewife and mother; they did not want to feel guilty if they did not read books or take part in community activities. But if education is not the cause of the problem, the fact that education somehow festers in these women may be a clue.

If the secret of feminine fulfillment is having children, never have so many women, with the freedom to choose, had so many children, in so few years, so willingly. If the answer is love, never have women searched for love with such determination. And yet there is a growing suspicion that the problem may not be sexual, though it must somehow be related to sex. I have heard from many doctors evidence of new sexual problems between man and wife—sexual hunger in wives so great their husbands cannot satisfy it. . . .

Can the problem that has no name be somehow related to the domestic routine of the housewife? When a woman tries to put the problem into words, she often merely describes the daily life she leads. What is there in this recital of comfortable domestic detail that could possibly cause such a feeling of desperation? Is she trapped simply by the enormous demands of her role as modern housewife: wife, mistress, mother, nurse, consumer, cook, chauffeur; expert on interior decoration, child care, appliance repair, furniture refinishing, nutrition, and education? . . .

If I am right, the problem that has no name stirring in the minds of so many American women today is not a matter of loss of femininity or too much education, or the demands of domesticity. It is far more important than anyone recognizes. It is the key to these other new and old problems which have been torturing women and their husbands and children, and puzzling their doctors and educators for years. It may well be the key to our future as a nation and a culture. We can no longer ignore that voice within women that says: "I want something more than my husband and my children and my home."

# 39

## THE STRUGGLE FOR POLITICAL RIGHTS

★═══★═══★

The modern civil rights movement began with *Brown* v. *The Board of Education* in 1954 and a successful boycott of the Montgomery, Alabama, bus company over seating rights in 1955. For the next few years, two groups provided the movement with leadership: the National Association for the Advancement of Colored People (NAACP), which worked mainly through the courts and enjoyed a national membership, and the Southern Christian Leadership Conference (SCLC), which was based in the African American churches of the South and used the tactics of nonviolent demonstrations and boycotts. Though differing in methods, the two organizations shared important characteristics. Their chief objective was the integration of public facilities, including schools. And although they both had predominantly black membership, they accepted white support and participation, as was evident at the 1963 "March on Washington," one of the last large multiracial gatherings of the era.

At this point the movement shifted gears. Its primary focus moved from efforts to integrate public facilities to efforts to secure black voting rights, which the NAACP and SCLC had until now largely avoided out of concern about the possible reaction to this kind of challenge to white power. And in fact the effort did provoke fierce resistance and much violence, particularly during the "freedom summers" of 1964 and 1965, when black and white college students ran voter registration campaigns in various part of the South, including ultra-segregationist Alabama and Mississippi. A new organization, the Student Non-Violent Coordinating Committee (SNCC), orchestrated the voter drives, holding meetings and recruiting people to try to register.

One recruit was Fannie Lou Hamer, a sharecropper's daughter and an agricultural worker from the Mississippi Delta, one of the most impoverished regions in the South. Hamer attended an SNCC meeting at a church near her home and was inspired to try to register to vote (which she managed in 1963). She became an SNCC field secretary, and in 1964, helped form the Mississippi Freedom Democratic Party (MFDP) to challenge the convention credentials of the white supremacist Democratic regulars of the state. One of 68 MFDP members to go to the convention, Hamer testified to the Credentials Committee in a televised presentation. The Committee turned down the MFDP's request to be seated at the convention instead of the regulars, or at least with them. But her testimony (below) generated waves of support from viewers, forcing negotiations that gave two seats to black Mississippians and access to the convention floor to several others. Hamer rejected this compromise and returned to Mississippi to run for Congress against a white incumbent. She lost.

The violent white reaction to the voter registration drives sparked an angry response among young black activists, who increasingly opposed any white participation in the movement. After 1966, the civil rights movement became more ethnocentric, militant, and fragmented. By 1970, SNCC no longer existed, and neither did the movement in its original form. Yet there had been political gains. In 1965, President Johnson pushed a landmark Voting Rights Act through Congress, one of the signal domestic accomplishments of his administration. Thereafter, Southern black registration rose steadily. And in 1968 Fannie Lou Hamer gained a regular delegate seat to the convention, becoming the first black Mississippian to do so since Reconstruction and the first Mississippi woman ever.

Fannie Lou Hamer was born in 1917 into a large Mississippi sharecropper family. She had to drop out of school after the sixth grade to work, but she continued to read and study the Bible with teachers from the local church. Following her work with SNCC and MFDP and her powerful convention testimony, she became a member of the Democratic National Committee, a developer of the nonprofit Delta Ministry and Freedom Farms Corporation, a policy council member of the National Women's Political Caucus, and a trustee of the Martin Luther King Center for Nonviolent Social Change. She died in Mound Bayou, Mississippi, in 1977.

**Questions to Consider.** What did Hamer do that led white Mississippians to retaliate against her and her associates? What was the nature of the retaliation? Did it change over time? Which type of retaliation was, in her account, most severe? Could Hamer have done anything to reduce white rage? What is the most likely explanation for the positive national response to Hamer's testimony?

❌══❌══❌

# Testimony at the Democratic Convention (1964)

## FANNIE LOU HAMER

Mr. Chairman, and to the Credentials Committee, my name is Mrs. Fannie Lou Hamer, and I live at 626 East Lafayette Street, Ruleville, Mississippi, Sunflower County, the home of Senator James O. Eastland, and Senator Stennis.

It was the 31st of August in 1962 that eighteen of us traveled twenty-six miles to the county courthouse in Indianola to try to register to become first-class citizens.

We was met in Indianola by policemen, Highway Patrolmen, and they only allowed two of us in to take the literacy test at the time. After we had taken this test and started back to Ruleville, we was held up by the City Police and the State Highway Patrolmen and carried back to Indianola where the bus driver was charged that day with driving a bus the wrong color.

After we paid the fine among us, we continued on to Ruleville, and Reverend Jeff Sunny carried me four miles in the rural area where I had worked as a timekeeper and sharecropper for eighteen years. I was met there by my children, who told me that the plantation owner was angry because I had gone down to try to register.

After they told me, my husband came, and said the plantation owner was raising Cain because I had tried to register. Before he quit talking the plantation owner came and said, "Fannie Lou, do you know—did Pap tell you what I said?"

And I said, "Yes, sir."

He said, "Well I mean that." He said, "If you don't go down and withdraw your registration, you will have to leave." Said, "Then if you go down and withdraw," said, "you still might have to go because we are not ready for that in Mississippi."

And I addressed him and told him and said, "I didn't try to register for you. I tried to register for myself."

I had to leave that same night.

On the 10th of September 1962, sixteen bullets was fired into the home of Mr. and Mrs. Robert Tucker for me. That same night two girls were shot in Ruleville, Mississippi. Also Mr. Joe McDonald's house was shot in.

And June the 9th, 1963, I had attended a voter registration workshop; was returning back to Mississippi. Ten of us was traveling by the Continental Trailway bus. When we got to Winona, Mississippi, which is Montgomery County, four of the people got off to use the washroom, and two of the people—to use the restaurant—two of the people wanted to use the washroom.

Fannie Lou Hamer, "Testimony at the Democratic Convention, 1964" from Testimony to the Credentials Committee, Democratic National Committee Convention, 1964. Reprinted by permission of Jacqueline Hamer.

The four people that had gone in to use the restaurant was ordered out. During this time I was on the bus. But when I looked through the window and saw they had rushed out I got off of the bus to see what had happened. And one of the ladies said, "It was a State Highway Patrolman and a Chief of Police ordered us out."

I got back on the bus and one of the persons had used the washroom got back on the bus, too.

As soon as I was seated on the bus, I saw when they began to get the five people in a highway patrolman's car. I stepped off of the bus to see what was happening and somebody screamed from the car that the five workers was in and said, "Get that one there." When I went to get in the car, when the man told me I was under arrest, he kicked me.

I was carried to the county jail and put in the booking room. They left some of the people in the booking room and began to place us in cells. I was placed in a cell with a young woman called Miss Ivesta Simpson. After I was placed in the cell I began to hear sounds of licks and screams, I could hear the sounds of licks and horrible screams. And I could hear somebody say, "Can you say, 'yes, sir,' nigger? Can you say 'yes, sir'?"

And they would say other horrible names.

She would say, "Yes, I can say 'yes, sir'"

"So, well, say it."

She said, "I don't know you well enough."

They beat her, I don't know how long. And after a while she began to pray, and asked God to have mercy on those people.

And it wasn't too long before three white men came to my cell. One of these men was a State Highway Patrolman and he asked me where I was from. I told him Ruleville and he said, "We are going to check this."

They left my cell and it wasn't too long before they came back. He said, "You are from Ruleville all right," and he used a curse word. And he said, "We are going to make you wish you was dead."

I was carried out of that cell into another cell where they had two Negro prisoners. The State Highway Patrolmen ordered the first Negro to take the blackjack.

The first Negro prisoner ordered me, by orders from the State Highway Patrolman, for me to lay down on a bunk bed on my face.

I laid on my face and the first Negro began to beat. I was beat by the first Negro until he was exhausted. I was holding my hands behind me at that time on my left side, because I suffered from polio when I was six years old.

After the first Negro had beat until he was exhausted, the State Highway Patrolman ordered the second Negro to take the blackjack.

The second Negro began to beat and I began to work my feet, and the State Highway Patrolman ordered the first Negro who had beat me to sit on my feet—to keep me from working my feet. I began to scream and one white man got up and began to beat me in my head and tell me to hush.

One white man—my dress had worked up high—he walked over and pulled my dress—I pulled my dress down and he pulled my dress back up.

I was in jail when Medgar Evers* was murdered.

All of this is on account of we want to register, to become first-class citizens. And if the Freedom Democratic Party is not seated now, I question America. Is this America, the land of the free and the home of the brave, where we have to sleep with our telephones off the hooks because our lives be threatened daily, because we want to live as decent human beings, in America?

Thank you.

---

*Medgar Evers was an NAACP officer who was assassinated in 1963, the first of a wave of American assassinations.

# 40

## HEALTH AND DIGNITY

Lyndon Johnson would have been "a tough can-do president," said a disappointed Lady Bird Johnson after her husband had lost the 1960 Democratic presidential nomination to John F. Kennedy. At that point Johnson stepped down as majority leader of the Senate, agreed to run for vice president with Kennedy, helped carry enough Southern states to put Kennedy in the White House—and became president himself in November 1963 when Kennedy was assassinated. Once in office, Johnson, confident of his ability to influence Congress and eager to pursue and expand Kennedy's unfinished initiatives, told his staff, "Get me those bills. We've got a window here that's going to close pretty quickly." The country was about to discover what Lady Bird was talking about.

In 1964 Johnson engineered, over bitter Southern objections, a historic Civil Rights Act banning public segregation and an Economic Opportunity Act authorizing funds for a "war on poverty," an office to coordinate Head Start and Upward Bound programs for children and adolescents, and VISTA, a kind of "domestic peace corps." The next year Johnson really hit his stride, with the Elementary and Secondary Education Act, the first general federal program for schools in U.S. history; the Voting Rights Act authorizing federal officials to register qualified African American voters in the South; a housing act to supplement low-income rents; a federal loan program for needy college students; and the establishment of the National Endowments for the Arts and the Humanities. These "Great Society" initiatives concluded in 1966 with unprecedented consumer safety legislation and subsidies for urban housing development, recreational facilities, and mass-transit projects.

Amid this welter of legislation, nothing (the voting rights act possibly excepted) was more important over the long term than the Medical Care Act of 1965 providing medical insurance for the elderly and health funds for welfare recipients. The Medicare Act represented the culmination of nearly three decades of Democratic political labor. The 1935 Social Security Act had left out health care except for minor provisions for the disabled—Roosevelt did not think Congress would support it—and future attempts to provide federal health insurance, beginning in the late 1940s with Harry Truman, foundered on the combined opposition of Republican conservatives and the American Medical Association. In 1960, John F. Kennedy made passage of a Medicare bill a part of his legislative agenda, as did Lyndon Johnson when he assumed office. The Democrats' landslide electoral victory of 1964 allowed its enactment. The document below is a transcript of remarks by Johnson and former President Truman at the signing of the bill on July 31, 1965, at the Truman Library in Independence, Missouri. Truman was 81 years old at the time.

**Questions to Consider.** What point was Johnson making when he arranged to hold the signing of the Medicare bill at the Truman Library? What other former presidents did he praise for promoting a program of this kind? Why was Johnson so scrupulous in thanking members of Congress? If good health was the main goal of the Medicare Act, why did Johnson emphasize other, less tangible aspects of the act? Neither Johnson nor Truman mentioned the "Medicaid" portion of the bill that subsidized low-income health care. Why not? What might have accounted for the vehement opposition of American doctors to federal health insurance?

★═══★═══★

# The Signing of the Medicare Bill (1965)

## LYNDON B. JOHNSON

*Harry S. Truman.* Thank you very much. I am glad you like the President. I like him too. He is one of the finest men I ever ran across.

Mr. President, Mrs. Johnson, distinguished guests:

You have done me a great honor in coming here today, and you have made me a very, very happy man.

This is an important hour for the Nation, for those of our citizens who have completed their tour of duty and have moved to the sidelines. These are the days that we are trying to celebrate for them. These people are our prideful responsibility and they are entitled, among other benefits, to the best medical protection available.

Not one of these, our citizens, should ever be abandoned to the indignity of charity. Charity is indignity when you have to have it. But we don't want these people to have anything to do with charity and we don't want them to have any idea of hopeless despair.

**Citation:** John T. Woolley and Gerhard Peters, *The American Presidency Project* [online]. Santa Barbara, CA: University of California (hosted), Gerhard Peters (database). Available from World Wide Web: http://www.presidency.ucsb.edu/ws/?pid=27123.

Mr. President, I am glad to have lived this long and to witness today the signing of the Medicare bill which puts this Nation right where it needs to be, to be right. Your inspired leadership and a responsive forward-looking Congress have made it historically possible for this day to come about.

Thank all of you most highly for coming here. It is an honor I haven't had for, well, quite awhile, I'll say that to you, but here it is:

Ladies and gentlemen, the President of the United States.

*Lyndon B. Johnson.* President and Mrs. Truman . . . and all of my dear friends in the Congress—both Democrats and Republicans:

The people of the United States love and voted for Harry Truman, not because he gave them hell—but because he gave them hope.

I believe today that all America shares my joy that he is present now when the hope that he offered becomes a reality for millions of our fellow citizens.

I am so proud that this has come to pass in the Johnson administration. But it was really Harry Truman of Missouri who planted the seeds of compassion and duty which have today flowered into care for the sick, and serenity for the fearful. . . .

It was a generation ago that Harry Truman said, and I quote him: "Millions of our citizens do not now have a full measure of opportunity to achieve and to enjoy good health. Millions do not now have protection or security against the economic effects of sickness. And the time has now arrived for action to help them attain that opportunity and to help them get that protection."

Well, today, Mr. President, and my fellow Americans, we are taking such action—20 years later. And we are doing that under the great leadership of men like John McCormack, our Speaker; Carl Albert, our majority leader; our very able and beloved majority leader of the Senate, Mike Mansfield; and distinguished Members of the Ways and Means and Finance Committees of the House and Senate—of both parties, Democratic and Republican.

Because the need for this action is plain; and it is so clear indeed that we marvel not simply at the passage of this bill, but what we marvel at is that it took so many years to pass it. . . .

There are more than 18 million Americans over the age of 65. Most of them have low incomes. Most of them are threatened by illness and medical expenses that they cannot afford.

And through this new law, Mr. President, every citizen will be able, in his productive years when he is earning, to insure himself against the ravages of illness in his old age.

This insurance will help pay for care in hospitals, in skilled nursing homes, or in the home. And under a separate plan it will help meet the fees of the doctors.

Now here is how the plan will affect you.

During your working years, the people of America—you—will contribute through the social security program a small amount each payday for hospital insurance protection. For example, the average worker in 1966 will contribute about $1.50 per month. The employer will contribute a similar amount. And this will provide the funds to pay up to 90 days of hospital care for each illness, plus diagnostic care, and up to 100 home health visits after you are 65. And beginning in 1967, you will also be covered for up to 100 days of care in a skilled nursing home after a period of hospital care.

And under a separate plan, when you are 65—that the Congress originated itself, in its own good judgment—you may be covered for medical and surgical fees whether you are in or out of the hospital. You will pay $3 per month after you are 65 and your Government will contribute an equal amount.

The benefits under the law are as varied and broad as the marvelous modern medicine itself. If it has a few defects—such as the method of payment of certain specialists—then I am confident those can be quickly remedied and I hope they will be.

No longer will older Americans be denied the healing miracle of modern medicine. No longer will illness crush and destroy the savings that they have so carefully put away over a lifetime so that they might enjoy dignity in their later years. No longer will young families see their own incomes, and their own hopes, eaten away simply because they are carrying out their deep moral obligations to their parents, and to their uncles, and their aunts.

And no longer will this Nation refuse the hand of justice to those who have given a lifetime of service and wisdom and labor to the progress of this progressive country.

And this bill, Mr. President, is even broader than that. It will increase social security benefits for all of our older Americans. It will improve a wide range of health and medical services for Americans of all ages.

In 1935 when the man that both of us loved so much, Franklin Delano Roosevelt, signed the Social Security Act, he said it was, and I quote him, "a cornerstone in a structure which is being built but it is by no means complete."

Well, perhaps no single act in the entire administration of the beloved Franklin D. Roosevelt really did more to win him the illustrious place in history that he has as did the laying of that cornerstone. And I am so happy that his oldest son Jimmy could be here to share with us the joy that is ours today. And those who share this day will also be remembered for making the most important addition to that structure, and you are making it in this bill, the most important addition that has been made in three decades.

And there is also John Fitzgerald Kennedy, who fought in the Senate and took his case to the people, and never yielded in pursuit, but was not spared to see the final concourse of the forces that he had helped to loose.

But it all started really with the man from Independence. And so, as it is fitting that we should, we have come back here to his home to complete what he began.

President Harry Truman, as any President must, made many decisions of great moment; although he always made them frankly and with a courage and a clarity that few men have ever shared. The immense and the intricate questions of freedom and survival were caught up many times in the web of Harry Truman's judgment. And this is in the tradition of leadership.

But there is another tradition that we share today. It calls upon us never to be indifferent toward despair. It commands us never to turn away from helplessness. It directs us never to ignore or to spurn those who suffer untended in a land that is bursting with abundance.

I said to Senator Smathers, the whip of the Democrats in the Senate, who worked with us in the Finance Committee on this legislation—I said, the highest traditions of the medical profession are really directed to the ends that we are trying to serve. And it was only yesterday, at the request of some of my friends, I met with the leaders of the American Medical Association to seek their assistance in advancing the cause of one of the greatest professions of all—the medical profession—in helping us to maintain and to improve the health of all Americans.

And this is not just our tradition—or the tradition of the Democratic Party—or even the tradition of the Nation. It is as old as the day it was first commanded: "Thou shalt open thine hand wide unto thy brother, to thy poor, to thy needy, in thy land.". . .

Because of this document—and the long years of struggle which so many have put into creating it—in this town, and a thousand other towns like it, there are men and women in pain who will now find ease. There are those alone in suffering who will now hear the sound of some approaching footsteps coming to help. There are those fearing the terrible darkness of despairing poverty—despite their long years of labor and expectation—who will now look up to see the light of hope and realization.

There just can be no satisfaction, nor any act of leadership, that gives greater satisfaction than this.

# 41

## SAVING THE ENVIRONMENT

★━━━★━━━★

Although occasionally writers such as Henry David Thoreau celebrated the beauty and power of nature, modern environmentalism began only late in the nineteenth century, as cities and industry grew so rapidly that they flattened and contaminated nature even as railroads increased access to it. In 1872 Congress created the first national park, Yellowstone, and twenty years later, after prodding by a new environmental organization, the Sierra Club, Congress enabled the president to set up wilderness areas. Theodore Roosevelt promoted more rational uses of scarce timber and mining resources after 1900. Franklin D. Roosevelt initiated important conservation projects, including the Tennessee Valley Authority and the Civilian Conservation Corps, during the Depression.

Environmentalism as a mass movement arose chiefly in the 1960s as people began to worry about not only the despoliation of wilderness but also the pollution of air, drinking water, and food and the wholesale annihilation of plant and animal species. In part this was because of a series of horror stories: polluted rivers spontaneously catching fire, poisons detected in human tissues and mothers' milk, acid rain destroying lakes and streams, massive coastal oil spills, air too "smoggy" to breathe safely. But the writings of scientists and naturalists, from Paul Erlich's *The Population Bomb* to Barry Commoner's *The Closing Circle* to Rechel Carson's *Silent Spring,* played a part as well.

President Richard Nixon responded to growing public anxiety by asking for a report from his Advisory Council on Executive Organization about what steps to take. The Council included Nixon stalwarts such as Roy Ash, president of Litton Industries and head of the Office of Management and Budget; John Connally, Nixon's Secretary of the Treasury; and Walter Thayer, Nixon's chief legal counsel. Given Nixon's reputation, environmental activists and liberals did not expect much and were therefore surprised at the Council's recommendation (excerpted below) to establish an Environmental Protection Agency (EPA) that would bridge government departments; possess broad powers, including powers to set standards and impose penalties; and have its own budget and significant autonomy.

Republicans were also surprised because EPA was precisely the kind of permanent regulatory agency that they associated with Lyndon Johnson and Franklin Roosevelt. But like his mentor Dwight Eisenhower, Nixon, though conservative in many ways, was comfortable with large, popular federal programs. In addition, suburban Republican women were among those most alarmed about pollution and pressure from Democrats was rising. And staunch Republicans had forwarded this proposal. Anyway, some kind of dramatic federal intervention to preserve and protect a deteriorating environment seemed imperative for the reasons discussed in the memorandum. In 1972, Congress followed up with the passage of the Clean Air Act and the Clean Water Act, the most sweeping environmental laws in the country's history; and in 1973, with an Endangered Species Act that enabled EPA to protect wildlife from hunters and habitat from builders.

These measures, though inadequate by some measures, worked fairly well. By the end of the century, although species and woodlands still vanished and cancer rates remained high, levels of DDT and other cancer-causing compounds were down, as were soot, carbon-monoxide, and sulfur-dioxide emissions. Energy usage grew more slowly than the overall economy. America's water supply, though not pristine, was the cleanest in the industrial world. And despite periodic antiregulation politics, the protection and cleansing of the world around us remained high on the nation's agenda.

**Questions to Consider.**  How did the Council defend its recommendation of a separate new agency rather than the strengthening of existing departmental environmental offices? What role would private business play? Why did the Council say that having EPA would actually benefit business? How did the Council expect a part of the problem of increased energy use to be addressed? What role was anticipated for transnational or global environmental action?

# President's Advisory Council
# Memorandum (1970)

## The Environmental Crisis

Pollution is essentially a by-product of our vastly increased per capita consumption, intensified by population growth, urbanization, and changing

http://www.epa.gov/history/org/origins/ash.htm.

industrial processes. In the coming years, problems of environmental degradation will rise exponentially.

While our population will increase from 200 to 260 million by the year 2000, pollution will increase much more rapidly. Even if 50 percent of the nation's electric generating capacity is nuclear-powered by the year 2000, pollutants resulting from fossil-fuel generation will double by 1980 and redouble by 2000.

Similarly, a seven-fold increase is expected in industrial wastes produced by the large water-using industries. These wastes are also expected to become more variable, more difficult to decompose, and more toxic. At the same time, our demand for fresh water will increase from 350 to 800 billion gallons a day—considerably exceeding the dependable supply of fresh water now available, some 650 billion gallons daily. More and more clean water will have to be retrieved from progressively dirtier waterways.

Even the fact that Americans annually junk 7 million cars, 100 million tires, 20 million tons of paper, 28 billion bottles, and 48 billion cans, does not reveal the dimensions of the problem. The 7 million cars, for example, represent less than 15 percent of the annual solid waste load. Each year we create 400 to 500 new chemicals. Many are toxic, but their exact ecological effects are not fully understood. We cannot even reliably forecast where or how they will turn up in our environment after they are used.

The enormous future needs for land, minerals, and energy require that the protection of our environment receive a powerful new impetus. In this, the nation will be on the "horns of a dilemma." The economic progress which we have come to expect, or even demand, has almost invariably been at some cost to the environment.

Pesticides have increased the yield of our crops and made it possible for less land to produce more food. They have also polluted the streams and lakes. Automobiles have broadened our economic and social opportunities, even as they have dirtied the air and jammed our highways. Some means must be found by which our economic and social aspirations are balanced against the finite capacity of the environment to absorb society's wastes.

## Inadequacy of Present Organization

Our National Government is neither structured nor oriented to sustain a well-articulated attack on the practices which debase the air we breathe, the water we drink and the land that grows our food. Indeed, the present departmental structure for dealing with environmental protection defies effective and concerted action.

The environment, despite its infinite complexity, must be perceived as a unified, interrelated system. Present assignments of departmental responsibilities do not reflect this primary characteristic.

Many agency missions, for example, are designed primarily along media lines—air, water, and land. Yet the sources of air, water, and land pollution are interrelated and often interchangeable. A single source may pollute the air with smoke and chemicals, the land with solid wastes, and a river or lake with chemical and other wastes. Control of the air pollution may convert the smoke to solid wastes that then pollute land or water. Control of the water-polluting effluent may convert it into solid wastes which must be disposed of on land.

Similarly, some pollutants—chemicals, radiation, pesticides—appear in all media. Successful interdiction now requires the coordinated efforts of a variety of separate agencies and departments. The result is a blurring of focus, and a certain Federally-sponsored irrationality.

A far more effective approach to pollution control, in our view, would:

- identify contaminates;
- trace them through the entire ecological chain, observing and recording changes in form as they occur;
- determine the total exposure of man and his environment;
- examine interactions among forms of pollution;
- and identify where in the ecological chain interdiction would be most effective.

Scientists we have consulted tell us that over the next ten years a geometric increase in our knowledge and ability to understand the problem will be required if we are to make wise and economic judgments concerning our environment. The Administration is on the threshold of a major Federal effort. It will not prosper without a sound organizational base. . . .

### Rationale for the Environmental Protection Administration (EPA)

Almost every part of government is concerned with and affects the environment. But since each agency has a job to do—resource development, transportation, health, defense, urban growth, or agriculture—its view of the environment is likely to be influenced accordingly. Sound environmental administration must reconcile divergent interests and serve the total public constituency. It must appreciate and take fully into account competing social and economic claims.

To bring together under one organizational roof all the Executive Branch entities dealing with the environment is impossible. This practical fact overwhelms the normally sound concept of building line organizations which can make trade-off decisions among competitor groups.

Nor would it help very much, given the large number of departments involved, to affiliate the environmental responsibility, particularly the critical standard-setting function, with any single existing department. That department would then be called upon to make decisions affecting other departments, when its own objectivity could be called into question. If in HEW, for example, a decision affecting DOT or HUD might well give primacy to HEW's health mission. If in Interior, a natural resource bias might well exist with respect to a matter involving the farmer or the city dweller. In short, no single agency encompasses more than a few of the perspectives requisite to environmental administration.

Given the nature and causes of environmental deterioration, programs to rectify pollution are largely geared to the great concentrations of urban population. The fact further weakens the argument for associating environmental protection with natural resources and less populated areas.

Since the Council believes that the key standard-setting function should be performed outside the agencies whose interests may affect those standards, we regard the EPA as the strongest organizational alternative. The question then becomes one of deciding what other functions such an agency should have to do its job.

We believe the standard-setting function cannot stand alone. We must know that standards are soundly based; thus, a research capability is necessary. We must know if standards are working; thus, we must be able to monitor the environment. And we must be able to offer incentives for compliance and to move against violators. These are the activities that will give effect to the standard-setting function.

The Council also believes that an independent EPA would offer distinct advantages to the business community and to state and local governments.

The Federal Government is not equipped solely or even primarily to effect a turnabout in our environmental situation through its own powers and resources. The business community is an indispensable partner in this process, even though enforcement is needed so that a business which cooperates will not be placed at a competitive disadvantage. The single agency would simplify the relationship of the private sector whose cooperation and ingenuity are essential if any real progress is to be made.

Federal anti-pollution programs must rely heavily on state and local efforts. The trend toward merger and coordination of environmental efforts at the state and local level is often inhibited by present Federal fragmentation. The EPA will simplify relationships with state and local governments and reduce the need to shop around for grant programs and other assistance.

# 42

## LIFE AND CHOICE

Except for a brief "baby boom" period after 1945, the number of children born to the average American woman has steadily decreased since the early nineteenth century. She had seven children on average in the early 1800s, four in the late 1800s, three in the early 1900s, two in the late 1900s. In the nineteenth century, the chief methods for limiting births were primitive contraception, abstinence, and, especially, abortion. In the early twentieth century, however, abortion became illegal in most states, and abstinence in marriage was less acceptable to husbands and wives. Improved contraception and delays in first marriages therefore became increasingly important birth-limiting measures. The falling birthrate since 1960 has come chiefly from a dramatic improvement in contraceptive techniques, especially contraceptive sterilization, the pill, the intrauterine device, and the vaginal sponge. Less important but still significant has been a rise in abortion rates, most notably in the five years that followed the historic 1973 Supreme Court decision in *Roe* v. *Wade,* which ruled restrictive state abortion laws unconstitutional.

*Roe* v. *Wade* reflected major changes in American society. These included advances in birth control technology, a desire to limit family size, and, especially, increased attention to the rights of women. One of these rights, according to modern feminists, is "reproductive freedom," of which abortion on demand was a crucial part. *Roe* v. *Wade* also typified a notable long-term shift in how the Supreme Court has viewed constitutional "rights"—or at least the question of which rights are the truly vital ones. In theory, all rights in the Constitution are of equal value, but over the years the Court, reflecting changes in social values, has always cherished some rights as more important than others. In the nation's early days, private property was given special consideration; later this came to include the rights of businesses and liberty of contract. Then, in the 1930s and 1940s, economic rights lost pride of place to the rights enumerated in the First Amendment. Later, the right to vote and to attend racially integrated schools was judged to be of fundamental importance. With the *Roe* v. *Wade* decision, so was the right to privacy.[1]

Justice Harry Blackmun's decision, which invalidated the statutes of thirty states that forbade abortions except to save the mother's life, sparked bitter controversy. "Prolife" forces, most affiliated with religious denominations and uncompromisingly opposed to abortion, denounced the ruling. They called for a constitutional amendment defining human life as beginning at conception, picketed abortion clinics, and successfully urged Congress to curtail most Medicaid funds for abortions. Meanwhile, "prochoice" advocates organized in support of the right of a woman (rather than the state) to choose whether or not to have an abortion. They also supported doctors' rights to perform abortions and poor women's rights to obtain them. By the 1980s, a political candidate's position on abortion could make or break a campaign, just as a Supreme Court nominee's position on *Roe* v. *Wade* could make or break a Court nomination.

Harry Blackmun, author of the *Roe* v. *Wade* decision, was born in Illinois in 1908. He grew up in the Minneapolis-St. Paul area and then headed east to attend Harvard College and Harvard Law School. Blackmun returned to Minneapolis to open a private practice before moving to Rochester, Minnesota, as legal counsel for the world-famous Mayo Clinic. A hard-working, serious-minded, moderate Republican, he was first appointed to the federal judiciary by President Dwight Eisenhower in 1959. Blackmun, a boyhood friend of Chief Justice Warren Burger, was promoted to the Supreme Court in 1970 after the Senate had rejected Richard Nixon's first two nominations to fill a recent vacancy. Although Blackmun was initially perceived as Burger's "Minnesota twin," the *Roe* v. *Wade* ruling (from which Justices Byron White and William Rehnquist dissented) marked the beginning of his drift away from the conservative Burger wing of the Court toward the more liberal wing associated with Justice William Brennan.

**Questions to Consider.** On what two constitutional grounds did the appellant seek to overturn restrictive Texas abortion laws? Of the three reasons commonly given to justify restricting abortions since the nineteenth century, which did Blackmun consider most important? Where in the Constitution did he find grounds for the right to privacy claimed by the appellant? Did Blackmun consider a woman's right to privacy a guarantee of an absolute right to abortion? The State of Texas (the appellee) argued that states could restrict abortion because the state has a "compelling interest" in protecting the right of an unborn

1. In *Rust* v. *Sullivan* (1991) the Supreme Court decided that medical personnel in family planning clinics receiving federal funds may not mention abortion or abortion facilities to clients.—*Eds.*

fetus under the provisions of the Fourteenth Amendment. How did Blackmun deal with this argument? Why did he call Texas's position "one theory of life"? Why did Blackmun discuss "trimesters" and "viability" at such length? If medical technology were to shift the point of viability from the third to the second trimester, would that undercut the force of *Roe* v. *Wade*?

⊞══⊞══⊞

## *Roe* v. *Wade* (1973)

### HARRY BLACKMUN

The principal thrust of appellant's attack on the Texas statutes is that they improperly invade a right, said to be possessed by the pregnant woman, to choose to terminate her pregnancy. Appellant would discover this right in the concept of personal "liberty" embodied in the Fourteenth Amendment's Due Process Clause; or in personal, marital, familial, and sexual privacy said to be protected by the Bill of Rights.

It perhaps is not generally appreciated that the restrictive criminal abortion laws in effect in a majority of States today are of relatively recent vintage. Those laws, generally proscribing abortion or its attempt at any time during pregnancy except when necessary to preserve the pregnant woman's life, are not of ancient or even of common law origin. Instead, they derive from statutory changes effected, for the most part, in the latter half of the nineteenth century. . . .

Three reasons have been advanced to explain historically the enactment of criminal abortion laws in the nineteenth century and to justify their continued existence.

It has been argued occasionally that these laws were the product of a Victorian social concern to discourage illicit sexual conduct. Texas, however, does not advance this justification in the present case, and it appears that no court or commentator has taken the argument seriously. . . .

A second reason is concerned with abortion as a medical procedure. When most criminal abortion laws were first enacted, the procedure was a hazardous one for the woman. . . . Modern medical techniques have altered this situation. Appellants refer to medical data indicating that abortion in early pregnancy, that is, prior to the end of first trimester, although not without its risk, is now relatively safe. . . . The State retains a definite interest in protecting the woman's own health and safety when an abortion is proposed at a late stage of pregnancy.

The third reason is the State's interest—some phrase it in terms of duty—in protecting prenatal life. Some of the argument for this justification rests on

*Roe* v. *Wade*, 410 U.S. 113 (1973).

the theory that a new human life is present from the moment of conception. The State's interest and general obligation to protect life then extends, it is argued, to prenatal life. Only when the life of the pregnant mother herself is at stake, balanced against the life she carries within her, should the interest of the embryo or fetus not prevail. Logically, of course, a legitimate State interest in this area need not stand or fall on acceptance of the belief that life begins at conception or at some other point prior to live birth. In assessing the State's interest, recognition may be given to the less rigid claim that as long as at least *potential* life is involved, the State may assert interests beyond the protection of the pregnant woman alone. . . .

The Constitution does not explicitly mention any right of privacy. In a line of decisions, however, going back perhaps as far as *Union Pacific R. Co. v. Botsford* (1891), the Court has recognized that a right of personal privacy, or a guarantee of certain areas or zones of privacy, does exist under the Constitution. . . . These decisions make it clear that only personal rights that can be deemed "fundamental" or "implicit in the concept of ordered liberty," are included in this guarantee of personal privacy. They also make it clear that the right has some extension to activities relating to marriage, procreation, contraception. . . .[1]

This right of privacy, whether it be founded in the Fourteenth Amendment's concept of personal liberty and restrictions upon state action, as we feel it is, or, as the District Court determined, in the Ninth Amendment's reservation of rights to the people, is broad enough to encompass a woman's decision whether or not to terminate her pregnancy. The detriment that the State would impose upon the pregnant woman by denying this choice altogether is apparent. Specific and direct harm medically diagnosable even in early pregnancy may be involved. Maternity, or additional offspring, may force upon the woman a distressful life and future. Psychological harm may be imminent. Mental and physical health may be taxed by child care. There is also the distress, for all concerned, associated with the unwanted child, and there is the problem of bringing a child into a family already unable, psychologically and otherwise, to care for it. In other cases, as in this one, the additional difficulties and continuing stigma of unwed motherhood may be involved. All these are factors the woman and her responsible physician necessarily will consider in consultation. . . .

On the basis of elements such as these, appellants argue that the woman's right is absolute and that she is entitled to terminate her pregnancy at whatever time, in whatever way, and for whatever reason she alone chooses. With this we do not agree. Appellant's arguments that Texas either has no valid interest at all in regulating the abortion decision, or no interest strong enough to support any limitation upon the woman's sole determination, is unpersuasive. The Court's decisions recognizing a right of privacy also acknowledge that some state regulation in areas protected by that right is appropriate.

---

1. References to prior court decisons have been omitted.—*Eds.*

As noted above, a State may properly assert important interests in safe-guarding health, in maintaining medical standards, and in protecting potential life. At some point in pregnancy, these respective interests become sufficiently compelling to sustain regulation of the factors that govern the abortion decision. The privacy right involved, therefore, cannot be said to be absolute. In fact, it is not clear to us that the claim . . . that one has an unlimited right to do with one's body as one pleases bears a close relationship to the right of privacy previously articulated in the Court's decisions. The Court has refused to recognize an unlimited right of this kind in the past.

We therefore conclude that the right of personal privacy includes the abortion decision, but that this right is not unqualified and must be considered against state interests in regulation. . . .

Appellee [the state of Texas] argues that the State's determination to recognize and protect prenatal life from and after conception constitutes a compelling state interest. We do not agree fully. . . .

The Constitution does not define "person" in so many words. Section 1 of the Fourteenth Amendment contains three references to "person." The first, in defining "citizens," speaks of "persons born or naturalized in the United States." The word also appears both in the Due Process Clause and in the Equal Protection Clause. "Person" is used in other places in the Constitution. . . . But in nearly all these instances, the use of the word is such that it has application only postnatally. None indicates, with any assurance, that it has any possible prenatal application. All this, together with our observation, that throughout the major portion of the nineteenth century prevailing legal abortion practices were far freer than they are today, persuades us that the word "person," as used in the Fourteenth Amendment, does not include the unborn. . . .

Texas urges that, apart from the Fourteenth Amendment, life begins at conception and is present throughout pregnancy, and that, therefore, the State has a compelling interest in protecting that life from and after conception. We need not resolve the difficult question of when life begins. When those trained in the respective disciplines of medicine, philosophy, and theology are unable to arrive at any consensus, the judiciary, at this point in the development of man's knowledge, is not in a position to speculate as to the answer.

In view of all this, we do not agree that, by adopting one theory of life, Texas may override the rights of the pregnant woman that are at stake. We repeat, however, that the State does have an important and legitimate interest in preserving and protecting the health of the pregnant woman, whether she be a resident of the State or a nonresident who seeks medical consultation and treatment there, and that it has still *another* important and legitimate interest in protecting the potentiality of human life. These interests are separate and distinct. Each grows in substantiality as the woman approaches term and, at a point during pregnancy, each becomes "compelling."

With respect to the State's important and legitimate interest in the health of the mother, the "compelling" point, in the light of present medical knowledge, is at approximately the end of the first trimester. This is so because of the now established medical fact, referred to above . . . that until the end of the first trimester mortality in abortion is less than mortality in normal childbirth. It follows that, from and after this point, a State may regulate the abortion procedure to the extent that the regulation reasonably relates to the preservation and protection of maternal health. Examples of permissible state regulation in this area are requirements as to the qualifications of the person who is to perform the abortion; as to the licensure of that person; as to the facility in which the procedure is to be performed, that is, whether it must be a hospital or may be a clinic or some other place of less-than-hospital status; as to the licensing of the facility; and the like.

This means, on the other hand, that, for the period of pregnancy prior to this "compelling" point, the attending physician, in consultation with his patient, is free to determine, without regulation by the State, that in his medical judgment the patient's pregnancy should be terminated. If that decision is reached, the judgment may be effectuated by an abortion free of interference by the State.

With respect to the State's important and legitimate interest in potential life, the "compelling" point is at viability. This is so because the fetus then presumably has the capability of meaningful life outside the mother's womb. State regulation protective of fetal life after viability thus has both logical and biological justifications. If the State is interested in protecting fetal life after viability, it may go so far as to proscribe abortion during that period except when it is necessary to preserve the life or health of the mother.

Measured against these standards, the Texas Penal Code, in restricting legal abortions to those "procured or attempted by medical advice for the purpose of saving the life of the mother," sweeps too broadly.

To summarize and to repeat:

A state criminal abortion statute of the current Texas type, that excepts from criminality only a *life saving* procedure on behalf of the mother, without regard to pregnancy stage and without recognition of the other interests involved, is violative of the Due Process Clause of the Fourteenth Amendment.

(a) For the stage prior to approximately the end of the first trimester, the abortion decision and its effectuation must be left to the medical judgment of the pregnant woman's attending physician.

(b) For the stage subsequent to approximately the end of the first trimester, the State, in promoting its interest in the health of the mother, may, if it chooses, regulate the abortion procedure in ways that are reasonably related to maternal health.

(c) For the stage subsequent to viability the State, in promoting its interest in the potentiality of human life, may, if it chooses, regulate, and even proscribe, abortion except where it is necessary, in appropriate medical judgment, for the preservation of the life or health of the mother.

# 43

## SPIRIT AND CULTURE

★━━★━━★

Writing in 1884, an American archbishop who understood the importance of wholehearted Roman Catholic participation in the nation's social and political life wrote the following:

Republic of America, receive from me the tribute of my love and my
loyalty. . . . *Esto perpetua*. Thou bearest in thy hands the hopes of the
human race, thy mission from God is to show to nations that men are
capable of [the] highest civil and political liberty. . . . Believe me, no
hearts love thee more ardently than Catholic hearts, . . . and no hands
will be lifted up stronger and more willing to defend, in war and peace,
thy laws and thy institutions than Catholic hands. *Esto perpetua*.

In an address written nearly a century later and reproduced in part in
the document below, Hispanic bishops echo these sentiments, affirming
their love for the United States, "although the struggle has been difficult."

Similarly to nineteenth-century Irish Catholics who endured years
of discrimination in America, Hispanic Catholics have been forced to
cope with the effects of racism and poverty. Recognizing this, the
Catholic church has addressed the particular difficulties that confront
Hispanic Americans, and Hispanic religious have led efforts to end the
suffering of the community.

In terms of the number of people who call themselves believers, and
also as a percentage of the total population, Christianity in America is
larger than it has ever been. The denominations showing the most
growth are Southern Baptists and Roman Catholics, and to a great
degree the increase in the latter is explained by the fact that Hispanics
are the fastest-growing immigrant group. As the document suggests,
the Catholic church has worked hard to establish a relationship with
Hispanics, organizing itself to deal with the most urgent problems of
the community and linking the foundations of the Christian gospel
with the historical identity and traditions of the Hispanic people.

**Questions to Consider.** What is meant by *mestizaje?* What special
problems of the Hispanic community do the pastors address? In their
view, what elements in American society endanger both the *mestiza*
tradition and religious convictions? Are there clues in the Message that

help explain why Hispanic Americans tend to be Democratic rather than Republican in their politics? How might Hispanic bishops respond to efforts to expel illegal Hispanic immigrants from the U.S.?

★═══★═══★

# Pastoral Message of the Hispanic Bishops (1982)

Four hundred fifty years after your apparition in our lands, we, your sons, come as the shepherds of our Hispanic people in the United States of North America. We come full of joy and hope, but we also come saddened and preoccupied with the suffering of our people.

We are the shepherds of a people on the march. Walking with our people, we come to you, Mother of God and our mother, so that we may receive a renewed spirit. We want to be filled with enthusiasm to go out and proclaim the wonders of God that have taken place in our history, that are taking place at this time in our lives and that will take place in the future. . . .

## I. Our Pilgrimage Throughout History

### A. The Birth of a New People

At a unique moment in the history of this world, three radically different and totally unknown worlds met: indigenous America, Africa and Europe.

The clash carried many of the indigenous people to slavery and death, and made them strangers in their own land. The Africans were violently wrenched from their lands and transplanted to far-off countries as slaves. This initiated a shock whose reverberations are experienced even today. There also began at that time a *mestizaje*, an intertwining of blood and culture that in effect brought about the birth of a new people.

The roots of our Latin American reality are grounded in their threefold inheritance. It is our identity, our suffering, our greatness and our future. . . .

### B. Our Faith

Our ancestors had a strong sense of religiosity. Their lives were centered in their God. They were a people of spiritual values, of wisdom and humanizing customs.

The missionaries brought us the knowledge of a personal God who, through his Son, invites us to a new life. The Gospel purified and enriched the beliefs of our lands.

"Pastoral Message of the Hispanic Bishops," *Origins Magazine*, August 12, 1982, pp. 145–152. Reprinted by permission.

Because of this our faith is personal and cultural, because the word was made flesh on our land when his mother arrived on the hill of Tepeyac. Little by little the Gospel has penetrated every aspect of our life and culture. It is the alpha and omega, the center of our very being. Faith penetrates our music, art, poetry, language, customs, fiestas—every expression of our life.

Faithful to our tradition we hope that the Gospel continues to transform our life and our culture.

### C. Our Mestizaje

The Hispanic people of the United States of North America is a people of *mestizaje*, an interlacing of the blood and culture of the indigenous, African and European peoples. In the present reality of our people we find a new intertwining: that of the Latin American people and those of the United States. From this second *mestizaje*, the Hispanic American people begin to emerge.

We are thus a new people and within our very being we combine the cultural riches of our parents. The Virgin of Guadalupe, our *madrecita mestiza*, comes to fill with joy and blessings the painful and difficult process of our *mestizaje*. . . .

## II. Our Reality

Much has been gained but the suffering continues. We are conscious of the oppression and exploitation of our people. We have seen bodies disfigured by hunger and saddened by the fear of the law; we have heard the cries of abandoned children mistreated by their own parents. We sense the loneliness of the elderly ignored by their relatives and the depression of prisoners whose greatest crime has been the lack of money to pay someone to defend them in court. We have shared the pain and the heat of farm workers and domestic laborers, the invisible slaves of modern society. In the jails and the detention camps there are some who have come to our country in search of work and freedom, yet who have been considered criminals. We have seen our youth with empty eyes because they have nothing to look forward to in life. We have been with the countless victims of the violence that grows daily in our neighborhoods and even in our families. We will not rest until all injustice is eliminated from our life.

We have shared with our people the fear that comes from racism and discrimination. The knowledge that we might be rejected, ridiculed or insulted paralyzes us. . . .

### A. Our Identity

Our parents taught us to love the United States, although the struggle has been difficult. Our people have always struggled to improve themselves. We love the peace founded on truth, justice, love and freedom (*Pacem in Terris*).

We have not taken up arms against our country but instead have defended it. We have fought to eliminate the injustices that rule our lives. The road has been long and difficult, littered with many obstacles, but we have made progress and will continue ahead with firmness and determination. . . .

## B. Challenges

There are certain challenges in our society which we must meet.

Our betterment in social life does not mean that we forget our roots—our Latin American *mestiza* tradition. The more we value our past, the more strength will we have to launch ourselves toward the building of our future.

Development of a more human life does not mean that we allow ourselves to be enslaved and destroyed by materialism, consumerism, social climbing, the desire for continuous pleasure and immediate gratification. All of this come from the idolatry of gold. These values are the cancer of society.

The modernization of the family does not mean that we abandon the greatest treasure of our Hispanic culture. The family is in great danger today. Divorce is on the rise, the elderly are forgotten and even cheated, children are abandoned and young people make the street their home. The spirit of individualism is killing the spirit of community that is the core of the family. . . .

## III. Artisans of a New Humanity . . .

### A. A Rebirth of the Church

The word of the Gospel takes human form the more it penetrates, encompasses and ennobles our culture. It is expressed by means of images, symbols, music, art and wisdom. The church is born out of our response to the word of Jesus. Today we are living a true rebirth of the Hispanic American *mestizo* church. . . .

### B. A More Authentic Following of Jesus

Christ is our only model and like him we ought to be ready to commit ourselves and to be steadfast in the proclamation of truth, always filled with compassion and mercy.

Our following of him demands us to raise our voice when life is threatened, defending and respecting everyone as persons created by God. We are obligated to fight for peace and justice.

Just as he opened up new horizons for us, so too must we raise up the farm worker, the migrant and the laborer. We must aid in the self-improvement of all in search of a better place in society.

**President Ronald Reagan.** Ronald Reagan gestures as he speaks to the National Association of Evangelicals. (© Bettmann/Corbis)

CHAPTER NINE

# Conservative Resurgence

# 44

## THE CONSERVATIVE SOUTH

★━━★━━★

Of all the strands of the vast and complex New Deal coalition of Franklin Roosevelt, the most restless was the "Solid South," the once Democratic former slave states that were in the process of rebelling over the issue of African American rights. In 1948, when the Democrats included pro-civil rights language in their platform, Strom Thurmond of South Carolina bolted the party and led a "Dixiecrat" white supremacist and states rights ticket that carried four states. In 1956, dozens of Southern Congressmen and Senators signed a Southern Manifesto opposing school desegregation. The manifesto omitted the open racism of 1948 but contained a ringing defense of states rights, understood at the time as code for continued segregation. Between 1960 and 1964, segregationist Harry Byrd of Virginia won most of Alabama and Mississippi's electoral votes, John Tower became the first Republican elected to the Senate from Texas since Reconstruction, and Thurmond switched parties and worked for Barry Goldwater against Lyndon Johnson. Goldwater carried only six states, but five of them were in the Deep South, where white voters liked his states rights rhetoric.

But no one upended party tradition like Governor George Wallace of Alabama. First elected governor in 1962, Wallace made himself a Southern hero the next year by pledging "Segregation forever!" and vowing to keep the state university segregated by "standing in the school house door." He did not, but white Southerners loved him anyway, and not just in Alabama. Wallace thought the battle against integration was not winnable at the state level alone. It had to be waged nationally, which Wallace proceeded to do by challenging Johnson for the 1964 Democratic nomination and winning a third of the primary votes in three Northern states. In 1968 Wallace ran for president on his own American Independent ticket. Enjoying the backing of numerous ultraconservative groups and making a powerful appeal to blue-collar Northerners, he carried five states and drew 10 million votes, half from outside the South. He made another strong showing in 1972 as a Democrat and won primaries in Michigan and Maryland. A day later, an assassin shot and crippled him, effectively ending his national political career.

Considered by liberal Democrats to be little more than a racist demagogue pandering to the lowest elements of the country, conservatives thought of Wallace very differently. As late as 1975, the readers of *Conservative Digest* voted him one of the three most significant conservative figures in the country, and many thought he would be a good running mate for Ronald Reagan. And although he ran his later races as a Democrat, Wallace said in 1981 that modern Republicans took "a lot of their thoughts and their words and their principles from George Wallace." The following excerpt is from his 1963 gubernatorial inaugural address.

Wallace was born in Alabama in 1919, graduated from the state university law school, and was elected to the Alabama House in 1946 with a moderate reputation on race, which he kept until vowing after a later loss that he would "never be out-segged again." He ran a tight, powerful, well-funded Alabama political machine. Blocked constitutionally from running for governor in 1966, he nominated his wife Lurleen to run instead. She won. Wallace regained the governorship in 1982 despite being wheelchair bound, garnering some black support by repudiating his earlier views. He died in 1998. By then, he had helped shatter the standing of the national Democratic party in the South, weakened it in the blue-collar North, and opened both to unprecedented Republican encroachment.

**Questions to Consider.** Although Wallace tried to avoid the crude white supremacist rhetoric that the Dixiecrats had used in 1948, he needed in this speech to make it clear that he was talking about race relations as well as constitutional government. What were the different ways he tried to accomplish this? What various code words and concepts did he use to convey his commitment to white supremacy? How did he link the struggles of Alabama with the Cold War? What groups in the anti-colonial conflicts of the time did he compare to the Southerners? What were Wallace's views on how the economy should operate? On what grounds did he attack centralized New Deal-type programs? Huey Long, the legendary Depression-era governor of neighboring Louisiana, rode to national prominence on a "Share Our Wealth" platform. Did Wallace support such egalitarian programs? What relation did Wallace see between the role of God and faith in society and the role of government and men?

# Governor's Inaugural Address (1963)

### GEORGE WALLACE

Today I have stood, where once Jefferson Davis stood, and took an oath to my people. It is very appropriate then that from this Cradle of the Confederacy, this very Heart of the Great Anglo-Saxon Southland, that today we sound the drum for freedom as have our generations of forebears before us done, time and time again through history. Let us rise to the call of freedom-loving blood that is in us and send our answer to the tyranny that clanks its chains upon the South. In the name of the greatest people that have ever trod this earth, I draw the line in the dust and toss the gauntlet before the feet of tyranny . . . and I say . . . segregation today . . . segregation tomorrow . . . segregation forever.

The Washington, D.C., school riot report is disgusting and revealing. We will not sacrifice our children to any such type school system—and you can write that down. The federal troops in Mississippi could be better used guarding the safety of the citizens of Washington, D.C., where it is even unsafe to walk or go to a ballgame—and that is the nation's capitol. I was safer in a B-29 bomber over Japan during the war in an air raid, than the people of Washington are walking to the White House neighborhood. A closer example is Atlanta. The city officials fawn for political reasons over school integration and THEN build barricades to stop residential integration—what hypocrisy!

Let us send this message back to Washington by our representatives who are with us today—that from this day we are standing up, and the heel of tyranny does not fit the neck of an upright man . . . that we intend to take the offensive and carry our fight for freedom across the nation, wielding the balance of power we know we possess in the Southland . . . that WE, not the insipid bloc of voters of some sections . . . will determine in the next election who shall sit in the White House of these United States. . . . That from this day, from this hour . . . from this minute . . . we give the word of a race of honor that we will tolerate their boot in our face no longer . . . and let those certain judges put that in their opium pipes of power and smoke it for what it is worth.

Hear me, Southerners! You sons and daughters who have moved north and west throughout this nation . . . we call on you from your native soil to join with us in national support and vote . . . and we know . . . wherever you are . . . away from the hearths of the Southland . . . that you will respond, for though you may live in the fartherest reaches of this vast country . . . your heart has never left Dixieland.

And you native sons and daughters of old New England's rock-ribbed patriotism . . . and you sturdy natives of the great Mid-West . . . and you descendants of the far West flaming spirit of pioneer freedom . . . we invite

www.archives.state.al.us/govs_list/inauguralspeech.html.

you to come and be with us . . . for you are of the Southern spirit . . . and the Southern philosophy . . . you are Southerners too and brothers with us in our fight.

What I have said about segregation goes double this day . . . and what I have said to or about some federal judges goes TRIPLE this day. . . .

And while the manufacturing industries of free enterprise have been coming to our state in increasing numbers, attracted by our bountiful natural resources, our growing numbers of skilled workers and our favorable conditions, their present rate of settlement here can be increased from the trickle they now represent to a stream of enterprise and endeavor, capital and expansion that can join us in our work of development and enrichment of the educational futures of our children, the opportunities of our citizens and the fulfillment of our talents as God has given them to us. To realize our ambitions and to bring to fruition our dreams, we as Alabamians must take cognizance of the world about us. We must re-define our heritage, re-school our thoughts in the lessons our forefathers knew so well, first hand, in order to function and to grow and to prosper. We can no longer hide our head in the sand and tell ourselves that the ideology of our free fathers is not being attacked and is not being threatened by another idea . . . for it is. We are faced with an idea that if a centralized government assume enough authority, enough power over its people, that it can provide a utopian life . . . that if given the power to dictate, to forbid, to require, to demand, to distribute, to edict and to judge what is best and enforce that will produce only "good" . . . and it shall be our father . . . and our God. It is an idea of government that encourages our fears and destroys our faith . . . for where there is faith, there is no fear, and where there is fear, there is no faith. In encouraging our fears of economic insecurity it demands we place that economic management and control with government; in encouraging our fear of educational development it demands we place that education and the minds of our children under management and control of government, and even in feeding our fears of physical infirmities and declining years, it offers and demands to father us through it all and even into the grave. It is a government that claims to us that it is bountiful as it buys its power from us with the fruits of its rapaciousness of the wealth that free men before it have produced and builds on crumbling credit without responsibilities to the debtors . . . our children. It is an ideology of government erected on the encouragement of fear and fails to recognize the basic law of our fathers that governments do not produce wealth . . . people produce wealth . . . free people; and those people become less free . . . as they learn there is little reward for ambition . . . that it requires faith to risk . . . and they have none . . . as the government must restrict and penalize and tax incentive and endeavor and must increase its expenditures of bounties . . . then this government must assume more and more police powers and we find we are become government-fearing people . . . not God-fearing people. We find we have replaced faith with fear . . . and though we may give lip service to the Almighty . . . in reality, government has become our god. It is, therefore, a basically ungodly government and its appeal to the psuedo-intellectual and the politician is to change their status from servant of the people to master of the people . . . to play at being God . . . without faith in God . . . and without the wisdom of God. It is a system that is the very opposite of Christ for it feeds and encourages everything degenerate and base in our people as it assumes the responsibilities that we ourselves should assume. Its pseudo-liberal spokesmen and some Harvard advocates have never examined the logic of its substitution of what it calls "human rights" for individual rights, for its propaganda play on words has appeal for the unthinking. Its logic is totally material and irresponsible as it runs the full gamut of human desires . . . including the theory that everyone has voting rights without the spiritual responsibility of preserving freedom. Our founding fathers recognized those rights . . . but only within the framework of those spiritual responsibilities. But the strong, simple faith and sane reasoning of our founding fathers has long since been forgotten as the so-called "progressives" tell us that our Constitution was written for "horse and buggy" days . . . so were the Ten Commandments.

Not so long ago men stood in marvel and awe at the cities, the buildings, the schools, the autobahns that the government of Hitler's Germany had built . . . Just as centuries before they stood in wonder of Rome's building . . . but it could not stand . . . for the system that built it had rotted the souls of the builders . . . and in turn . . . rotted the foundation of what God meant that men should be. Today that same system on an international scale is sweeping the world. It is the "changing world" of which we are told . . . it is called "new" and "liberal." It is as old as the oldest dictator. It is degenerate and decadent. As the national racism of Hitler's Germany persecuted a national minority to the whim of a national majority . . . so the international racism of the liberals seeks to persecute the international white minority to the whim of the international colored majority . . . so that we are footballed about according to the favor of the Afro-Asian bloc. But the Belgian survivors of the Congo cannot present their case to a war crimes commission . . . nor the Portuguese of Angola . . . nor the survivors of Castro . . . nor the citizens of Oxford, Mississippi. . . .

We intend, quite simply, to practice the free heritage as bequeathed to us as sons of free fathers. We intend to re-vitalize the truly new and progressive form of government that is less that two hundred years old . . . a government first founded in this nation simply and purely on faith . . . that there is a personal God who rewards good and punishes evil . . . that hard work will receive its just deserts . . . that ambition and ingenuity and incentiveness . . . and profit of such . . . are admirable traits and goals . . . that the individual is encouraged in his spiritual growth and from that growth arrives at a character that enhances his charity toward others and from that character and that charity so is influenced business, and labor and farmer and government. We intend to renew our faith as God-fearing men . . . not government-fearing men nor any other kind of fearing-men. We intend to roll up our sleeves and pitch in to develop this full bounty God has given us . . . to live full and useful lives and in absolute freedom from all fear. Then can we enjoy the full richness of the Great American Dream.

We have placed this sign, "In God We Trust," upon our State Capitol on this Inauguration Day as physical evidence of determination to renew the faith of our fathers and to practice the free heritage they bequeathed to us. We do this with the clear and solemn knowledge that such physical evidence is evidently a direct violation of the logic of that Supreme Court in Washington, D.C., and if they or their spokesmen in this state wish to term this defiance . . . I say . . . then let them make the most of it.

This nation was never meant to be a unit of one . . . but a united of the many . . . that is the exact reason our freedom loving forefathers established the states, so as to divide the rights and powers among the states, insuring that no central power could gain master government control.

In united effort we were meant to live under this government . . . whether Baptist, Methodist, Presbyterian, Church of Christ, or whatever one's denomination or religious belief . . . each respecting the others' right to a separate denomination . . . each, by working to develop his own, enriching the total of all our lives through united effort. And so it was meant in our political lives . . . whether Republican, Democrat, Prohibition, or whatever political party . . . each striving from his separate political station . . . respecting the rights of others to be separate and work from within their political framework . . . and each separate political station making its contribution to our lives. . . .

And so it was meant in our racial lives . . . each race, within its own framework has the freedom to teach . . . to instruct . . . to develop . . . to ask for and receive deserved help from others of separate racial stations. This is the great freedom of our American founding fathers . . . but if we amalgamate into the one unit as advocated by the communist philosophers . . . then the enrichment of our lives . . . the freedom for our development . . . is gone forever. We become, therefore, a mongrel unit of one under a single all powerful government . . .

The true brotherhood of America, of respecting the separateness of others . . . and uniting in effort . . . has been so twisted and distorted from its original concept that there is a small wonder that communism is winning the world. . . .

But we warn those, of any group, who would follow the false doctrine of communistic amalgamation that we will not surrender our system of government . . . our freedom of race and religion . . . that freedom was won at a hard price and if it requires a hard price to retain it . . . we are able . . . and quite willing to pay it.

The liberals' theory that poverty, discrimination and lack of opportunity is the cause of communism is a false theory . . . if it were true the South would have been the biggest single communist bloc in the western hemisphere long ago . . . With all trouble with communists that some sections of this country have . . . there are not enough native communists in the South to fill up a telephone booth . . . and THAT is a matter of public FBI record.

Southerners played a most magnificent part in erecting this great divinely inspired system of freedom . . . and as God is our witness, Southerners will save it. . . .

I will apply the old sound rule of our fathers, that anything worthy of our defense is worthy of one hundred percent of our defense. I have been taught that freedom meant freedom from any threat or fear of government. I was born in that freedom, I was raised in that freedom . . . I intend to live in that freedom . . . and God willing, when I die, I shall leave that freedom to my children . . . as my father left it to me.

My pledge to you . . . to "Stand up for Alabama," is a stronger pledge today than it was the first day I made that pledge. I shall "Stand up for Alabama," as Governor of our State . . . you stand with me . . . and we, together, can give courageous leadership to millions of people throughout this nation who look to the South for their hope in this fight to win and preserve our freedoms and liberties.

# 45

## THE NEW REPUBLICANS

★━━★━━★

The Voting Rights Act of 1965 led to the registration of two-thirds of eligible African American voters, millions in all, most of them in the South. When they voted, they overwhelmingly deserted the party of Lincoln for the party of Lyndon Johnson—which drove angry white voters the other way, a process that the urban riots and black nationalism of the 1960s accelerated. The third-party candidacy in 1968 of George Wallace, Alabama's segregationist governor, finally shattered the Democrats' hold on the South. A huge opportunity therefore beckoned to the Republicans, but one they had difficulty exploiting because many Republican voters as of the late 1960s had little stomach for the racism and states rights doctrines of a George Wallace or Strom Thurmond. Richard Nixon won the presidency in 1968 by a narrow margin because he lost most of the Southern states to Wallace, a worse showing than Goldwater's in 1964. Analysts showed, however, that combining Wallace's vote with Nixon's would produce winning majorities. The challenge, as a Nixon campaign memo argued, was to develop "a racial policy conservative enough to entice the South from Wallace" without forfeiting traditional Republicans or blue-collar Northern workers, a task to which high-level staffers devoted themselves.

The result was that Nixon and his running mate, Spiro Agnew, pounded two broad traditional themes in the run-up to 1972. One was that the Republican party, which traditionally opposed big government, redistributive economics, liberal critics, and crime was a natural home for alienated white Southerners. An example of this kind of appeal is the Agnew address (excerpted below) to a group of Jackson, Mississippi, businessmen. A second theme, embodied in Nixon's 1972 radio address, was that Republicans opposed welfare and welfare free loaders and the redistributive taxation that supported them. White voters, both Southern and non-Southern, thought instinctively of welfare recipients as people of color. Attacks on welfare therefore became, logically and almost as a matter of course, a staple of Republican politics. States rights largely vanished from Republican rhetoric; anti-welfare rhetoric flourished.

The Agnew-Nixon strategy largely worked. Many national concerns—taxes, Vietnam, crime—contributed to the post-1968 Republican resurgence. But so did the sophisticated exploitation of white Southern and blue-collar anxieties. One end product was the creation of a new "Solid South." The Republicans carried all 11 former Confederate states in 1972 (Nixon), 1980 and 1984 (Ronald Reagan), 1988 (George H. W. Bush), and 2000 (George W. Bush), and 7 of the 11 in 1992 and 1996, and they did so without forfeiting their opportunity to hold and extend their Northern support. And as white Southerners changed their party affiliation and started to win most elections, they also came to dominate Republican party machinery, Congress, and much of the judiciary—one of the most remarkable political realignments in American history.

Spiro Agnew, the governor of Maryland when Nixon chose him for vice president, was a pro-business Greek American whose assignment was to help Nixon carry the West and the border states. Agnew became a key player in efforts to exploit a backlash against black power and racial and cultural disorder. He resigned the vice presidency in 1973 after being accused of taking bribes. Nixon's reputation has come to rest positively on his diplomatic overtures to China and Russia and negatively on his disgrace and resignation following the Watergate scandal. But his contributions to the ascendance of his party may have been equally important.

**Questions to Consider.** How did Agnew attempt to disavow a "Southern Strategy," but still convey sympathy with the white South? How did Agnew connect concerns about desegregation and anti-Southern attitudes with concern about Vietnam? Why would white Southerners have responded to attacks on liberal intellectuals?

How did Nixon use the welfare issue, which had deep roots among Republicans, for his electoral purposes? How did he tailor his message to business men and the affluent as well as workers? How did he link his anti-welfare message to the war? Why did he take care to say that he was not anti-union? In what ways would his message have appealed to Northerners as well as white Southerners?

★══★══★

# Speech in Jackson, Mississippi  (1969)

### SPIRO AGNEW

Very shortly the Supreme Court will consider a case involving desegregation of Mississippi schools. President Nixon is convinced that your public officials have made a strong case for additional time to implement the law without

From John R. Coyne Jr., *The Impudent Snobs*, 1972, pp. 253–261. Published by Arlington House.

destroying quality education. The NAACP disagrees and has brought this case to compel immediate action. It is hoped that the result will provide a sensible solution.

Much has been made of the Nixon administration's attitude toward the Southern states—mostly by the Northeastern liberal community. They've accused us of something, as you heard tonight, they call "The Southern Strategy." We have no Southern Strategy. We do have a conviction that the people of the United States, irrespective of their point of geographic residence, have an inherent right to be treated even-handedly by their government.

For too long the South has been the punching bag for those who characterize themselves as liberal intellectuals. Actually, they are consistently demonstrating the antithesis of intelligence. Their reactions are visceral, not intellectual; and they seem to believe that truth is revealed rather than systematically proved. These arrogant ones and their admirers in the Congress, who reach almost for equal arrogance at times, are bringing this nation to the most important decision it will ever have to make. They are asking us to repudiate principles that have made this country great. Their course is one of applause for our enemies and condemnation for our leaders. Their course is a course that will ultimately weaken and erode the very fibre of America. They have a masochistic compulsion to destroy their country's strength whether or not that strength is exercised constructively. And they rouse themselves into a continual emotional crescendo—substituting disruptive demonstration for reason and precipitate action for persuasion.

This group may consider itself liberal, but it is undeniable that it is more comfortable with radicals. These people use the word "compassion" as if they invented it. "Compassion" is their weapon and their shield. But they apply compassion selectively. Crime is excused only when the criminal is "disadvantaged."

They're equally selective as reformers. Waste in the Pentagon is a national outrage. Waste in welfare and poverty programs is a matter to be overlooked. . . .

This is the group that believes in marching down the streets of America to protest the war in Vietnam to our President. They would never think of protesting the continuation of this war to the government that is actually continuing it—the government of Hanoi. . . .

In my judgment, the principles of most of the people of Mississippi are the principles of the Republican Party. Since the policy makers of the other party have repudiated these principles, does it not make sense that Mississippi should become a strong state in the Republican column? It not only makes sense, but it's happening. The success of this gathering proves beyond question that it is happening.

# Labor Day Radio Address (1972)

### RICHARD M. NIXON

## The Worker's Values under Fire

On this Labor Day, I would like to discuss with you some of the decisions you will be facing this year—decisions that will affect your job, your paycheck, and your future.

Today, this Nation is operating under a system that is rooted in the values that built America:

> —We believe that an able-bodied person should earn what he gets and keep most of what he earns. We must stop increases in taxes before they reach the point that the American wage earner is working more for the Government than he is for himself.
> —We believe it is wrong for someone on welfare to receive more than someone who works.
> —We believe that a person's ability and ambition should determine his income, and that his income should not be redistributed by Government or restricted by some quota system.
> —We believe that when Government tampers too much with the lives of individuals, when it unnecessarily butts into the free collective bargaining process, it cripples the private enterprise system on which the welfare of the worker depends.

Because we have held fast to those values, the American worker has a higher standard of living and more freedom than any worker in the world today.

## Work Ethic or Welfare Ethic?

We are faced this year with the choice between the "work ethic" that built this Nation's character and the new "welfare ethic" that could cause that American character to weaken.

Let's compare the two:

The work ethic tells us that there is really no such thing as "something for nothing," and that everything valuable in life requires some striving and some sacrifice. . . .

The welfare ethic, on the other hand, suggests that there is an easier way. It says that the good life can be made available to everyone right now, and that this can be done by the Government. . . .

Richard M. Nixon, "Labor Day Radio Address," *The Clearest Choice* (n.p., 1972), 3–7.

The choice before the American worker is clear: The work ethic builds character and self-reliance, the welfare ethic destroys character and leads to a vicious cycle of dependency.

The work ethic builds strong people.

The welfare ethic breeds weak people. . . .

## The Fallacy of Income Redistribution

Let me give you three specific examples of the difference between the work ethic and the welfare ethic, and how the choice directly affects your life.

The believers in the welfare ethic think it is unfair of some people to have much more income than others. They say we should begin right away to re-distribute income, so that we can reduce the number of poor and bring about that day when everybody has much closer to the same income.

I believe that a policy of income redistribution would result in many more Americans becoming poor, because it ignores a human value essential to every worker's success—the incentive of reward.

It's human nature for a person who works hard for a living to want to keep most of what he earns, and to spend what he earns in the way he wants. Now, some may call this work ethic selfish or materialistic, but I think it is natural for a worker to resent seeing a large chunk of his hard-earned wage taken by Government to give to someone else who may even refuse to work. . . .

## Quotas: Anti-ability, Anti-opportunity

A third traditional value that is coming under attack today by the welfare ethic has to do with ability, the great American idea that a person should be able to get ahead in life not on the basis of how he looks or who he knows, but rather on what he can do.

In employment and in politics, we are confronted with the rise of the fixed quota system—as artificial and unfair a yardstick as has ever been used to deny opportunity to anyone. . . .

## Labor's Choice

Does the American workingman want to turn over a large part of his eco-nomic freedom, including much of his freedom to bargain collectively, to eco-nomic theorists who think they can permanently manage the economy?

Does the American workingman want to trade away opportunity for the false promise of government security?

Does the American workingman want his country to become militarily weak and morally soft?

I call upon working men and women across the Nation to make this Labor Day commitment: to understand all that is at stake for them and their fami-lies and to make their decision out of a conviction of what is best for them-selves and best for all the people of America.

# 46

## STOPPING THE EQUAL RIGHTS AMENDMENT

★▬▬★▬▬★

The small National Women's Party first proposed an Equal Rights Amendment (ERA) to the Constitution in 1923. The Nineteenth Amendment had given women the vote; the ERA, which declared that "men and women shall have equal rights through the United States and in every place subject to its jurisdiction," aimed for equality in all areas, not just voting. But the proposal stirred much opposition, including from other political women, because it seemed to threaten the important body of Progressive-era state legislation that protected women workers. Supporters continued to push for its adoption, picking up the endorsement of the 1940 Republican convention, but the effort went nowhere.

In the 1960s, the ERA took on a new life as feminists acting under the aegis of the National Organization for Women sought to build on the successes of the civil rights movement. Initially, this new version of the ERA—that "equal rights under the law shall not be abridged or denied by the United States or any state on account of sex"—attracted broad bipartisan support, including President Nixon's endorsement. Congress approved it in 1972, and 30 state legislatures ratified it within a few months, just eight shy of the number needed to amend. With polls showing nearly three-fifths of Americans in favor, the ERA appeared to have irresistible momentum. Given 1972 legislation requiring equal sports expenditures for women and men and the Supreme Court's *Roe* v. *Wade* abortion rights decision, so did contemporary feminism.

But opposition was mounting. The first 20 legislative ratifications came quickly, but the next few came only after bruising political battles, and from 1974 to 1977 only four states ratified. The opposition came from different directions: Christians following Biblical teaching about female subordination, lawmakers alienated by strident ERA lobbying, men dubious of the whole idea, Southerners resisting social change. Women, especially conservative women, also began to raise questions and battle back in the legislatures. By 1975, more men than women supported the amendment. Five ratifying states voted to rescind their vote; in seven states where one legislative chamber had ratified, the other chamber refused to approve. Of the 11 Southern states, only Texas ratified; of the 13 mountain and plains states, fewer than half ratified. Ratification topped out at 30 states before the deadline for approval passed. In 1980 the Republican party reversed its long-standing support for the amendment.

The key figure in turning the ERA tide was Phyllis Schlafly, a devout Midwestern Catholic and militant anti-Communist who had championed Goldwater in 1964 and, with her husband, directed an anti-Soviet foundation in St. Louis. Blocked by Republican moderates in a run for head of the Federation of Republican Women, Schlafly organized the Eagle Trust and published a newsletter that hammered feminists and Communists. The push to pass the ERA was a galvanizing moment. Schlafly formed a new organization, STOP ERA, persuaded other ex-Goldwaterites to raise funds, acquired mailing lists, and recruited hundreds of concerned Mormons, Southern Baptists, Methodists, and members of the Churches of Christ, most of them women, to contact legislators. This was a major accomplishment given the historic animosity among these denominations. By 1975, STOP ERA's 50,000 members had halted the ratification movement in its tracks, and affiliates such as Women Who Want to Be Women were fighting against state-funded child care and other threats, as they saw them, to the traditional family. STOP ERA was one of the earliest multidenominational church-based conservative crusades, a precursor of the Moral Majority and Christian Coalition of later years. It was also one of the earliest single-issue campaigns, anticipating the anti-gun control, anti-affirmative action, pro-capital punishment, pro-school prayer movements that fed the conservative tide. The following Schlafly interview appeared in the *Washington Star* in 1976 and later in *Conservative Digest*.

The death of the ERA did not mark the death of the women's rights movement. Occupational opportunities continued to increase, especially in the medical, legal, and academic professions and in corporate, municipal and educational administration. More women played sports; held political office; served in the military, including in command positions; became police officers, fire fighters, construction workers, and Protestant ministers. Abortion rights remained a contentious and divisive subject everywhere, all but displacing race as a rallying cry even in the South. But within 20 years, even Southerners tended to accept the notion of equal educational and economic opportunity for women.

**Questions to Consider.** Why did Schlafly argue that ERA was a fraud? Were her main points economic or cultural and moral? To what extent did her economic arguments assume that men should support and protect women? What role did abortion play in her thinking? What role did scripture and religion play? Why was she opposed to "state nurseries"? Do you find her argument that ERA would be anti-family persuasive?

# Interview with the *Washington Star* (1976)

### PHYLLIS SCHLAFLY

*Question:* What do you make of the recent setbacks of the Equal Rights Amendment and the defeat of the state equal rights amendments in New York and New Jersey?

*Schlafly:* I think they show that despite the fact that the proponents had nearly 100 percent of the press on their side, and despite the fact that they had nearly 100 percent of the politicians who cared to commit themselves on their side, nevertheless the voters recognized ERA as a fraud, and they're against it. They recognize it as a takeaway of women's rights; they recognize it won't do anything good for women, and so they're against it.

*Q:* Why do you feel that if women got legal equality, say in New York, it would take away their rights?

*Schlafly:* The New York state support law is a beautiful law. It says the husband must support his wife, and the husband must support their minor children under age 21. It's perfectly obvious that when you apply the ERA to that law, it becomes immediately unconstitutional.

So ERA will take away the right of the wife to be supported and to have her minor children supported. Obviously, this is an attack on the rights of the wife and on the family. The principal thing that ERA does is to take away the right of the wife in an ongoing marriage, the wife in the home.

*Q:* Do you think that that is the reason men support their wives, because it's the law?

*Schlafly:* Yes, I do. Because it is their duty, and I think duty is an honorable word. When men get married they know that they are taking on the duty of supporting their wives.

*Q:* Do you think that women today really are getting married to be supported?

*Schlafly:* Even if you think that in the future the law should be changed, I think it is a gross invasion of the property rights of women in existing marriages to come along and say, "Now as a new principal of law—no matter that you went into marriage 10, 20, 30, 40 years ago, thinking that the marriage contract meant a definite relationship—too bad, sister. You're on your own now." And that's what they're saying.

Phyllis Schlafly, Interview with *Washington Star,* January 18, 1976. Reprinted by permission of Phyllis Schlafly.

*Q:* You see it happening that the wife at some point would have to support the husband?

*Schlafly:* She would be equally liable for the financial support.

*Q:* What's wrong with that?

*Schlafly:* What's wrong with that? Because you can't make the having of babies equally shared. I think our laws are entitled to reflect the natural differences and the role assigned by God, in that women have babies and men don't have babies.

Therefore, the wife has the right to support, and the husband has the duty to pay for the groceries on the table. Anything that ERA does to that is a takeaway of what she has now. It's a reduction in those rights. And even if you want to discuss alimony or child support or divorced women, in any state where alimony is something that goes only from husband to wife, which is half the states, ERA knocks it out, because it isn't equal.

*Q:* You mean the women might have to pay alimony.

*Schlafly:* Sure, that's right. And the proponents say this is what they want.

*Q:* Well, do you really see anything wrong with a woman paying alimony if she has the money and her husband doesn't?

*Schlafly:* The thing that's so fraudulent about ERA is that it is presented as something which will benefit women, which will lift women out of this second-class citizenship, this oppression that they've allegedly been in for the last 200 years. The proponents cannot show any single way that ERA is going to benefit women.

*Q:* You are also against the women's movement?

*Schlafly:* I certainly am.

*Q:* Why is that?

*Schlafly:* I think it is destructive and antifamily. I think their goals can be summed up as, first, for ERA, which is a takeaway of the legal rights that wives now have. Second, it is pro-abortion on demand, and government-financed abortion and abortion in government hospitals or any hospitals. Third, it's for state nurseries, to get the children in the nurseries and off the backs of the mothers.

Fourth, it is for prolesbian legislation, which is certainly an antimarriage movement. And fifth, it is for changing the school textbooks in order to eliminate what they call the stereotype of woman in the home as wife and mother. So I consider that all five of their principle objectives are antifamily.

*Q:* Do you think that women would be as well off today were it not for the women's movement?

*Schlafly:* I certainly do. There were more women in Congress prior to the women's movement than there are today.

*Q:* Well, haven't there been a lot of other gains, though? There are many more women working today and a lot of them are getting better salaries too.

*Schlafly:* And a lot of them who are working would prefer to be in the home. They are working for economic reasons.

*Q:* But if they have to work then it's important that they make as much money as they can, at least as much as men, for what they are doing.

*Schlafly:* I believe in equal pay for equal work. I do not believe in hiring unqualified women over qualified men to remedy some alleged oppression of 25 years ago.

*Q:* Do you think that people are being forced to hire this way?

*Schlafly:* Yes, we had a good example of that recently in a federal court, a ruling that has ordered the Chicago Police Department to hire 16 percent women, on a quota. Now in order to do this they have got to throw out the physical qualifications that are required to be a policeman on the Chicago police force. And I feel this is absolutely wrong.

It's hurtful to men, it's hurtful to women and it's hurtful to the community. And it will do nothing but demoralize and destroy the police force.

*Q:* You think the women will not be able to perform the job as well as men?

*Schlafly:* That's correct. The same thing's true in the military. There is an honorable place for women in the military. They have the best of both worlds in the military today. They are protected from combat service and from some of the dangerous and unpleasant jobs in the military.

I feel that ERA, which would require identical treatment in combat, and in the draft the next time we have one of these wars, is hurtful to everybody. It's hurtful to the defense of our country, it's terribly hurtful to our young women, it's hurtful to the women who want to make a career in the military and it's hurtful to the men.

*Q:* Don't you think that the women who want to be in the service should be the ones to make that decision?

*Schlafly:* You mean the decision as to whether they go into combat? No, I certainly don't. I think the purpose of the military is to defend our country in battle. The purpose is not to provide on-the-job training for somebody who thinks she wants a fun career with a lot of men around.

*Q:* You feel that women need to be protected in many ways?

*Schlafly:* I feel that there are physical differences between men and women. The women's lib movement establishes as dogma that there is no difference between men and women except the sex organs. I think this is nonsense.

# 47

## Business Unleashed

Ronald Reagan first made his mark in politics with a televised appeal in 1964 on behalf of conservative Senator Barry Goldwater, the Republican presidential candidate. Reagan argued a position popular with the Sunbelt and the suburbs, where Republicans were beginning to show strength—that high taxes, social programs, and regulations were strangling individual freedom and threatening to drag the country "down to the ant heap of totalitarianism." He also showed himself to be a brilliant speaker—relaxed, confident, earnest, and poised, with a warm voice, a gift for turning a phrase, and a knack for seeming simultaneously friendly and determined. The speech failed to rescue Goldwater's foundering campaign, but it did launch Reagan's own political career, which led first to the California governor's mansion and then to the White House.

Reagan's major victory in the presidential election of 1980 can be traced to several sources. The Democratic candidate, incumbent Jimmy Carter, was widely perceived as a weak president, unable to lift the country from a lingering economic slump or to rescue American diplomatic hostages from the clutches of Moslem fundamentalists in Iran. But Reagan was himself a strong candidate, promising repeatedly (as he had on Goldwater's behalf sixteen years before) to cut taxes, deregulate business, balance the federal budget, and increase military spending—in brief, to restore unregulated capitalism and global supremacy, the twin pillars of the American system. That some of these promises appeared contradictory, mutually exclusive, or impossible was no problem, Reagan argued. According to "supply-side economics," which Reagan popularized, the country could accomplish these ends simply by cutting taxes enough to trigger massive investment and rapid growth, thus generating higher tax revenues despite lower tax rates. Reagan's Republican rival, George Bush, dismissed this notion as "voodoo economics." Nevertheless, Reagan's form of voodoo proved enormously popular with the American business community, which aggressively supported and financed his candidacy. President Reagan's inaugural address, excerpted below, signaled his determination to follow through on his campaign promises.

Born in 1911, Ronald Reagan won initial fame in Hollywood, where he worked in films and was president of the Screen Actors' Guild. During the 1950s he appeared on television and did publicity for General Electric Company. A two-term governor of California, he was by 1980 both a seasoned politician and a seasoned actor—photogenic, comfortable before the cameras, and possessing a mellifluous, compelling voice. No president since Franklin D. Roosevelt, with whom Reagan often compared himself, used the electronic media so effectively or to such political advantage. His critics labeled him "the Teflon president" because he managed for years to escape unscathed from scandal or policy gaffes. But his friends called him "the Great Communicator," perhaps the finest of the century.

**Questions to Consider.** What was the nature of the "crisis" that Reagan saw in the United States in 1981? How did this crisis manifest itself at the government level? Why did Reagan say "government is the problem"? Did the president propose specific steps to deal with this? What steps did he propose for forcing government to live "within its means"? How, given these principles, was it possible for Reagan to oversee the biggest increase in the federal deficit to that date in American history?

★━━★━━★

# First Inaugural Address  (1981)

### RONALD REAGAN

These United States are confronted with an economic affliction of great proportions. We suffer from the longest and one of the worst sustained inflations in our national history. It distorts our economic decisions, penalizes thrift, and crushes the struggling young and the fixed-income elderly alike. It threatens to shatter the lives of millions of our people.

Idle industries have cast workers into unemployment, causing human misery and personal indignity. Those who do work are denied a fair return for their labor by a tax system which penalizes successful achievement and keeps us from maintaining full productivity.

But great as our tax burden is, it has not kept pace with public spending. For decades, we have piled deficit upon deficit, mortgaging our future and our children's future for the temporary convenience of the present. To continue this long trend is to guarantee tremendous social, cultural, political, and economic upheavals.

*The New York Times,* January 21, 1981.

You and I as individuals can, by borrowing, live beyond our means, but only for a limited period of time. Why, then, should we think that collectively, as a nation, we are not bound by that same limitation? . . .

In this present crisis, government is not the solution to our problem. Government is the problem.

From time to time, we have been tempted to believe that society has become too complex to be managed by self-rule, that government by an elite group is superior to government for, by, and of the people. But if no one among us is capable of governing himself, then who among us has the capacity to govern someone else?

All of us together, in and out of government, must bear the burden. The solutions we seek must be equitable, with no one group singled out to pay a higher price.

We hear much of special interest groups. Our concern must be for a special interest group that has been too long neglected. It knows no sectional boundaries or ethnic and racial divisions, and it crosses political party lines. It is made up of men and women who raise our food, patrol our streets, man our mines and our factories, teach our children, keep our homes, and heal us when we are sick—professionals, industrialists, shopkeepers, clerks, cabbies, and truckdrivers. They are, in short, "We the people," this breed called Americans. . . .

So, as we begin, let us take inventory. We are a nation that has a government—not the other way around. And this makes us special among the nations of the earth. Our government has no power except that granted it by the people. It is time to check and reverse the growth of government, which shows signs of having grown beyond the consent of the governed.

It is my intention to curb the size and influence of the federal establishment and to demand recognition of the distinction between the powers granted to the federal government and those reserved to the states or to the people.

All of us need to be reminded that the federal government did not create the states; the states created the federal government.

So there will be no misunderstanding, it is not my intention to do away with government. It is, rather, to make it work—work with us, not over us; to stand by our sides, not ride on our backs. Government can and must provide opportunity, not smother it—foster productivity, not stifle it.

If we look to the answer as to why, for so many years, we achieved so much, prospered as no other people on earth, it was because here, in this land, we unleashed the energy and individual genius of man to a greater extent than has ever been done before. Freedom and the dignity of the individual have been more available and assured here than in any other place on earth. The price for this freedom has been high at times. But we have never been unwilling to pay that price.

It is no coincidence that our present troubles parallel and are proportionate to the intervention and intrusion in our lives that result from unnecessary and excessive growth of government. . . .

So with all the creative energy at our command, let us begin an era of national renewal. Let us renew our determination, our courage, and our strength. And let us renew our faith and our hope. We have every right to dream heroic dreams. . . .

In the days ahead, I will propose removing the roadblocks that have slowed our economy and reduced productivity. Steps will be taken aimed at restoring the balance between the various levels of government. Progress may be slow—measured in inches and feet, not miles—but we will progress. It is time to reawaken this industrial giant, to get government back within its means, and to lighten our punitive tax burden. And these will be our first priorities; on these principles there will be no compromise.

# 48

## The Evil Empire

The main theme of Ronald Reagan's first inaugural address was the need to stimulate the American economy by cutting taxes and getting the government "off our backs." This position was dear to the hearts of the "Old Right"—traditional business conservatives concerned chiefly with economic policies. But Reagan's triumphant campaign of 1980 had also energized the so-called "New Right"—groups concerned chiefly with restoring traditional morality by combating abortion, pornography, homosexuality, and women's liberation and by returning prayer to the public schools and the death penalty to American justice.

The heartland of the New Right was the Old South, where the liberalism of the Democratic party had alienated white voters and where Protestant fundamentalism, strengthened by television evangelists, was growing rapidly. Long a target of Republican strategists, the South became a natural base for Ronald Reagan, who skillfully tailored his appeals to the region by couching them in terms of morality rather than race. Such appeals would in turn attract all voters wanting to restore traditional authority and morals. One of Reagan's great political achievements was to bring these New Right voters decisively into the Republican camp.

Increasingly, moreover, the president linked the new morality to the old struggle against Communism. In part, he did this to forge a connection between his domestic agenda and the immense military build-up undertaken during his administration. He also knew that both old and new conservatives could unite behind an aggressive foreign policy. Perhaps the most famous instance of his linking diplomacy with moral conservatism came in a speech, excerpted below, to the National Association of Evangelicals. In this speech Reagan called Soviet Communism "the focus of evil in the modern world." Ironically, during his second administration Ronald Reagan met with Soviet Premier Mikhail Gorbachev on several occasions and signed a path-breaking treaty with the USSR banning intermediate-range nuclear forces in Europe.

**Questions to Consider.** What were the "tried and time-tested values" Reagan referred to early in his speech? Were they only the "concern for others and respect for the rule of law under God" that he had mentioned earlier, or did he mean something more? How did he think government support for birth-control services for girls would undermine the values of concern for others and the rule of law under God? What did Reagan's efforts to cut funds for teenage birth control share with the struggle against abortion? What did he mean when he called the Soviets the "focus of evil in the modern world"? Do you think Reagan really meant to imply that proponents of a freeze on building and deploying nuclear weapons were under the influence of Satan ("old Screwtape")?

★━━━★━━━★

# Speech to the National Association of Evangelicals (1983)

### RONALD REAGAN

This administration is motivated by a political philosophy that sees the greatness of America in you, her people, and in your families, churches, neighborhoods, communities—the institutions that foster and nourish values like concern for others and respect for the rule of law under God.

Now, I don't have to tell you that this puts us in opposition to, or at least out of step with, a prevailing attitude of many who have turned to a modernday secularism, discarding the tried and time-tested values upon which our very civilization is based. No matter how well intentioned, their value system is radically different from that of most Americans. And while they proclaim that they're freeing us from superstitions of the past, they've taken upon themselves the job of superintending us by government rule and regulation. Sometimes their voices are louder than ours, but they are not yet a majority.

An example of that vocal superiority is evident in a controversy now going on in Washington. And since I'm involved, I've been waiting to hear from the parents of young America. How far are they willing to go in giving to government their prerogatives as parents?

Let me state the case as briefly and simply as I can. An organization of citizens, sincerely motivated and deeply concerned about the increase in illegitimate births and abortions involving girls well below the age of consent, sometime ago established a nationwide network of clinics to offer help to these girls and, hopefully, alleviate this situation. Now, again, let me say, I do not fault their intent. However, in their well-intentioned effort, these clinics

*The New York Times,* March 9, 1983.

have decided to provide advice and birth control drugs and devices to underage girls without the knowledge of their parents.

For some years now, the Federal Government has helped with funds to subsidize these clinics. In providing for this, the Congress decreed that every effort would be made to maximize parental participation. Nevertheless, the drugs and devices are prescribed without getting parental consent or giving notification after they've done so. Girls termed "sexually active"—and that has replaced the word "promiscuous"—are given this help in order to prevent illegitimate birth or abortion.

Well, we have ordered clinics receiving Federal funds to notify the parents such help has been given. One of the nation's leading newspapers has created the term "squeal rule" in editorializing against us for doing this, and we're being criticized for violating the privacy of young people. A judge has recently granted an injunction against an enforcement of our rule. I've watched TV panel shows discuss this issue, seen columnists pontificating on our error, but no one seems to mention morality as playing a part in the subject of sex.

Is all of Judeo-Christian tradition wrong? Are we to believe that something so sacred can be looked upon as a purely physical thing with no potential for emotional and psychological harm? And isn't it the parents' right to give counsel and advice to keep their children from making mistakes that may affect their entire lives? . . .

More than a decade ago, a Supreme Court decision literally wiped off the books of fifty States statutes protecting the rights of unborn children. Abortion on demand now takes the lives of up to 1.5 million unborn children a year. Human life legislation ending this tragedy will some day pass the Congress, and you and I must never rest until it does. Unless and until it can be proven that the unborn child is not a living entity, then its right to life, liberty, and the pursuit of happiness must be protected.

You may remember that when abortion on demand began, many, and, indeed, I'm sure many of you, warned that the practice would lead to a decline in respect for human life, that the philosophical premises used to justify abortion on demand would ultimately be used to justify other attacks on the sacredness of human life—infanticide or mercy killing. Tragically enough, those warnings proved all too true. Only last year a court permitted the death by starvation of a handicapped infant. . . .

Now, I'm sure that you must get discouraged at times, but you've done better than you know, perhaps. There's a great spiritual awakening in America, a renewal of the traditional values that have been the bedrock of America's goodness and greatness.

One recent survey by a Washington-based research council concluded that Americans were far more religious than the people of other nations; 95 percent of those surveyed expressed a belief in God and a huge majority believed the Ten Commandments had real meaning in their lives. And another study has found that an overwhelming majority of Americans disapprove of adultery, teenage sex, pornography, abortion, and hard drugs. And this same study showed a deep reverence for the importance of family ties and religious belief. . . .

And this brings me to my final point today. During my first press conference as President, in answer to a direct question, I pointed out that, as good Marxist-Leninists, the Soviet leaders have openly and publicly declared that the only morality they recognize is that which will further their cause, which is world revolution. I think I should point out I was only quoting Lenin, their guiding spirit, who said in 1920 that they repudiate all morality that proceeds from supernatural ideas—that's their name for religion—or ideas that are outside class conceptions. Morality is entirely subordinate to the interests of class war. . . .

They must be made to understand we will never compromise our principles and standards. We will never give away our freedom. We will never abandon our belief in God. And we will never stop searching for a genuine peace. But we can assure none of these things America stands for through the so-called nuclear freeze solutions proposed by some.

The truth is that a freeze now would be a very dangerous fraud, for that is merely the illusion of peace. The reality is that we must find peace through strength. . . .

Yes, let us pray for the salvation of all of those who live in that totalitarian darkness—pray they will discover the joy of knowing God. But until they do, let us be aware that while they preach the supremacy of the state, declare its omnipotence over individual man, and predict its eventual domination of all peoples on the Earth, they are the focus of evil in the modern world. . . .

So, I urge you to speak out against those who would place the United States in a position of military and moral inferiority. You know, I've always believed that old Screwtape reserved his best efforts for those of you in the church. So, in your discussions of the nuclear freeze proposals, I urge you to beware the temptation of pride—the temptation of blithely declaring yourselves above it all and label both sides equally at fault, to ignore the facts of history and the aggressive impulses of an evil empire, to simply call the arms race a giant misunderstanding and thereby remove yourself from the struggle between right and wrong and good and evil.

# 49

## MASCULINITY AND WAR

The Southern Baptist Convention (SBC) was born when Baptist congregations in the South separated from their Northern brethren over the issue of slavery. The SBC continued to go its own way after the Civil War. Highly emotional and intensely evangelical, Southern Baptist ministers preached scriptural inerrancy, anti-Catholicism, the separation of church and state, and the autonomy of local congregations. While their true passion was calling individual souls to Christ, they also opposed gambling, drinking, and dancing. By the mid-twentieth century, the SBC was the country's largest, fastest-growing Protestant denomination, with some of its biggest congregations and television audiences.

Race mattered. Strom Thurmond, George Wallace, and other arch-conservatives were Southern Baptists, and Southern Baptists organized many private white Christian academies after the Supreme Court's 1954 school desegregation decision. But eventually race faded as a major obsession, and the SBC passed few resolutions on any social issue except drinking until the 1970s, when it expressed alarm over crime rates and efforts to undermine parental rights and male prerogative. Abortion was addressed, but unlike anti-abortion activists, most of whom were Catholic, the Southern Baptists in their first statement on the issue in 1971 affirmed not only "a high view of life, including fetal life," but also the right to abortion "under such conditions as rape, incest, clear evidence of severe fetal deformity" and likely damage to the "emotional, mental and physical health of the mother," a position not markedly different from the *Roe* v. *Wade* decision. A significant shift occurred in 1980, however, when the Convention opposed taking the life of a "developing human being" except to save the mother's life. A 1982 resolution called abortion the killing of 4,000 "persons" daily, a position that aligned Southern Baptists with the Catholic hierarchy and with churches such as the Lutheran Church-Missouri Synod, the Mormons, the Churches of Christ, and numerous unaffiliated evangelical bodies.

The SBC also went on record against the Equal Rights Amendment, the ordination of women, "secular humanism," and assisted suicide. Other resolutions endorsed Scriptural infallibility, scientific creationism, capital punishment, and tax cuts. A 1996 resolution condemning homosexual marriage was one of the longest in SBC history. And there were startling reversals of doctrine. The Convention redefined the concept of the "priesthood of the believer"—holy Baptist doctrine since the days of founder Roger Williams in the seventeenth century—to mean ministerial and executive rather than individual prerogative, a stance that strengthened the disciplinary powers of the Convention and its officers at the expense of worshippers. It also modified its ancient enmity to Catholicism in order to facilitate joint action against abortion, gay marriage and pornography and for the traditional family. These positions were close to those of the post-1980 Republican party, and Southern Baptists fought for them through Moral Majority, which was created in 1979 to facilitate evangelical collaboration with Catholics, Mormons, and Orthodox Jews, and through the Christian Coalition, which replaced Moral Majority in the 1990s. The leaders of both these organizations were dedicated Republicans. The Convention passed a resolution mourning the death of non-Baptist Ronald Reagan, the first SBC motion commemorating any president.

Below are resolutions on homosexuals and women in military service. These were important issues because President Bill Clinton, against the advice of high-ranking commanders, had ordered a "Don't ask, don't tell" policy with regard to homosexuals joining the military and because women, despite persistent prejudice, were attending the military academies and enlisting in the ranks in unprecedented numbers.

**Questions to Consider.** What kinds of evidence did the resolutions offer in support of these stances? Why did the Convention argue that homosexual politics was "masquerading" as civil rights? Why did the second resolution condemn the "unbiblical social agenda" of ideological feminism? Were the argument against homosexual soldiers and against women in combat essentially the same, or were they different? Which resolution best conveys the underlying ideal of Southern Baptists? Which stance was most likely to gain traction with the American public?

■━━■━━■

# On Homosexuality, Military Service and Civil Rights (1993)

WHEREAS, Homosexuality is immoral, contrary to the Bible (Lev. 18:22; 1 Cor. 6:9–10) and contrary to traditional Judeo-Christian moral standards, and the open affirmation of homosexuality represents a sign of God's surrendering a society to its perversions (Rom. 1:18–32); and

From http://www.sbc.net/resolutions/amResolution.asp?ID=613 and http://www.sbc.net/resolutions/amResolution.asp?ID=1089. Reprinted by permission of the Southern Baptist Convention.

WHEREAS, Open and avowed homosexuality is incompatible with the requirements of military service according to high ranking military leaders and most military personnel; and

WHEREAS, Homosexual conduct is inconsistent with the Uniform Code of Military Justice and is detrimental to morale, unit cohesion, good order, discipline, and mission accomplishment; and

WHEREAS, Homosexuality in the military would endanger the life and health of military personnel by the increased exposure to sexually transmitted diseases and by enhanced danger of tainted blood in battlefield conditions; and

WHEREAS, Open homosexuality in the military would have significant adverse impact on the Pentagon's budget including medical, legal and social costs; and

WHEREAS, Southern Baptist and other evangelical military chaplains may be pressured to compromise the essential gospel message, withhold their biblical convictions about this sexual perversion and submit to "sensitivity training" concerning homosexuality if openly declared homosexuals are permitted to serve; and

WHEREAS, Southern Baptists and other evangelical members of the armed forces will be placed in compromising environments which will violate their conscience if the ban is lifted and will discourage other potential evangelical recruits from serving in the armed forces; and

WHEREAS, Homosexual politics is masquerading today as "civil rights," in order to exploit the moral high ground of the civil rights movement even though homosexual conduct and other learned sexual deviance have nothing in common with the moral movement to stop discrimination against race and gender; and

WHEREAS, Government should not give special legal protection and endorsement to homosexuality, nor impose legal sanctions against those who believe homosexual conduct to be immoral.

Therefore, Be It RESOLVED, That we, the messengers to the Southern Baptist Convention, meeting at Houston, Texas, June 15–17, 1993, affirm the biblical truth that homosexuality is sin, as well as the biblical promise that all persons, including homosexuals, can receive abundant, new and eternal life by repenting of their sin and trusting Jesus Christ as Savior and Lord (1 Cor. 6:11).

Be it further RESOLVED, That we oppose all effort to provide government endorsement, sanction, recognition, acceptance, or civil rights advantage on the basis of homosexuality; and

Be it further RESOLVED, That we oppose lifting the ban on homosexuals serving in the armed forces, and that we support passage of any legislation before Congress which restores and inforces the ban; and

Be it further RESOLVED, That we deplore acts of hatred or violence committed by homosexuals against those who take a stand for traditional morality as well as acts of hatred or violence committed against homosexuals; and

Be it finally RESOLVED, That we express our profound pride in and support of those who serve in the United States military, and for our chaplains in the military as they perform their ministry based on biblical principles and moral convictions, in an increasingly tumultuous environment.

★━━★━━★

# On Women in Combat (1998)

### RESOLUTIONS OF THE SOUTHERN BAPTIST CONVENTION

WHEREAS, The President and Congress have moved the United States military services to abandon their historic policy of limiting combat military service to males, and are now recruiting, training, and assigning women to combat roles; and

WHEREAS, God created male and female with specific and complementary characteristics (Genesis 1:27), declaring them "good" (Genesis 1:31) so that male and female in relationship constitute a complete expression of the divine order for humanity, yet without blurring or denying the meaning or significance of gender-based distinctions established by God in the created order; and

WHEREAS, The equality of male and female as to dignity and worth, following from their creation in the image of God (Genesis 1:27), is fully consistent with gender-based distinctions as to roles and responsibilities which are also established in the created order; and

WHEREAS, God, by creating Adam first (Genesis 2:18; 1 Corinthians 11:8) and also by creating woman "an help meet for him" (Genesis 2:18, 20, 22; 1 Corinthians 11:9), has set the gender-based role and responsibility of males in the most basic unit of society (the family) to be that of leader, provider and self-sacrificial protector (also cf. Ephesians 5:25; 1 Peter 3:70), and likewise has set the gender-based role and responsibility of females to be that of help and nurture (Genesis 2:18) and life-giving (Genesis 3:20) under male leadership and protection (cf. 1 Peter 3:7); and

WHEREAS, The purpose of military combat is to inflict deadly harm upon an enemy, and the essence of combat is to use force against an enemy in order to kill, damage or destroy—a purpose and essence aligned with the male role but opposed to the female role; and

WHEREAS, The moral justification for combat service is the duty to protect and defend vital national interests, including the welfare, security, and good order of families, which justification is essentially linked to the divinely as-signed role and responsibilities of self-sacrificial male headship of the family (Ephesians 5:23–24); and

WHEREAS, The pattern established by God throughout the Bible is that men, not women, bear responsibility to serve in combat if war is necessary (Genesis 14:14; Numbers 31:3, 21, 49; Deuteronomy 20:5–9; 3:14; Joshua 1:14–18; 6:3, 7, 9; 8:3; 10:7; 1 Samuel 16:18; 18:5; 2 Samuel 11:1; 17:8; 23:8–39; Psalm 45:3–5; Song of Solomon 3:7–8; Isaiah 42:13); and

WHEREAS, Biblical examples that record women serving in combat (Judges 4:4–23) are presented as contrary to proper and normal gender-based distinc-tions, and result from a shameful failure of male leadership (Judges 4:9–10; Nahum 3:13); and

WHEREAS, Willful rejection of a gender-based role distinction that limits combat military service to males is a foolish social experiment that: (1) threat-ens good military order and discipline by unnecessarily escalating sexual ten-sions among combat warriors, (2) weakens unit cohesion, (3) exposes female warriors taken as P.O.W.s to the special trauma of rape and sexual abuse, (4) places a major new strain on marital fidelity, and (5) risks the nation's military security by scrambling the moral framework defining male/female relationships.

Therefore, be it RESOLVED, That the messengers to the Southern Baptist Convention, meeting June 9–11, 1998, in Salt Lake City, Utah, do, with loyal respect and deep concern, warn against and oppose the training and assign-ing of females to military combat service because: it rejects gender-based dis-tinctions established by God in the order of creation; it undermines male headship in the family by failing to recognize the unique gender-based responsibility of men to protect women and children; and it subordinates the combat readiness of American troops, and the national security of the United States, to the unbiblical social agenda of ideological feminism; and

Be it further RESOLVED, That we give deepest gratitude and honor to those courageous women who have served their country in military support roles; and

Be it further RESOLVED, That we commit our prayer support to all military members and families serving this great nation around the world.

Be it finally RESOLVED, That we call upon the President, Congress, and all military leaders to reverse the present policy and to restore the historic limitation of military combat service to males only.

# 50

## RESPONSE TO TERROR

On September 11, 2001, terrorists belonging to Al Qaeda, a global network of Islamic extremists, crashed hijacked passenger planes into the
World Trade Center in New York City and the Pentagon in Washington,
D.C. The attacks killed nearly 3,000 people, most of them U.S. citizens, making this the most deadly attack on continental American soil
since the days of the Civil War. With Afghanistan as a command and
training base, Al Qaeda had cells in dozens of countries from North
America to the Philippines. There was therefore no "return address" on
this attack; no nation was responsible, so there was no nation on which
to declare war.

President George W. Bush, in office less than a year, made this clear
in a radio message shortly after the assault, asserting that "this is a conflict
without battlefields or beachheads," against opponents "who believe
they are invisible." Victory, said the president, would come in a series of
actions against terrorist organizations "and those who harbor and support
them." Bush quickly mobilized U.S. military strength and deployed it
against the ruling Taliban regime in Afghanistan—a radical Islamic theoc-
racy that provided training and staging areas for Al Qaeda. American
special forces and air power, supported by dissident Afghan warlords,
overthrew the Taliban in a matter of weeks and restored a more sympathetic government in the capital, Kabul. It has not been possible, however, to pacify the country or prevent a Taliban resurgence in some areas.

The president's objective to "eradicate the evil of terrorism" meant
that the conflict would not end with the Afghan campaign, since neither
Al Qaeda nor its leader, Osama bin Laden, a wealthy Saudi citizen, had
been eliminated. There were other Islamic militants in Lebanon, Pales-
tine, Chechnya, Indonesia, Pakistan, and elsewhere who posed threats to
the United States and its interests. Bush specifically denounced three
other countries—Iran, Iraq, and North Korea—as an "axis of evil" that
hid terrorists or presented other threats. Iraq became a particular focus of
administration enmity. Bush accused Iraq—against which his father had
waged a limited war a decade earlier to safeguard Middle Eastern oil
reserves—of assisting Al Qaeda and possessing biological, chemical,
and nuclear weapons of mass destruction. He threatened American

military intervention, alone if necessary, to cripple terrorism and eliminate the weapons.

In September 2002, Bush enunciated a new foreign policy doctrine, framed by the war on terror and the confrontation with Iraq—but with broader significance. This "Bush Doctrine," excerpted below, stressed a commitment to human rights and free trade as well as opposition to terrorism. More profoundly, it asserted a right to strike preemptively, or preventively, against "rogue states and their terrorist clients before they are able to threaten or use weapons of mass destruction," a claim that no previous administration had ever made. It further committed the United States to building a military force that no potential adversary could hope to equal, a decision that abandoned the "sufficiency" or "parity" doctrines that had long guided American military policy. In referencing the need for "homeland security," the Bush Doctrine had clear domestic implications as well, as shown with the passage of the U.S.A. Patriot Act, permitting the collection of immense amounts of data—from bank transactions to library use to air travel to medical records—on both U.S. citizens and visitors to the United States, and the establishment of a new federal Department of Homeland Security.

Acting on his newly enunciated preemptive strategy, in 2003 Bush ordered the invasion of Iraq, without United Nations, authorization, for the purpose of unseating the dictator Saddam Hussein. Some 150,000 U.S. troops, assisted by 45,000 British and Australians, waged the three-week campaign, which shattered the power of the government. The occupation of the country did not go well, however, with more Americans dying after the end of formal combat operations than before. Most European countries, many of whom had opposed unilateral U.S. action, refused to send supporting occupation troops, as did allies such as Turkey, Pakistan, and Canada. Significant parts of the country remained dangerous to U.S. occupying troops and dysfunctional. The U.S. forces found no evidence of Iraqi weapons of mass destruction or ties to Al Qaeda. This led some to question the Bush administration's wisdom, even its honesty, in justifying the invasion. Others saw invasion as a natural extension of the Bush security strategy articulated in the document below. As of the end of 2007, some 4,000 U.S. troops had died in the occupation and nearly five times that many were wounded.

George W. Bush was born in New Haven, Connecticut, in 1946. The eldest son of President George H. W. Bush and the grandson of U.S. Senator Prescott Bush, George W. grew up in Texas and, like his father, attended Phillips Andover Academy in Massachusetts and then Yale University, where he graduated in 1968. After serving as a fighter pilot in the Texas Air National Guard during the Vietnam War, Bush earned a Harvard MBA in 1975, worked in the Texas oil and gas industry for a decade, and helped manage his father's successful presidential campaign in 1988. From 1989 to 1994 he was managing partner of the Texas Rangers baseball team. He was the first Texas governor to be elected to two four-year terms and in 2000 became the second son of a president to win the presidency, in part through a contested ballot situation in Florida, where his brother Jeb was governor. Bush, a Methodist, has been called the most religious president in American history and also the most conservative since the nineteenth century.

**Questions to Consider.** Of the seven main parts of the doctrine given below, which strike you as the most original or novel? Which seem to mark the biggest break from previous U.S. doctrine? In the part on "Terror Alliance," the final sentence has raised alarms among other countries' leaders. Why might they have concerns about the formulation? How is "terrorism" defined here? In the "Deadliest Weapons" section, how does the doctrine differentiate between trustworthy and "rogue" regimes possessing weapons of mass destruction? The section seems to equate the possessing of such weapons with seeking to possess them. Is this reasonable? The section on "Strike First" has become one of the most controversial parts of the Bush Doctrine. Why do you think this is so? Similarly controversial is the final section, "Military," which argues that no "potential adversary" should equal the United States in military power, implying a permanent objective of military supremacy. Again, why might this have raised such concern? Does this section further suggest that the intelligence community as well as the military would need to grow dramatically, and perhaps even expand its surveillance to within the United States itself? If so, would this represent a dramatic departure?

★━━★━━★

# The Bush Strategic Doctrine (2002)

### GEORGE W. BUSH

The United States possesses unprecedented and unequaled strength and influence in the world. Sustained by faith in the principles of liberty, and the value of a free society, this position comes with unparalleled responsibilities, obligations, and opportunity. The great strength of this nation must be used to promote a balance of power that favors freedom.

**Human Rights:** In pursuit of our goals, our first imperative is to clarify what we stand for: The United States must defend liberty and justice because

*The Boston Globe,* September 21, 2002.

A World Trade Center tower in ruins shortly after planes crashed into and destroyed it in the nightmarish terrorist attack of September 11, 2001. (AP/Wide World Photos)

these principles are right and true for all people everywhere. No nation owns these aspirations and no nation is exempt from them. Fathers and mothers in all societies want their children to be educated and to live free from poverty and violence. No people on earth yearn to be oppressed, aspire to servitude, or eagerly await the midnight knock of the secret police.

America must stand firmly for the nonnegotiable demands of human dignity: the role of law, limits on the absolute power of the state, free speech, freedom of worship, equal justice, respect for women, religious and ethnic tolerance, and respect for private property.

**Terror Alliance:** The enemy is not a single political regime or person or religion or ideology. The enemy is terrorism premeditated, politically motivated violence perpetrated against innocents. In many regions, legitimate grievances prevent the emergence of a lasting peace. Such grievances deserve to be, and must be, addressed within a political process. But no cause justifies terror. The United States will make no concessions to terrorist demands and strike no deals with them. We make no distinction between terrorists and those who knowingly harbor or provide aid to them.

**Regional Conflicts:** Concerned nations must remain actively engaged in critical regional disputes to avoid explosive escalation and minimize human suffering. In an increasingly interconnected world, regional crisis can strain our alliances, rekindle rivalries among the major powers, and create horrifying affronts to human dignity. When violence erupts and states falter, the United States will work with friends and partners to alleviate suffering and restore stability. No doctrine can anticipate every circumstance in which U.S. action, direct or indirect, is warranted. We have finite political, economic, and military resources to meet our global priorities.

**Deadliest Weapons:** At the time of the Gulf War, we acquired irrefutable proof that Iraq's designs were not limited to the chemical weapons it had used against Iran and its own people, but also extended to the acquisition of nuclear weapons and biological agents. In the past decade North Korea has become the world's principal purveyor of ballistic missiles and has tested increasingly capable missiles while developing its own [weapons of mass destruction] arsenal. Other rogue regimes seek nuclear, biological, and chemical weapons as well. These states' pursuit of, and global trade in, such weapons has become a looming threat to all nations.

**Strike First:** We must be prepared to stop rogue states and their terrorist clients before they are able to threaten or use weapons of mass destruction against the United States and our allies and friends. Our response must take full advantage of strengthened alliances; the establishment of new partnerships with former adversaries; innovation in the use of military forces; modern technologies, including the development of an effective missile-defense system; and increased emphasis on intelligence collection and analysis.

The United States will not use force in all cases to preempt emerging threats, nor should nations use preemption as a pretext for aggression. Yet in an age where the enemies of civilization openly and actively seek the world's most destructive technologies, the United States cannot remain idle while dangers gather.

**Global Economy:** We will promote economic growth and economic freedom beyond America's shores. All governments are responsible for creating their own economic policies and responding to their own economic challenges. We will use our economic engagement with other countries to underscore the benefits of policies that generate higher productivity and sustained economic growth.

**Military:** We will maintain the forces sufficient to support our obligations and to defend freedom. Our forces will be strong enough to dissuade potential adversaries from pursuing a military buildup in hopes of surpassing, or equaling, the power of the United States.

We must strengthen intelligence warning and analysis to provide integrated threat assessments for national and homeland security. Since the threats inspired by foreign governments and groups may be conducted inside the United States, we must also ensure the proper fusion of information between intelligence and law enforcement. Initiatives in this area will include strengthening the authority of the director of Central Intelligence to lead the development and actions of the nation's foreign intelligence capabilities.